Canon® EOS 6D

FOR
DUMMIES®

A Wiley Brand

Canon® EOS 6D

FOR DUMMIES®

A Wiley Brand

by Doug Sahlin

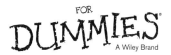

Canon® EOS 6D For Dummies®

Published by
John Wiley & Sons, Inc.
111 River Street
Hoboken, NJ 07030-5774

www.wiley.com

Copyright © 2013 by John Wiley & Sons, Inc., Hoboken, New Jersey

Published by John Wiley & Sons, Inc., Hoboken, New Jersey

Published simultaneously in Canada

For general information on our other products and services, please contact our Customer Care Department within the U.S. at 877-762-2974, outside the U.S. at 317-572-3993, or fax 317-572-4002.

For technical support, please visit www.wiley.com/techsupport.

Wiley publishes in a variety of print and electronic formats and by print-on-demand. Some material included with standard print versions of this book may not be included in e-books or in print-on-demand. If this book refers to media such as a CD or DVD that is not included in the version you purchased, you may download this material at http://booksupport.wiley.com. For more information about Wiley products, visit www.wiley.com.

Library of Congress Control Number: 2013932106

ISBN 978-1-118-53039-9 (pbk); ISBN 978-1-118-53065-8 (ebk); ISBN 978-1-118-53059-7 (ebk); ISBN 978-1-118-53041-2 (ebk)

Manufactured in the United States of America

10 9 8 7 6 5 4 3 2 1

About the Author

Doug Sahlin is an author and photographer living in Venice, Florida. He's written books on computer applications, such as Adobe Flash and Adobe Acrobat. He's also written books on digital photography and co-authored 13 books on various applications, such as Adobe Photoshop and Photoshop Elements. Recent titles include: *Digital Landscape and Nature Photography For Dummies, Digital SLR Shortcuts and Settings For Dummies,* and *Canon EOS 7D For Dummies.* Many of his books have been bestsellers on Amazon.

Doug is president of Doug Plus Rox Photography, a wedding and event photography company. Doug teaches Adobe Acrobat to local businesses and government institutions. He also teaches Adobe Photoshop and Adobe Photoshop Lightroom at local photography stores.

Dedication

Dedicated to my wife Roxanne, the love of my life and one of the best photographers on the planet.

Author's Acknowledgments

Thanks to Acquisitions Editor Steve Hayes for making this book a possibility. Special thanks to Project Editor Blair Pottenger, and Copy Editor Barry Childs-Helton for making sure my text is squeaky clean with no grammatical errors. Thanks to Technical Editor Scott Proctor for making sure the book is technically accurate. Many thanks to the other members of the Wiley team for taking the book from concept to fruition.

Thanks to agent extraordinaire Margot Hutchison for ironing out the contractual details. Many thanks to Canon for creating some of the greatest cameras on the planet. Special thanks to my friends and family. Kudos to my wife Roxanne for putting up with my late nights and occasional mood swings when I'd written one more page than I should for the day. And thanks to our furry kids, Niki and Micah, for their love, affection, and comic relief.

Publisher's Acknowledgments

We're proud of this book; please send us your comments at http://dummies.custhelp.com. For other comments, please contact our Customer Care Department within the U.S. at 877-762-2974, outside the U.S. at 317-572-3993, or fax 317-572-4002.

Some of the people who helped bring this book to market include the following:

Acquisitions and Editorial

Project Editor: Blair J. Pottenger

Executive Editor: Steve Hayes

Senior Copy Editor: Barry Childs-Helton

Technical Editor: Scott Proctor

Editorial Manager: Kevin Kirschner

Editorial Assistant: Annie Sullivan

Sr. Editorial Assistant: Cherie Case

Cover Photo: © KirbusEdvard / iStockphoto. Camera image courtesy of Canon.

Composition Services

Project Coordinator: Patrick Redmond

Layout and Graphics: Jennifer Creasey, Amy Hassos, Joyce Haughey

Proofreader: Lindsay Amones

Indexer: Potomac Indexing, LLC

Publishing and Editorial for Technology Dummies

Richard Swadley, Vice President and Executive Group Publisher

Andy Cummings, Vice President and Publisher

Mary Bednarek, Executive Acquisitions Director

Mary C. Corder, Editorial Director

Publishing for Consumer Dummies

Kathleen Nebenhaus, Vice President and Executive Publisher

Composition Services

Debbie Stailey, Director of Composition Services

Contents at a Glance

Table of Contents

Part II: Going Beyond Point-and-Shoot Photography ... 107

Chapter 5: Shooting Pictures and Movies with Live View.........109

Chapter 6: Getting the Most from Your Camera 131

Introduction

Your Canon EOS 6D is the latest and greatest digital camera on the market — with a stunning 20.2-megapixel capture, Live View, high-definition video, and much more. But all this technology can be a bit daunting, especially if this is your first real digital SLR (single-lens reflex). You no longer have modes like Portrait, Sport, Landscape, and so on. You've graduated to the big leagues. All you have to do is master the power you hold in your hands.

I've been using Canon digital SLRs since the EOS 10D, and I've learned a lot about the cameras since then. In addition to the EOS 6D I'm using to write this book, I also own an EOS 5D MKII and EOS 7D, which has a lot of the features found on your EOS 6D. My goal is to show you how to become one with your camera. I don't get overly technical in this book, even though your camera is very technical. I also do my best to keep it lively. So if you want to master your EOS 6D, you have the right book in your hands.

About This Book

If you find the buttons and menus on your shiny new EOS 6D a tad intimidating, this book is for you. In the chapters of this book, I take you from novice point-and-shoot photographer to one who can utilize all the bells and whistles your camera offers. You'll find information about every menu and button on your camera, as well as when to use them, and what settings to use for specific picture-taking situations. I also show you how to use the software that ships with your camera.

Foolish Assumptions

Ah yes. Assume. When broken down to its lowest common denominator . . . Okay, I won't go there. But as an author, I have to make some assumptions. First and foremost, you should now own, or have on order, a Canon EOS 6D. If you own one of those cute little point-and-shoot Canon cameras, good for you, but this book won't help you with that camera. You should also have a computer to download your images to. A basic knowledge of photography is also helpful. I know, you probably meet all assumptions. But my editor assumes I'll put this section in this part of the book.

Conventions Used in This Book

To make life easier, this book has several conventions that are used to identify pertinent information — stuff you should know. So to help you navigate this book easily, I use a few style conventions:

- Terms or words that you might be unfamiliar with in the context of photography, I have *italicized* — and I also define these.

- Numbered steps that you need to follow and characters you need to type are set in **bold.**

- Margin art is used to identify camera buttons. When you see one of these icons, it shows you what button to push, or dial to rotate.

- The Canon EOS 6D menu has pretty little icons for each tab, but no text to describe what each tab does. I name the tabs to make things easier for you, dear reader, and for my editor and me. You'll find a table with tab names in Chapter 2.

The Long and Winding Road Ahead

I divide this book into four parts, with each devoted to a specific aspect of your camera. The chapters flow logically from one subject to the next, to take you from shooting in Full Auto mode to becoming a seasoned photographer who knows what mode to choose and what settings to use for taking pictures of specific subjects. You can read the book from cover to cover — or, if you need quick information about a specific topic, peruse the Table of Contents or Index until you find the desired topic. Most of the sections in this book don't require reading additional material.

The following sections offer a brief overview of each part of the book.

Part 1: Getting Started with Your Canon EOS 6D

Part I contains four chapters that help you get up and running with your EOS 6D:

- Chapter 1 introduces you to the camera and shows you how to do some basic tasks.

- Chapter 2 shows you how to take pictures using the two Automatic modes. I show you how to go fully automatic and how to use the Creative Auto mode.

✔ Chapter 3 shows you how to specify the image format. I show you how to choose JPEG and RAW format, discuss different sizes, and offer my recommendation for the ideal format.

✔ Chapter 4 shows you how to use the LCD monitor for a myriad of purposes. I show you how to review your images, use the histogram, and more.

Part II: Going Beyond Point-and-Shoot Photography

In this part of the book, I cut to the chase and show you how to master the advanced features of your camera.

✔ Chapter 5 shows you how to use Live View mode. I show you how to take pictures with Live View, change Autofocus modes, and more. I also show you how to capture movies with Live View. So you're live in Chapter 5.

✔ Chapter 6 shows you how to use the Creative shooting modes. In this chapter, I also show you how to modify camera exposure, bracket exposure, and more.

✔ Chapter 7 shows you how to use the advanced features of your camera. I show you how to set ISO, set white balance, and much more. I also show you how to use your EOS 6D with Canon Speedlites.

✔ Chapter 8 shows you how to use your EOS 6D in specific shooting situations. I discuss sport photography, wildlife photography, landscape photography, and more.

Part III: Editing and Sharing Your Images

This part of the book shows you how to organize and edit your images with Canon's ImageBrowser EX and Digital Photo Professional software.

✔ Chapter 9 introduces you to Canon's ImageBrowser EX and Digital Photo Professional. I show you how to download and organize your work, plus show you how to do some basic editing tasks.

✔ Chapter 10 shows you how to print your images from ImageBrowser EX and Canon Digital Photo Professional. I also show you how to make contact sheets in both applications.

Part IV: The Part of Tens

The book concludes with two top ten lists, written by yours truly, who happens to have a gap between his teeth like David Letterman, who happens to be famous for his top ten lists. The lists are grouped according to subject matter, and a splendid time is guaranteed for all. And tonight Mr. Kite is topping the bill.

- ✐ Chapter 11 shows you how to create a custom menu and register your favorite settings. I also show you how to add copyright information to the camera and much more.
- ✐ Chapter 12 shows you how to create a makeshift tripod, create abstract images, create multiple exposures in camera, and more.

Icons and Other Delights

For Dummies books have icons that indicate important bits of information. You can hopscotch from icon to icon and discover a lot. But when in doubt, read the text associated with the icon. In this book, you find the following icons:

- ✐ A Tip icon contains information designed to save you time and, in some instances, your very sanity.

- ✐ This icon warns you about something you should not do; something your fearless author has already done and decided it's not a good thing to do again.

- ✐ When you see this icon, it's the equivalent of a virtual piece of string tied around your finger. This is information you want to commit to memory.

- ✐ When you see this icon, it's for the geeks in the group who like to know all manner of technical stuff.

You'll also find icons in the margin that show you controls on your camera, and menu tabs.

Shoot Lots of Pictures and Enjoy!

Your EOS 6D is a digital photography powerhouse; use it and use it often. The old adage "practice makes perfect" does apply, though. The only way to become a better photographer and master your equipment is to apply what you know and shoot as many pictures as you can. While you're working your way through this book, keep your camera close at hand. When your significant other pokes his or her head into the room, grab your camera and start practicing your craft. Take one picture, then another, and another, and so on. With practice, you'll know your camera like the back of your hand. You'll also know which rules of photography and composition work for you — and you'll start to develop your own style. For that matter, you'll probably amaze yourself, too.

Part I

getting started with your **Canon EOS 6D**

In this part . . .

- ✔ Get to know the lay of the land and familiarize you with the controls of your EOS 6D.

- ✔ Find out how to take great pictures automatically as well as how to specify image size and format.

- ✔ Understand how to get around in the menu.

- ✔ Learn to master your LCD monitor.

- ✔ Visit www.dummies.com for great Dummies content online.

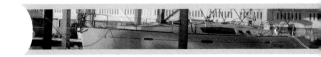

Exploring Your EOS 6D

In This Chapter

- ► Getting to know the camera controls
- ► Using the LCD panel
- ► Using the viewfinder
- ► Introducing wireless and GPS
- ► Attaching and removing a lens
- ► Using image stabilization
- ► Using a zoom lens
- ► Changing camera settings
- ► Using SD cards
- ► Accessorizing your EOS 6D

The Canon EOS 6D is a camera many people have been waiting for. Combining a full frame sensor in an ergonomic body with other bells and whistles at a fraction of the cost of the Canon EOS 5D MKIII makes this a very desirable camera for photographers who shoot landscapes and want to get the maximum amount of real estate in the frame. This camera has the best features of the cropped-frame sensor cameras such as the EOS 60D and EOS 7D with the new, all-singing all-dancing DIGIC 5 sensor. It doesn't get any better than this unless you fork over the cold hard cash for an EOS 5D MKIII. And the camera comes with a dual-axis level built into the viewfinder, which means that as long as you use this feature, you never have to deal with a defective horizon line (technical-speak for slanted horizon line) again. The fact that you have this book in your hands means you already know that, but want to master the features of the new camera.

The camera comes with a shooting mode for every photographer. If you're new to digital photography, or this is your first digital SLR, Canon has given you several modes to create great photographs automatically. Think of these as your training wheels. If you're a seasoned photographer, Canon also gives you quite a few modes where you can take the reins and create the type of photograph you want. Add WiFi, GPS, multiple exposures, and HDR in-camera, and you've got a potent tool for creating cool images.

Getting familiar with all this new technology can seem daunting even to a seasoned photographer. I was impressed, albeit a tad flummoxed, when I saw the first reviews for this camera. Even though I'm a seasoned Canon digital single-lens reflex (DSLR) user — my first digital SLR was the EOS 10D — I still had to flatten a learning curve when I first had the EOS 6D in hand, chomping at the bit to take some pictures. But it's my job to get down to brass tacks with new technology and show you how to master this technology. The fact that you're reading this probably means that you want to know how to use all the bells and whistles Canon has built into the camera. In this chapter I begin at the beginning: the buttons, knobs, and other controls on the outside of the camera. Getting to know the camera controls like the back of your hand is the first step to taking gorgeous pictures with this awesome new edition to Canon's line of digital SLR cameras.

Getting in Touch with the Camera Controls

If you're a longtime Canon user, you know that you can do an awful lot with the camera by using external controls, which saves you from having to use pesky menus that other camera manufacturers are so fond of. The controls for this camera are easy to reach and give you access to many powerful camera features. Although you may think it's a daunting task to know which button does what, after you use the camera for a while, you'll automatically know which control gives you your desired result and then reach for it instinctively, without taking your eye from the viewfinder. But first, you need to know what each control does. I explain the controls you find on the outside of the camera in the upcoming sections.

Exploring the top of the camera

The top of the camera (as shown in Figure 1-1) is where you find the controls you use most when creating images. The top of the camera is where you change settings like ISO (International Organization for Standards), aperture, and shutter speed, choose a shooting mode, and press the shutter button to take a picture. You can do lots of other things from the top of the camera, which in my humble opinion is the most important piece of real estate on the camera, except of course for the lens, which is your window to your world as you photograph it. I suggest you get to know the controls on the top of your camera intimately, like the back of your hand. Many photographers, including me, make it a point to memorize where the controls are and access them without taking an eye off the viewfinder. If you do this, you'll instinctively be able to dial in the right settings when a photo opportunity appears. If you have to fumble and take your eyes away from the viewfinder, you'll miss a lot of shots. Here's what you find on the top of the camera:

- **Shutter button:** This button pre-focuses the camera and takes a picture. I discuss this button in greater detail in Chapter 2.

- **Main dial:** This dial changes a setting after you press a button. For example, after you press the ISO Speed button, you move this dial to change the ISO speed setting. I show you how to use this button as the need arises.

- **LCD Panel Illumination button:** Press this button when you're in dim or dark conditions and you need to shed a little light on the LCD panel.

- **Metering mode button:** This button changes the Metering mode (see Chapter 6 for more on the Metering mode).

- **ISO speed-setting button:** This button sets the ISO speed setting (see Chapter 6 for more on the ISO speed setting). Canon has instituted a nice feature on this button. This is the only button on the top of the camera that is concave with a little dimple on it, which makes it easy to find this button by feel.

- **LCD panel:** This panel shows you all the current settings. I show you how to read the information in this panel in the section, "Decoding the LCD Panel," later in this chapter.

- **Drive button:** This button changes the drive mode from single shot to multi-shot.

- **AF button:** This button changes the Auto Focus Operation.

- **Hot shoe:** Slide a compatible flash unit (a Canon flash unit is dubbed a *Speedlite*) into this slot. The contacts in the hot shoe communicate between the camera and the flash unit. (I discuss flash photography in Chapter 6.)

- **Mode dial:** This button determines which shooting mode the camera uses to take the picture. (I show you how to use this dial to choose specific shooting modes in Chapter 6, and in Chapter 8, I show you how to choose optimal settings for specific picture-taking situations.)

- **Mode Dial Lock Release button:** Push this button to unlock the Mode Dial and then rotate the Mode Dial to choose a different shooting mode. This new feature ensures you'll never accidentally select a different shooting mode than the one that you've chosen for the type of pictures you're taking.

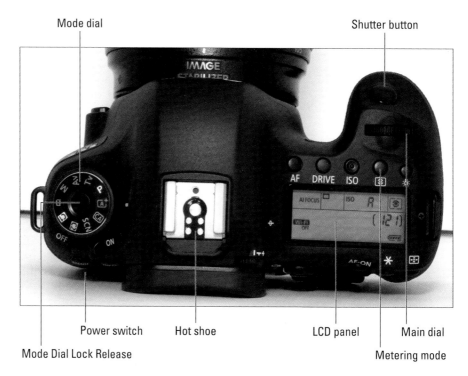

Figure 1-1: On top of your camera, all covered with dials and buttons.

Exploring the back of the camera

The back of the camera is also an important place. Here you find controls to power up your camera, access the camera menu, and much more. The following is what you find on the back of your EOS 6D (see Figure 1-2):

- **Access lamp:** Flashes when the camera writes data to the inserted memory card.

- **AF Point Selection button:** This button enables you to change from multiple autofocus points to a single autofocus point (see Chapter 6).

- **AE Lock/FE Lock button:** This button locks exposure to a specific part of the frame (see Chapter 6). When used with a dedicated Canon flash, this button is used to lock flash exposure to a specific part of the frame.

- **AF-ON button:** This button, in certain shooting modes, establishes focus. You also use this button to establish focus on a specific part of the person, place, or thing you're photographing (see Chapter 6).

✔ **Live View Shooting/Movie Shooting switch:** This switch serves one function: It switches from Live View Still Mode to Live View Movie mode (for those of you who aspire to be the next great indie filmmaker), which I explain in detail in Chapter 5.

✔ **Live View/Movie Start/Stop button:** You use this switch to engage Live View mode, and when you switch to movie shooting mode, this button starts and stops recording a movie (see Chapter 5).

✔ **Index/Magnify/Reduce button:** This button displays multiple images on the LCD monitor, or zooms in or out on a single image displayed on the LCD monitor.

✔ **Playback button:** This button displays the last image captured, or the last image viewed.

✔ **Quick Control button:** Press this button to display the Quick Control menu on the LCD monitor. (I show you how to use the Quick Control menu in Chapter 4.) You can also use the Quick Control button in conjunction with the SCN modes, Scene Intelligent Auto, and the CA (Creative Auto) mode.

✔ **Quick Control dial:** This button selects a setting or highlights a menu item. This dial is used when performing various tasks, and I discuss it throughout this book as needed.

✔ **Multi-controller button:** Use this button for a myriad of tasks, such as changing the autofocus point, selecting an option when using the Quick Control Menu instead of the camera menu, navigating to a menu item or switching from one camera menu to the next. (I explain this button in detail when it's associated with a specific task throughout this book.)

✔ **Set button:** Press this button to confirm a task, such as erasing an image from your card or setting a menu option. I show you how to use this button in conjunction with specific tasks throughout this book.

✔ **Erase button:** This button deletes a single image, or multiple images. (I show you how to delete images in Chapter 4.)

✔ **Multi-Function Lock switch:** This switch prevents a setting from being accidentally erased. Flick the switch to the right to lock the Quick Control dial when you're in shooting mode. Flick the switch left to unlock the Quick Control dial and enable setting changes.

✔ **Dioptric adjustment knob:** This control fine-tunes the viewfinder to your eyesight (see Chapter 2).

✔ **Viewfinder/eyepiece:** Use the viewfinder to compose your pictures. Shooting information, battery status, and the amount of shots that can be stored on the memory card is displayed in the viewfinder. The eyepiece cushions your eye when you press it against the viewfinder and creates a seal that prevents ambient light from having an adverse effect on the exposure.

✔ **Info button:** Press this button to display shooting information on the LCD monitor. You can choose from many different information screens. (I inform you about the different screens in Chapter 4.)

✔ **Menu:** Press this button to display the last used camera menu on the LCD monitor. (I introduce you to the camera menu in Chapter 2 and refer to the menu throughout this book.)

✔ **Power switch:** Okay, so this is a no-brainer. This switch powers the camera on and off.

Live View/Movie Start/Stop   AF-ON button

Live View/Movie switch   AE Lock/FE Lock

Dioptric adjustment knob   AF Point Selection

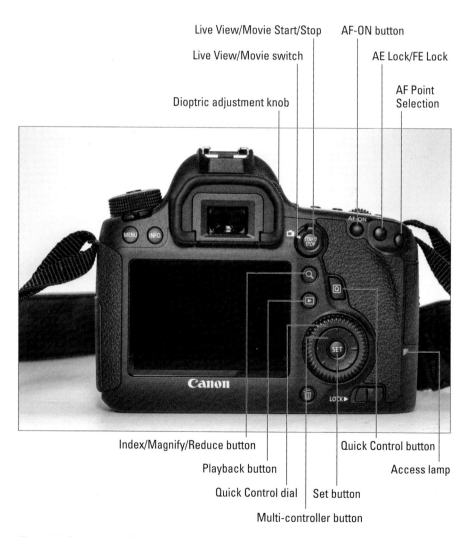

Index/Magnify/Reduce button   Quick Control button

Playback button   Access lamp

Quick Control dial   Set button

Multi-controller button

Figure 1-2: Buttons and dials and switches; oh my.

Exploring the front of the camera

The front of your camera (see Figure 1-3) has a couple controls you can use and other gizmos that the camera uses. Here you'll find a couple buttons that you use every day and some features you rarely use. The following is on the front of your camera:

- **Remote control sensor:** Senses the infrared beam from an RC-6 remote controller (sold separately) to actuate the shutter. Note that if you plan to purchase the RC-6 remote, it is line of sight only; you must point the remote at the front of the camera in order for it to be functional.

- **DC coupler cord hole:** The DR-E6 power adapter (sold separately) can be used to power the camera without a battery. This hole allows you to close the battery door when the DC coupler is installed properly.

- **Self-timer lamp:** This button flashes when you've enabled the self-timer. The lamp flashes quicker before the shutter is released.

- **Body cap:** Use the body cap to protect the interior of the camera when the lens isn't attached.

- **EF index mount:** In Figure 1-3 it's hidden behind the body cap, but you'll see it in all it's glory when I show you how to align an EF lens with this mark when attaching it to the camera (see the section, "Attaching a Lens," later in this chapter).

- **Depth-of-Field Preview button:** Press this button to preview the *depth of field* (the amount of the image in front of and behind your subject that's in apparent focus) at the current f-stop.

- **Lens-Release button:** Press this button when releasing a lens from the camera. I show you how to attach and remove lenses in the sections, "Attaching a Lens" and "Removing a Lens," later in this chapter.

- **Microphone:** Records monaural sound when recording movies.

- **Speaker:** Technically, this is actually on the side of the camera above the ports from which you connect the camera to external devices like the TV. Plays back sound when previewing video.

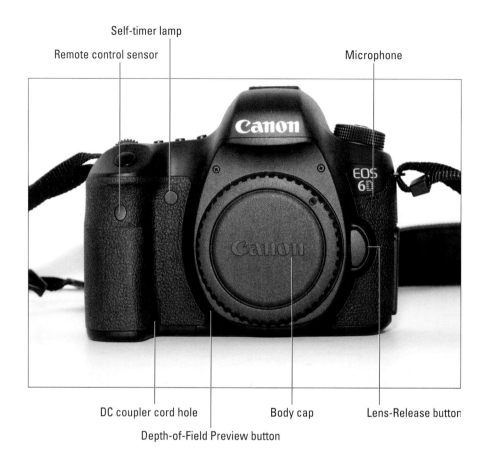

Self-timer lamp

Remote control sensor

Microphone

DC coupler cord hole

Body cap

Lens-Release button

Depth-of-Field Preview button

Figure 1-3: The front of the camera is an ergonomic wonder.

Decoding the LCD Panel

The LCD panel on the top of the camera displays a lot of information, such as the shutter speed, aperture, ISO speed setting, and more. Figure 1-4 shows all the possible options that can appear on the LCD panel. However, you'll never see this much information when you photograph a picture. I show you the type of information you can expect to see on the LCD panel during specific picture-taking scenarios I discuss throughout this book. With the LCD panel, you can see the current settings for white balance, ISO, Metering mode, and much more. Here's a road map for the information you'll find on the LCD panel:

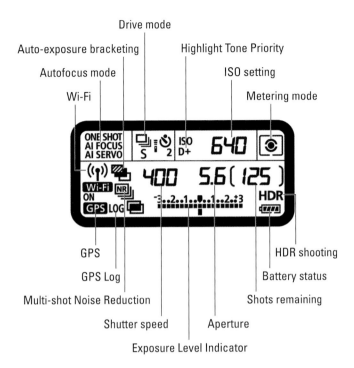

Figure 1-4: You find lots of useful information on the LCD panel.

- ✔ **Autofocus mode:** Displays M Focus when you choose to focus the lens manually.

- ✔ **Drive mode:** Displays the icon for the currently selected Drive mode (see Chapter 7).

- ✔ **Highlight Tone Priority:** Displays the D+ icon when you've enabled Highlight Tone Priority.

- ✔ **ISO speed setting:** The currently selected ISO speed setting displays here. You can also use this information when setting the ISO speed (see Chapter 2).

- ✔ **Metering mode:** Displays the icon for the metering mode you're currently using.

- ✔ **Wi-Fi mode:** This spot shows whether you have Wi-Fi on or off. It also displays signal strength, when connected to a wireless server.

- ✔ **GPS:** This spot on the panel shows whether you have GPS enabled.

- ✔ **Log:** This spot on the panel shows whether or not you are logging GPS locations for each image and creating a virtual map of the locations you've visited.

✔ **AEB:** This icon displays when you enable auto-exposure bracketing (see Chapter 7).

✔ **Multi-shot Noise Reduction:** This spot on the panel shows when you have multi-shot noise reduction enabled.

✔ **Multiple Exposure Shooting:** This spot on the panel shows when you have multiple exposure shooting enabled.

✔ **Shutter speed:** Displays the shutter speed, as metered by the camera or set by you, that will be used to shoot the next picture. If you're taking pictures with Shutter Priority mode or Manual mode (see Chapter 7), you can use the LCD panel to set the shutter speed.

✔ **Aperture:** Displays the f-stop that will be used to take the next picture. You can use this information to change the aperture when shooting in Manual mode or Aperture Priority mode (see Chapter 7).

✔ **Shots remaining/Self-timer countdown:** This spot on the panel does double duty. When you're using the self-timer, the time remaining until the picture is taken displays here. Otherwise, the display shows the number of shots remaining that you can fit on the SD (Secure Digital) card you insert in the camera to capture your images. An SD card is the digital equivalent of reusable film. But you probably already know that, don't you?

✔ **Exposure Level Indicator:** This tool indicates whether exposure compensation or auto-exposure bracketing has been enabled; it is also used to set flash compensation and when you manually set the shutter speed and aperture when shooting in M (Manual) mode. (See Chapter 6 for more on auto-exposure bracketing and see Chapter 7 for flash compensation.)

✔ **HDR:** This icon is displayed when you're capturing images in HDR mode.

✔ **Battery status:** This icon displays the amount of charge remaining in the battery. You can also get detailed information on the camera battery from the camera menu as I discuss in Chapter 7.

You see examples of different scenarios on the LCD panel throughout this book as I discuss various picture-taking situations.

Peering into the Viewfinder

The viewfinder, or *information central* as I like to call it, is another place you find a plethora of information. In the viewfinder, you see the image as it will be captured by your camera (see Figure 1-5). Use the viewfinder to compose your picture and view camera settings while you change them. Figure 1-5 shows all the possible icons that can be displayed while taking a picture and displays all the autofocus points. You never see this much information displayed while taking a picture. (I show you different viewfinder scenarios when I discuss different picture-taking scenarios throughout the book.) When you peer into the viewfinder, you find the current shooting settings, icons for battery status, shots remaining, and much more. Here's the info displayed (from left to right) in your viewfinder:

✔ **Warning symbol:** This icon appears when the Monochrome picture style is enabled or when White Balance has been modified or bracketed, but will not be displayed if you've changed from AWB (Automatic White Balance) to one of the presets such as Cloudy. The warning symbol is your warning to change your settings after you've taken all of the black and white photos you want to take, or you're finished capturing images that require white balance modification.

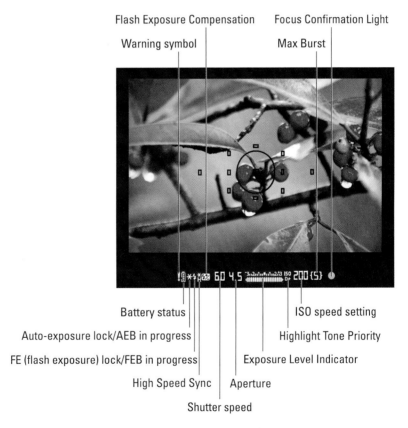

Figure 1-5: Lots of useful information is in the viewfinder.

You can modify Custom Function C.FnIII-4 to also display the warning icon when you've enabled ISO expansion, or when you've enabled spot metering. For more information on Custom Functions, see Chapter 6.

✔ **Battery status:** This icon shows you the amount of charge left in your battery.

✔ **AE lock/AEB in progress:** This icon indicates that you've locked the auto-exposure to a specific point in the frame or that auto-exposure bracketing is being performed (see Chapter 6).

✔ **Flash ready:** This icon indicates that the flash has recycled to full power and is ready for use (see Chapter 7).

✔ **FE (flash exposure) lock/FEB in progress:** This icon indicates that you've locked the flash exposure to a specific point in the frame or that flash exposure bracketing is being performed (see Chapter 6).

✔ **High-speed sync:** This icon indicates that you've changed the Flash mode to high speed sync (see Chapter 7).

✔ **Flash Exposure Compensation:** This icon indicates that you've employed Flash Exposure Compensation (see Chapter 7).

✔ **Shutter speed:** Displays the shutter speed that will be used to take the next picture. You can also use this information to manually set the shutter speed when shooting in Shutter Priority mode or Manual mode (see Chapter 6).

✔ **Aperture:** Displays the f-stop that will be used to take the next picture. You can use this information to manually set the aperture when shooting in Aperture Priority mode or Manual mode (see Chapter 6).

✔ **Exposure Level Indicator:** This tool indicates whether exposure compensation or auto-exposure bracketing has been enabled; it is also used to set flash compensation and when you manually set the shutter speed and aperture when shooting in M (Manual) mode. (See Chapter 6 for more on auto-exposure bracketing and see Chapter 7 for flash compensation.)

✔ **Highlight Tone Priority:** This icon displays when you enable Highlight Tone Priority (see Chapter 6).

✔ **ISO speed setting:** This icon shows the currently selected ISO speed setting. You can also use this information when setting the ISO speed (see Chapter 7).

✔ **Max burst:** Shows the maximum number of shots you can take when shooting in Continuous mode. If fewer shots are remaining on the card than the maximum burst, the shots remaining display.

✔ **Focus confirmation light:** Lights when you achieve focus.

About the Multi-Controller and Multi-function Lock

On the back of your camera to the lower right of the LCD monitor is one button surrounded by two rings. The Set button is used to confirm a menu command that you navigate to with the Multi-controller and the Quick Control Dial. The Multi-controller is the ring with eight arrows nestled around the Set button. The Multi-controller is used to navigate to menu commands, and to navigate within an image when you use the Index/Magnify/Reduce button to zoom in on an image. When you are navigating an image that you've magnified, you can use all of the arrows to precisely navigate to the desired spot within the image. When you are navigating to a menu, or menu command you can only use the top and bottom arrows to navigate vertically to a menu item, or the left and right middle arrows to navigate horizontally to a menu item.

When I refer to the Multi-controller in conjunction with the menu, I tell you to use the control to navigate to the menu item. When you see the menu, you'll instinctively know which part of the controller to press to get to where you need to go. Think Joy Stick and you've got the Multi-controller nailed. In some instances, you can use the Multi-controller or the Quick Control dial to navigate to a menu item. When you have that option, I mention both controls. Like anything else in your life, when you have a choice, use the one that is most comfortable to you.

To the right of the Set button is a Multi-function Lock Switch. This switch is used to lock the Quick Control dial to avoid inadvertently changing settings when taking pictures. Slide the switch to the right to lock the Quick Control dial. Slide the switch to the left to release the lock and return functionality to the Quick Control dial.

You can also use the switch to lock the Main Dial and Multi-controller by navigating to the Custom Function C.FnIII-3. For more information on Custom Functions, see Chapter 6.

Exploring Camera Connections

On the right side of the camera, you find two flaps that can be lifted. The flaps are weather-resistant to protect the connections under the flaps. Under the flaps you find a plethora of connections. This is where you connect various sundry connectors to your camera as shown in Figure 1-6. You have the following connections available on your camera:

- ✓ **Remote Control:** Connect an N3 type remote control device to this port and you can trigger the shutter remotely. Canon also makes an N3 type interval timer that you can connect to this port to create time-lapse images.

✔ **Microphone port:** Connect an external microphone to this port to capture audio with your video. When you connect a microphone to this port, the onboard microphone is disabled. This port will capture stereo sound from a stereo microphone.

✔ **A/V Out / Digital:** Connect an A/V out cord to this port to view video on a TV set that does not have an HDMI port. The AV out cord supplied with the camera has three color coded connectors that plug into color coded ports on your TV for video plus left and right channel audio. Connect the cord with the Digital Out plug to a male USB port on a printer and you can print directly from the camera to your printer. This port can also be used to download images and movies directly from your camera to computer using the EOS Utilities.

✔ **HDMI Out:** Connect an HDMI cable from this port to an HDMI cable on your TV to watch high-definition video on your TV that you captured on your camera.

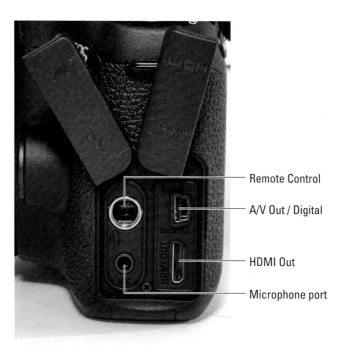

Remote Control

A/V Out / Digital

HDMI Out

Microphone port

Figure 1-6: Ports just looking to be plugged.

Modifying Basic Camera Settings

Your camera ships with default settings for the country in which the camera was purchased. You also have default settings for the amount of time it takes the camera to power off when no picture taking or menu activity has occurred. You can modify these settings to suit your taste, as I show you in the upcoming sections.

Adjusting the date and time

Adjusting your camera to the current date and time is important because your camera records the date and time of every picture you take. Note that the time is based on a 24-hour military clock. To set the date and time:

1. **Press the Menu button.**

   The previously used menu appears on the LCD monitor.

2. **Use the Multi-controller to navigate to the Camera Settings 2 tab (shown at the left of Figure 1-7).**

   The menu with the date and time options is displayed on your LCD monitor.

3. **Use the Multi-controller or Quick Control dial to highlight Date/Time/ Zone and then press the Set button.**

   The Date/Time/Zone dialog box is displayed and the month is selected (shown at the right of Figure 1-7).

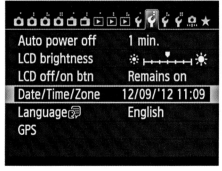
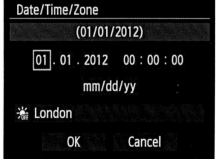

Figure 1-7: Adjusting the date and time.

4. **Press Set.**

   An up and down arrow appears above the current setting.

5. **Use the Multi-controller to set the month and then press Set.**

   The change is applied and the up and down arrows disappear.

6. **Use the Multi-controller to navigate to the date setting and then repeat Steps 4 and 5 to set the date.**

7. **Continue setting the year, hour, minute and second in the same manner as you set the month and date.**

8. **Use the Multi-controller to navigate to the box that shows the default manner in which the date is displayed.**

   The default setting is mm/dd/yy. You can, however, press Set to display an up and down arrow. Use the Multi-controller to highlight the method you prefer for the date and time to be displayed, and then press Set to apply the changes.

9. **Use the Multi-controller to navigate to the Daylight Savings option box.**

   Daylight Savings Time changes are disabled by default. If the time zone in which you live observes Daylight Savings Time, press set to display and up and down arrow, and then use the Multi-controller to select the Daylight Savings Time option (an icon that looks like the sun).

10. **Use the Multi-controller to select the Time Zone box.**

    The default time zone when the camera ships is London.

11. **Press Set to display an up and down area around the Time Zone Box, and then use the Multi-controller to select the applicable time zone.**

    The time zones are listed as cities.

12. **Highlight the city that is in your time zone and then press Set.**

    Review the settings to make sure you've got everything correct. If you goofed on a setting, you can use the Multi-controller to navigate to the setting and change it.

13. **Use the Multi-controller to highlight OK and then press Set.**

    The time changes are applied. Figure 1-8 shows the settings for your friendly author's EOS 6D.

If you photograph events with another photographer, make sure the time and dates are the same on both cameras. When you combine images from the photo shoot and edit them, you'll be able to accurately sort them by time and date.

Modifying the Auto Power Off time

Your camera powers off automatically after one minute of non-operation. You can specify a period of time from 1 minute to 30 minutes for auto power off, or you can disable the feature. However, your camera will automatically power off after 30 minutes of non-activity even if you choose to disable this feature. If you choose a power-off time that's a short duration, you'll conserve your battery. After your camera powers off, press the shutter button and the camera powers on again. To change the power-off time:

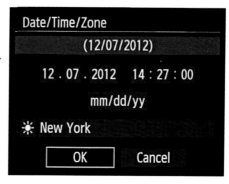

Figure 1-8: Time has come today.

1. **Press the Menu button.**

   The previously used menu appears on the LCD monitor.

2. **Press the Multi-controller button to navigate to the Camera Settings 2 tab (see the left image in Figure 1-9).**

3. **Use the Quick Control dial to highlight Auto Power Off (see the right image in Figure 1-9) and then press the Set button.**

   The Auto Power Off options display (see the right image in Figure 1-9).

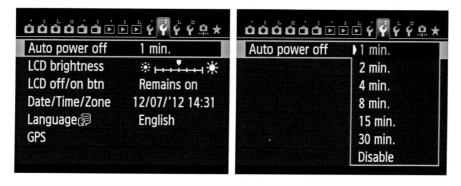

Figure 1-9: Changing the power-off time.

4. **Use the Quick Control dial to highlight the desired setting and then press Set.**

   The change is applied.

I recommend that you choose the shortest duration for auto-power that you're comfortable with. This helps conserve battery power. As long as the power button is in the On position, your camera wakes almost instantaneously when you press the shutter button halfway.

To restore the camera to its default settings, press the Menu button, and then use the Multi-controller to navigate to the Camera Settings 3 tab, choose Clear All Camera Settings, and press Set.

Adjusting the Viewfinder for Maximum Clarity

If you wear glasses, or your vision's not perfect, you can adjust the viewfinder clarity, which makes it easier to compose your images and focus manually. After all, if what you see in the viewfinder isn't what you get, you won't be a happy camper. To adjust viewfinder clarity:

1. **Attach a lens to the camera.**

2. **Look into the viewfinder and turn the dioptric adjuster knob (see Figure 1-10) left or right until the autofocus points look sharp and clear.**

   If the knob is hard to turn, remove the eyepiece cup.

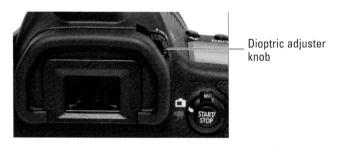

Dioptric adjuster knob

Figure 1-10: I can see clearly now . . .

Introducing Wireless and GPS

Canon has introduced new features not currently available on other cameras in this price range. The Wireless feature enables you to download images from your camera to your computer over a Wi-Fi network. You can also use this feature to send pictures to other Canon cameras with this feature, upload pictures to your smart phone with the Apple iOS 5.0 or later, and the Android OS 2.33 or later. There is also a Remote app available for the iPhone and Android which enables you to wirelessly control your camera from your phone.

The GPS (Global Positioning System) feature gives you the option of embedding the GPS coordinates of the location where you photograph an image as image metadata. This metadata can be used in applications like Abode Photoshop Lightroom 4 or Apple Aperture 3. In Adobe Photoshop Lightroom's Map module, images in your Library that have GPS data can be precisely positioned on the world map. The GPS feature also makes it possible for you to create a log of all the places where you photographed images.

If you're not using the Wireless or GPS feature, disable them to conserve battery life.

Attaching a Lens

The beauty of a digital SLR is that you can attach lenses with different focal lengths to achieve different effects. Your EOS 6D accepts a wide range of lenses from super wide-angle lenses that capture a wide view angle, to long telephoto lenses that capture a narrow view angle and let you fill the frame with objects that are far away. Your camera can only use EF lenses. If you've recently graduated from a cropped frame sensor camera and have a camera bag full of EF-S lenses, put them up for sale on eBay; they will not work with your new toy. To attach a lens to your camera:

1. **Remove the body cap from the camera.**

   Twist the cap counterclockwise to remove it. Alternatively, you'll remove the lens currently on the camera with the steps I outline in the upcoming "Removing a Lens" section.

2. **Remove the rear cap from the lens you're attaching to the camera.**

   Twist the cap clockwise to remove it.

3. **Align the dot on the lens with the mounting dot on the camera body (see Figure 1-11).**

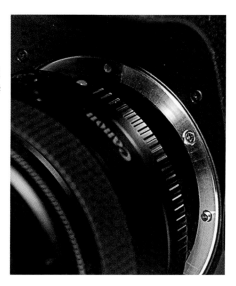

Figure 1-11: Aligning the lens.

Align the red dot on your lens with the red dot on the camera body.

4. **Twist the lens clockwise until it locks into place.**

Don't force the lens. If the lens doesn't lock into place with a gentle twist, you may not have aligned it properly.

Removing a Lens

When you want to use a different lens or store the camera body, remove the lens. Removing a lens and attaching another lens can be a bit of a juggling act. To remove a lens from your camera:

1. **Power off the camera.**

Never change lenses with the power on, because the charge of electricity can turn your sensor into a dust magnet.

2. **Press the Lens-Release button.**

This button unlocks the lens from the camera.

3. **Twist the lens counterclockwise until it stops and then gently pull the lens out of the body.**

4. **Quickly attach another lens to the camera.**

When you remove a lens, the inside of your camera is exposed to the elements. Dust can adhere to the sensor.

To minimize the chance of dust getting on your sensor, always turn off the camera when changing lenses. If you leave the power on, the sensor has a slight charge, which can attract dust floating in the air. Do not change lenses in a dusty environment, as dust may inadvertently blow into your camera. I also find it's a good idea to point the camera body down when changing lenses. Dust on the sensor shows up as little black specks on your images, which is not a good thing.

Never store that camera without the lens or body cap attached, because pollutants may accidentally get into the camera, harming the delicate mechanical parts, and possibly fouling the sensor.

Using Image Stabilization Lenses

Many Canon and third-party lenses that fit your camera offer *image stabilization* — a feature that enables you to shoot at a slower shutter speed than you'd normally be able to use and still get a blur-free image. The actual number of stops you can gain depends on how steady you are when handling the camera. To enable image stabilization:

1. **Locate the Stabilizer switch on the side of your lens.**

   On Canon lenses, you'll find the switch on the left side of the lens when the camera is pointed toward your subject (see Figure 1-12). If you're using a third-party lens, look for a switch the reads IS, or refer to the lens manual.

2. **Push the Stabilizer switch to On to enable image stabilization.**

   Image stabilization uses the camera battery to compensate for operator movement. Therefore, a good idea is to shut off this feature when you need to conserve battery power and don't need image stabilization. Note that some lenses have two image stabilization switches. The second switch changes between stabilizer modes. Mode 1 stabilizes the lens in a horizontal and vertical plane, and Mode 2 and Mode 3 (on super-telephotos) stabilize the lens when you pan to follow a moving object.

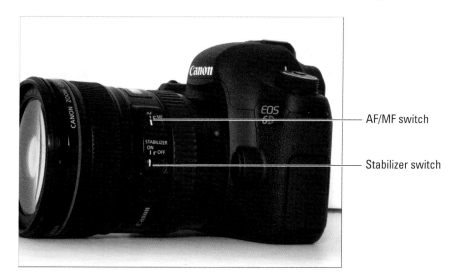

AF/MF switch

Stabilizer switch

Figure 1-12: Slide the Stabilizer switch to enable image stabilization.

When you take pictures with your camera mounted on a tripod, disable image stabilization. If you don't disable this feature, you may get a less-than-crystal-clear shot because the lens is trying to stabilize motion that is not present (the tripod stabilizes the camera).

Using a Zoom Lens

If you purchased your EOS 6D as a kit, the included lens is probably a 24-105 f/4.0 L series zoom lens. You can purchase additional Canon or third-party zoom lenses from your favorite camera supplier. Zoom lenses come in two flavors: twist to zoom, or push/pull to zoom in or out, respectively.

To use a zoom lens with a barrel that twists to change focal length:

1. **Grasp the lens barrel with your fingers.**

2. **Twist the barrel to zoom in or out.**

To use a push/pull zoom lens:

1. **Grasp the lens barrel with your fingers.**

2. **Push the barrel away from the camera to zoom in; pull the barrel toward the camera to zoom out.**

Working with SD Cards

Your camera uses SD (Secure Digital) cards to store the pictures you take. An *SD Card* is an electrical device similar to a flash drive. You insert a new SD card when you begin shooting and remove the card when it's full.

To insert an SD card:

1. **Open the SD card cover on the right side of the camera as you look from the back.**

   To open the cover, slide it away from the camera until it stops and then rotate it away from the camera.

2. **Insert the card in the slot.**

   As shown in Figure 1-13, the card label is facing you and the end with the contacts is facing the camera slot.

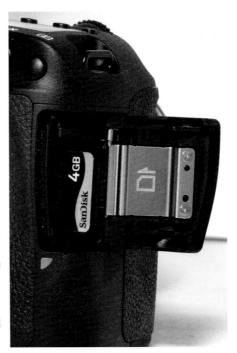

Figure 1-13: Inserting a SD card.

3. Gently push the card into the slot.

Never force a card because you may damage the contacts in the camera and the card. The card slides easily into the camera when aligned properly.

4. Close the SD card cover.

You're ready to shoot up a storm.

When an SD card is full, remove it from the camera and insert a new one. To remove an SD Card:

1. Turn the camera power switch to Off.

2. Open the SD card cover.

To open the cover, slide it away from the camera until it stops and then rotate it away from the camera.

3. Gently push the card in, then let go to eject it.

The SD card pops loose from the card mechanism.

4. Gently pull the SD card from the slot.

You're now ready to insert a new SD card and start shooting.

You may be tempted to pick up a 32GB or 64GB card, thinking you can store a gazillion images on one card and not worry about running out of room. But memory cards are electrical devices that are subject to failure — and will fail when you least expect it. If a large card fails, you lose lots of images. I carry a couple 16GB SD cards in my camera bag. Although I hate to lose any images, I'd rather lose 16GB worth of images than 32 or 64 GB. I advise you to purchase smaller memory cards.

It bears repeating: A memory card is a mechanical device that will fail when you least expect. If the worst happens, and your computer cannot read a card, you can purchase a data recovery program to retrieve the data from the card. Data recovery programs also work if you accidentally erase the card before downloading the images to your computer. A program called Card Recovery, which works with Windows applications, retails for $39.99 (www.cardrecovery.com), or you can purchase Card Rescue for the Mac, which retails for $39.99 (www.cardrescue.com). Both applications offer trial versions, which you can use to scan a corrupted card to see if there is data that can be recovered. After you perform a preview scan, you can purchase the applicable application for your operating system to recover the data.

Formatting an SD Card

After you download images to your computer and back them up (see Chapter 8), it's a good idea to format your cards before using them again, even if you didn't fill them. Doing this ensures you'll have a full card to work with and won't download duplicate images when you download them to your computer. To format an SD card:

1. **Insert the card into the camera, as I outline in the preceding section.**

2. **Press the Menu button.**

   The last used camera menu displays on the LCD monitor.

3. **Press the Multi-controller to navigate to the Camera Settings 1 tab.**

4. **Use the Multi-controller or the Quick Control dial to highlight Format.**

   The Format Card option is selected (see the left image in Figure 1-14).

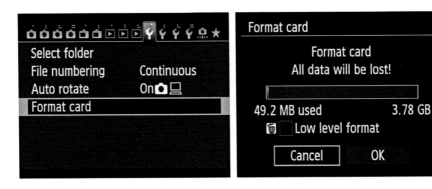

Figure 1-14: Formatting a card.

5. **Press the Set button.**

   The menu changes to show the amount of data on the card and displays a warning that all data will be lost (see the right image in Figure 1-14).

6. **Rotate the Quick Control dial to highlight OK and press Set.**

   The card is formatted. After formatting, you have a blank card that's ready to capture images from the camera.

There is also an option called a Low-Level format, which totally erases all data on the card and resets it to its default condition. To enable Low-Level format, press the Erase button that looks like a garbage can to enable the feature and then perform Step 6. It's a good idea to do a Low-Level format every now and again to restore your cards to an almost-new condition.

The only way you can restore images from a card that's been formatted is with a data recovery program. Make sure you've downloaded all images to your computer before you format a card.

7. **Press the shutter button halfway to exit the menu and resume taking pictures.**

About Your Camera Battery

The LP-E6 battery in your EOS 6D is a rechargeable lithium-ion battery that is engineered for a long life and enables you to capture about 1000 images when you use the camera in warm weather. When you photograph in colder climates, the amount of images you can capture decreases. Here are some recommendations for getting the best performance from your camera battery:

Here are a few recommendations for camera batteries:

- **After you charge a battery, replace the cover so you can see blue through the battery icon.** This signifies that you have a fully charged battery under the cover, useful information if you own more than one battery.

- **Remove the battery from the camera after you've finished shooting for the day.** The battery loses a bit of its charge if you store it in the camera.

- **When replacing the cover over a partially used or fully discharged battery, place the cover so that the blue does not show through the battery icon.** This is your indication that the battery is partially discharged.

- **In cold conditions, place the spare battery in your coat pocket.** This keeps it warm and extends the life of the battery charge.

- **Replace the battery immediately when you see the low battery warning.** If you deplete the power completely when your camera is writing data to the memory card, the card may be corrupted.

- **Never remove the battery when the data access light is blinking.** This indicates your camera is writing data to the card. Removing the battery prematurely can damage the memory card and cause loss of data.

- **Beware of third-party batteries that fit your EOS 6D.** They may not be compatible with your camera's battery information system, which means you won't know how much charge remains in the battery. If the battery runs out of charge while the camera is writing data to the memory card, you may damage the memory card, the battery, or both. Batteries that don't work with your camera typically come with their own charging units.

Charging Your Camera Battery

When you notice the battery-status icon is blinking, it's time to charge the battery. Charge the battery using the charger supplied with the camera. To recharge the battery, follow these steps:

1. **Plug the battery charger into a wall outlet.**

   You can use the battery charger in foreign countries as well as the United States. The battery charger works with 110 and 240 volt AC 50/60 Hz power sources.

2. **Insert the battery (see Figure 1-15).**

   After you insert the battery, three lights may flash. This indicates the battery has less than 25 percent of a full charge.

3. **Continue charging the battery until the light is green.**

   The battery has a 100 percent charge.

4. **Leave the battery in the charger for another hour to top off the battery.**

   Do not leave the battery in the charger and connected to a power outlet for more than two hours after the battery achieves a full charge, because you may damage the battery if you do.

5. **Replace the protective cover over the battery (see Figure 1-16).**

When you purchase your camera, the battery is not fully charged. Run your battery through one recharge cycle before using the camera.

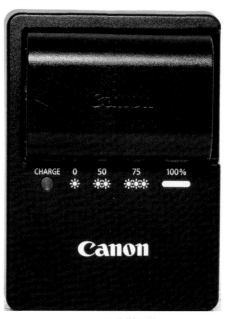

Figure 1-15: Charging the battery.

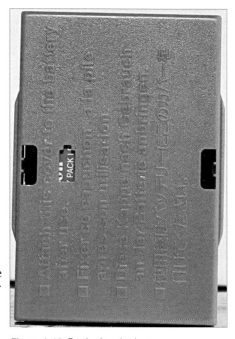

Figure 1-16: Replacing the battery cover.

About Sensor Cleaning

When you power off your Canon EOS 6D, the sensor is automatically cleaned (see Figure 1-17). The camera accomplishes this by jiggling the sensor to dislodge any dust particles. This works well, but sometimes stubborn particles of dust don't fall off the sensor with the automatic cleaning. You can, however, manually clean your sensor as outlined in the next section.

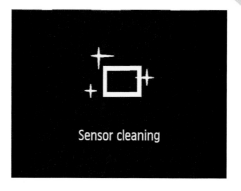

Figure 1-17: Shake it up baby, now. Shake it up baby. Clean me off.

Cleaning your sensor on command

If you notice black specks in areas of your image that are one solid color, such as the sky, you have dust on your sensor. Your camera will automatically clean the sensor as outlined in the previous section. However, sometimes that's not enough. If you consistently see dust spots in the same area on several images, you'll be happy to know there's a menu command you can use to clean your sensor, whenever you feel the need, by following these steps:

1. **Press the camera Menu button.**

   The camera menu is displayed on the LCD monitor.

2. **Use the Multi-controller to navigate to Camera Settings 4 tab (see the left image in Figure 1-18).**

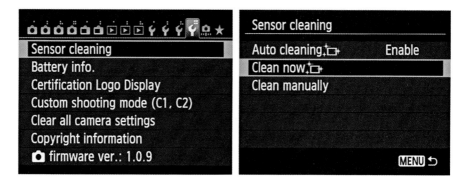

Figure 1-18: Cleaning the camera sensor.

3. **Use the Quick Control dial or Multi-controller to highlight Sensor Cleaning and then press Set.**

   The Sensor Cleaning options are displayed as shown in the right image in Figure 1-18.

4. **Use the Multi-controller or Quick Control dial to highlight Clean Now, and then press Set.**

5. **A dialog box appears, asking you whether you want to clean your sensor now.**

   OK is selected by default.

6. **Press Set.**

   Your camera performs a sensor cleaning cycle.

After using the Clean Now menu command, put a lens on your camera, manually set the focus to the closest distance at which the lens will focus, and then take a picture of the clear blue sky. Open the image in your image-editing program and zoom in to 100-percent magnification. Sensor dust shows as dark spots. If you have stubborn specks of sensor dust on your camera, run the Clean Now menu command a couple of times. If the dust is still there, you can manually clean the sensor (as outlined in the next section).

Manually Cleaning Your Sensor

Your camera has a self-cleaning sensor, and you can run a cleaning cycle whenever you want; however, you may inadvertently get a stubborn piece of dust that develops a magnetic attraction to your sensor and needs to be cleaned manually. To determine whether you have dust on your sensor, follow these steps:

1. **Switch to Av (Aperture Priority) mode and choose your smallest aperture.**

   For further information on using Aperture Priority mode and manually setting your aperture, see Chapter 6.

2. **Switch the lens to manual focus and rack the focus to its nearest point.**

   That's right, you want the sky to be out of focus. That way the dust specks will show up as black dots.

3. **Take a picture of a clear blue sky, download the picture to your computer, and review it in your image-editing program at 100 percent magnification.**

   If you see black specks in the image, you have dust on your sensor.

The best way to clean dust off your sensor is to blow it off with a powerful bulb blower. Several blowers are on the market with generic names like Hurricane or Rocket. The Giottos Rocket Blaster is shown in Figure 1-19. A good blower is made of natural rubber and features a small opening at the tip that enables you to direct a strong current of air with pinpoint accuracy.

To clean the sensor manually:

1. **Switch to one of the Creative Zone modes and then take the lens off the camera.**

   The option to clean manually is not available in the Basic Zones.

2. **Press the camera Menu button.**

   The camera menu is displayed on the LCD monitor.

3. **Use the Multi-controller to navigate to Camera Settings 4 tab (see the left image in Figure 1-20).**

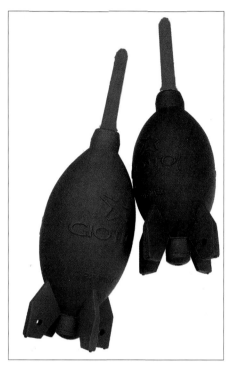

Figure 1-19: Use a bulb blower to clean your camera sensor.

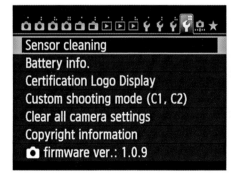
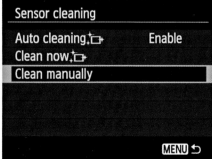

Figure 1-20: I'm gonna get this sensor squeaky clean.

4. **Use the Multi-controller or Quick Control dial to highlight Sensor Cleaning and then press Set.**

   The Sensor Cleaning options are displayed as shown in the right image in Figure 1-20.

5. **Use the Multi-controller or Quick Control dial to highlight Clean Manually, and then press Set.**

   The camera mirror opens and you have access to the camera sensor.

6. **Point the camera at the ground and place the air blower inside the sensor chamber being careful not to touch the sensor.**

   When you point the camera at the ground, any dust you dislodge off the sensor falls to the ground. Gravity works.

7. **Squeeze the bulb repeatedly.**

8. **When you've finished blowing dust off the sensor, power off the camera.**

   When you flip the camera switch to off, the mirror closes. Make sure you put a lens on the camera or a body cap on the camera immediately. After thoroughly cleaning the sensor, you don't want dust getting back in the chamber.

Never touch the sensor with the blower. Never use a blower with a CO_2 cartridge. CO_2 cartridges contain propellants that can foul your sensor.

Keeping your sensor clean

The best way to keep your sensor clean is to never change a lens. However, this defeats the purpose of a digital SLR. But if you are meticulous about changing lenses, and follow a bit of sage advice, you'll keep your sensor as squeaky-clean as possible. I first learned about sensor dust when I owned my first digital SLR, the Canon EOS 10D. I was on a business trip/vacation to California. When I was reviewing some images of the Golden Gate Bridge, I noticed some horrible dust specks on the image. Since then I've learned that doing the following minimizes the chances of dust adhering to the sensor:

- **Power off the camera before changing lenses.** If you leave the power on, the sensor maintains a charge that can attract dust.

- **Never change lenses in a dusty environment.** If you're photographing in a dry, dusty environment, find a sheltered area in which to change lenses. When all else fails, the inside of your car is a better place to change lenses than in a dry, dusty area.

- **Never change lenses when it's windy.** In windy conditions, find a sheltered environment in which to change lenses.

Using sensor cleaning equipment

If you're a DIY (do-it-yourself) kind of photographer, you may want to consider cleaning your sensor with commercially available products. Lots of products — brushes, swabs, and chemicals — that you use to manually clean the camera sensor are on the market. Yes, that does mean you physically touch the sensor with a product. Therefore the product you choose needs to be made from material that can't scratch the camera sensor. You must also have a very steady hand when using these products.

I've used sensor-cleaning products manufactured by VisibleDust (www.visibledust. com). VisibleDust manufactures a lighted sensor loupe that you place over the lens opening to examine the sensor for any visible dust — hence, the company name. The loupe is made of glass and makes it easy to see any specs of dust on your lens. VisibleDust also manufactures an Arctic Butterfly brush, which runs on two AAA batteries. To use this brush:

1. **Push a button to spin the brush.**

   This gives the brush a static electricity charge.

2. **Brush the sensor once with the charged brush.**

   Dust particles are attracted to the brush.

3. **Remove the brush from the camera body and then press the button to spin the brush again.**

This discharges the particles into the air.

4. **Use the brush as needed to remove any dust that may have accumulated on the sensor.**

I've used both products with a good outcome on my cameras. For more information, visit www.visibledust.com or ask your favorite camera retailer for information about these products.

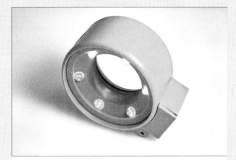

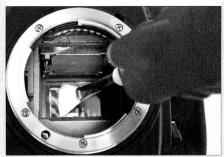

✔ **Point the camera down when changing lenses.** This minimizes the chances of dust blowing into the sensor.

✔ **Have the other lens ready.** When I change lenses, it's a juggling act. I keep the lens I'm going to put on the camera in one hand with the rear cap off. I point the camera at the ground and grasp the lens I'm going to remove with one hand, and press the lens release button with a finger from the other hand. I then quickly remove one lens and replace it with the other. With practice, you can do this quickly and minimize the chance of dust fouling your sensor.

The sensor chamber of your camera is lubricated. Sometimes lubricant can get on the sensor and cause a spot to appear on your images. If conventional methods of cleaning the sensor don't work, send the camera to Canon for sensor cleaning, or to a local camera shop that offers this service.

Accessorizing Your EOS 6D

Your EOS 6D is a mechanical and technological masterpiece. But the camera comes with a nice cardboard box, which is great for shipping the camera, but not so great for storing the camera on a day-to-day basis. And the camera ships with this nice strap that tells the world you're shooting with a Canon EOS camera, but the strap is thin — and with a long telephoto lens, it will feel like you're carrying a brick on your neck. So, first and foremost, you need a decent camera case and you need a good strap. There are lots of other goodies you can invest in that will make using your camera more enjoyable.

Useful Canon accessories

Canon sells lots of goodies in their online store that may also be available from other sources such as your local camera retailer or your favorite online camera store. Here are a couple of items you may consider purchasing:

- **Extra LP-E6 battery pack:** If you shoot lots of pictures, having an extra fully-charged battery in your camera bag can save the day.

- **Car Battery Charger CBE-E6:** If you do a lot of remote shooting from your car, this accessory enables you to charge your camera battery from the car's 12 volt outlet, which was formerly known as the receptacle for the cigarette lighter.

- **BGE 13 Battery Grip:** This accessory is attached to the bottom of your camera and extends your shooting time. The battery grip houses one or two LP-E6 batteries and six AA batteries. The grip also features a variety of operating controls such as shutter button, Main Dial, AF point selection button, AE lock/FE lock button, AF start button, multi-controller, and multi-function button. This is the ideal accessory if you're a high-volume shooter.

- **LC-5 Wireless Controller:** This accessory enables you to trigger the shutter of your EOS 6D wirelessly.

- **Dedicated Canon Flash:** Your EOS 6D does not have an onboard pop-up flash unit. Canon, however, makes several flash units that are compatible with your camera. The beauty of using a dedicated flash is that the camera communicates with the flash unit. The following flash units will work with your EOS 6D: 240EX, 430EXII and 600 EX. I discuss flash photography with your EOS 6D in Chapter 6.

- **RS-80N remote switch:** This accessory plugs into the side of your EOS 6D and enables you to trigger the shutter by pushing a button. This accessory is ideal if you use your camera on a tripod. If you press the camera shutter button, vibration is transmitted to the camera, which may cause the image to be less than sharp. The remote switch prevents the vibration.

- **TC-80N3 timer remote controller:** This accessory also plugs into the side of your EOS 6D. You use it to trigger the camera remotely, but you can also program this accessory to capture multiple images over a period of time. You determine the amount of time between images. With the camera mounted on a tripod, you can create time-lapse photographs of an object or area and record the climate change, cloud movement, and such. You bring the captured images into a program like Photoshop and create a time-lapse movie.

Useful 3rd party accessories

Canon makes great accessories for your camera, but there are other accessories you need, such as tripods, camera cases, camera bags, and so on. Canon does offer some of these accessories, but your friendly author has been at this photography game for some time and offers the following list for you to consider:

- **Camera strap:** This is the first item I suggest you replace. In fact, I suggest you don't even use the strap that came with the camera. Leave it in pristine condition in its little plastic snuggie. Then, if you ever decide to sell the camera on eBay, you can offer it with an unused camera strap. I suggest you purchase a sling strap such as those offered by CarrySpeed (www.carryspeed.com) or Black Rapid (www.blackrapid.com). A sling strap distributes the weight of the camera and lens over your shoulder and places the camera at your hip. When you need to use your camera, you can quickly grab it from your side and bring it to your eye. The CarrySpeed strap features a mounting system that does not let the strap touch the camera, which could possibly mar the finish. Another great thing about the CarrySpeed strap is the actual strap; it's wide and has a neoprene backing which holds the strap in place. A sling strap comfortably distributes the weight of the camera and lens. If you shoot for long periods of time and with long lenses, a comfortable camera strap is a must-have accessory.

- **Camera case:** If you end up purchasing lots of accessories for your camera (such as additional lenses, additional batteries, and so on), you'll need a place for your stuff. A hard-shell camera case is the ideal place to store your gear when you're not using it. Pelican (www.pelicancase.com), makes a wide variety of cases that you can customize to fit your gear. Nanuk (www.nanukcase.com) also sells a line of customizable hard-shell cases. I own both and can vouch for the fact that they are quality products.

✔ **Camera bag:** A camera bag is a place to put your stuff when you're out on a photo shoot. If you don't own a lot of gear, you can get by with a small camera bag. However, if you do end up owning a lot of gear, plus the obligatory kitchen sink, you'll need a bag that can hold lots of stuff, or perhaps two bags: one that will hold most of your gear and accessories, and a smaller bag to use when you're going commando (shooting with just your camera, one or two lenses, and a minimum of accessories). My favorite bags are the Speed Freak (the top of Figure 1-21) and ChangeUp (the bottom of Figure 1-21), both made by Think Tank Photo (www.think tankphoto.com). The bags are made of durable material, have bullet-proof zippers, and lots of hidey holes for your accessories.

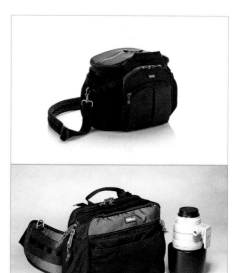

Figure 1-21: A comfortable camera bag is a must for any serious photographer.

LowePro (www.lowepro.com), also makes a good camera bag. A rain hood is another good option to look for when purchasing a camera bag. Rain and digital equipment are like oil and water; they don't mix.

✔ **Tripod:** If you shoot landscapes, HDR (High Dynamic Range), or shoot in low light, a tripod is a useful accessory. A tripod steadies your camera when you shoot at low shutter speeds. When you shoot with a tripod, it's advisable to have a remote-control device to trigger the shutter (as mentioned in the previous section). When you purchase a tripod, buy a device that will support the weight of your camera body, plus the heaviest lens you anticipate purchasing or using. Add fifty percent to that figure. If you purchase a tripod that will only handle the weight of your camera and its heaviest lens, you'll run into an issue known as *tripod creep*. This is when the tripod slowly sinks. You also need a sturdy tripod when photographing in windy conditions. Most tripods have a hook underneath the tripod head to which you can attach a sand bag, which helps steady the tripod in windy conditions. You also have to consider the weight of the tripod. If you use your car as a base of operations, or photograph in studio conditions, tripod weight is not that much of a factor. However, if you photograph wildlife and nature and do a lot of hiking, lugging a heavy tripod will quickly wear you out. If this is the case, consider purchasing an aluminum or carbon-fiber tripod. I purchased a carbon-fiber tripod as a gift for my wife and she loves it. The tripod will support her camera plus a 400 mm lens. The light weight makes it possible for her to hike several miles with the tripod and a camera bag in absolute comfort. Another useful option for a tripod is a built-in spirit level. Even though your camera has a built in dual-axis level, sometimes it's easier to take a quick look at the tripod. A good tripod head is also a must. If you can afford a lightweight tripod with a ball head, you'll have everything you need to capture blur-free photos with ease.

✔ **Hot-shoe level:** This is yet another way of making sure your camera is straight. Sometimes I like to get a low vantage point, but don't feel like being prone on the ground. When I run into this scenario, I use a small dual-axis bubble level that slides into the camera's hot shoe.

Even though your camera has a built-in dual-axis level, it will be hard to use in scenarios like this.

✔ **Extra memory cards:** Memory cards are cheap. Buy a couple of extra SD cards so you have a fresh card when you're photographing your favorite place, or a place you've never been to before.

✔ **Lens-cleaning kit:** Purchase a micro-fiber cloth that is designed to clean optical equipment. You can also purchase lens-cleaning fluid to use in conjunction with your micro-fiber cloth.

✔ **LCD protector:** Your LCD monitor is a vulnerable part of your camera. It can be chipped or otherwise damaged. Consider purchasing a screen to protect your LCD monitor from damage. Zagg makes a shield that is transparent and scratch-resistant. As of this writing, they have not made a screen for your camera, but have screens for every other popular Canon camera, so I'm sure one will be available for the EOS 6D in short order.

Accessories for video

Video is a whole different kettle of fish. Digital SLRs were not designed to capture video, so they're not user-friendly for videographers, but on the other hand, digital SLRs can capture incredible video that rivals conventional video recorders. Here are a few options to consider if you're going to create video with your Canon EOS 6D:

✔ **Tripod:** Review the information about tripods in the previous section. You can use the same tripod for still images and video. The only difference will be that you'll need to purchase a fluid ball head like the Manfrotto 504 HD Fluid Video Head. When you purchase a video head, make sure it will support the weight of your camera body, plus the heaviest lens you anticipate using for shooting video, plus 50 percent.

✔ **Video shoulder rig:** In addition to shooting from a tripod, you can shoot video using a rig that mounts the camera on your shoulder, or you can purchase a device that will hold the camera steady while you move. There are lots of rigs available in all different price ranges. My advice is to get one you can afford, and one that will hold your camera steady.

This may involve considerable research. I don't personally own a video rig, so I'm not in a position to make a recommendation. However, if you visit an online camera store like BH Photo or Adorama, look at the various models that are available. If there are reviews posted by users, read them as well. When you've narrowed it down to a couple of devices, call the camera store and ask them for their opinions.

- **Video viewfinder:** When you shoot video with your EOS 6D, the LCD monitor is your viewfinder. However, the LCD monitor can be difficult to view in bright light. Therefore a video viewfinder is a useful accessory. Hoodman makes an affordable video viewfinder called the Hoodloupe. You can combine this with an item called Hoodstrap that will mount the Hoodloupe to your camera to create a fairly inexpensive video viewfinder.

- **High-speed memory card:** When you capture video with your EOS 6D, your camera is capturing video at the rate of 24 to 30 frames per second. A standard memory card may not be able to keep up with the fast frame rate. For video, it's recommended that you use a card with a data-transfer rate of 90 mbs. Sandisk offers a memory card series called Extreme Pro that is ideal for capturing video.

Keeping It Clean

You've invested a considerable amount of money in your EOS 6D and accessories. To maintain your investment, and keep the camera in top operating condition, you need to take care of your purchase. As mentioned previously, you can clean your lenses with a lens-cleaning fluid and micro-fiber cloth. However, you should never use a solvent on your camera body. When you want to clean your camera body, wet a soft cloth, and then wring it almost dry. Gently rub the cloth over the camera body to remove any residue from skin oil or airborne pollutants. Some areas of your camera (such as the Quick Control dial) have ridges that are traps for dirt and debris from your skin. You can clean these areas with a soft toothbrush. It is also recommended that you clean your camera body with a soft, almost-dry cloth whenever you're photographing near the ocean when there's a salty mist in the air.

2

Creating Great Pictures Automatically

*Y*ou can do some pretty amazing things with your EOS 6D. You have lots of control over the camera to create awesome pictures. But if all the control seems a bit daunting when you're getting to know your new toy, you can let the camera make most of the decisions for you. If you're thinking point and shoot, yup, that's what you get when you let the camera take the reins. However, you can still create some great pictures with your EOS 6D when you take pictures using one of the automatic modes.

If you're an experienced photographer, breeze through this chapter and you can show someone else how to get great pictures with your high-tech camera — that is, if you can part company with it long enough for someone else to use it. In this chapter, I show you how to get the most out of your camera's auto modes. I also show you how to use the Self-Timer in case you want to take a self-portrait, and show you how to use the on-camera flash automatically.

One of the exciting features of the EOS 6D is *Live View mode,* which lets you compose your image with the LCD monitor. In this chapter, I deal exclusively with creating pictures through the viewfinder. If you're chomping at the bit to find out how to shoot with Live View, fast-forward to Chapter 5.

Ordering from Your Camera Menu

In spite of all the buttons and knobs on your camera, some of your picture-taking tasks involve using the camera menu. For example, when you format an SD card, you use the menu. You also use the menu to specify image size and quality as well as to set the parameters for tasks such as automatic exposure bracketing. I give you a brief introduction to the camera menu in Chapter 1 when I show you how to format an SD card and set the date and time. In this section, I give you a brief overview of the menu system. Throughout this book, I show you how to use the menu to perform specific tasks. To access the camera menu:

1. **Press the Menu button.**

   The last-used menu displays.

2. **Press the Mode Lock button and then rotate the Mode dial to P (see Figure 2-1).**

   P on the Mode dial stands for *Programmed Auto Exposure mode.* When you access the menu in one of the Creative shooting modes (P, Tv, Av, M, or B), you have access to all the menu items, which is extensive — 15 tabs in all. Alternatively, you can choose one of the Basic Zone options: A+, CA, or SCN, in which case you have a limited menu; 11 tabs to be exact. The latter might be considered training wheels for a beginning photographer who absolutely has

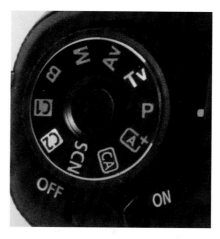

Figure 2-1: You have access to all menu options when you shoot in Programmed Auto Exposure mode.

to have a full-frame digital SLR, but for the purpose of getting familiar with the menu, stick with the P mode.

3. **Press the Multi-controller left or right to access the Shooting Settings 1 tab on the left (see the left image in Figure 2-2).**

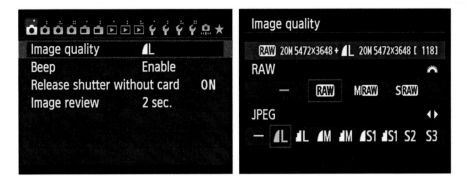

Figure 2-2: This menu has shooting options.

This tab, which is called Shooting Settings 1, is your first set of shooting options. You also have access to many of these menu options when you shoot in Creative Auto mode. Certain menu options, such as changing image format, aren't available when taking pictures with one of the Basic Zone shooting modes.

When you access a menu, the last command used is highlighted.

4. **Use the Quick Control dial or Multi-controller to highlight Image Quality and then press Set.**

Your menu display changes to reveal the image-quality options (see the right image in Figure 2-2). Notice the icon to the right of the RAW options. This signifies that you use the Main dial to specify this setting. Notice the icon to the right of the JPEG settings. This signifies that you use the Quick Control dial to specify this setting. Your camera can capture JPEG and RAW images simultaneously. This is handy when you're shooting an event where you need to deliver or post images almost immediately. Use the JPEG images to satisfy immediate client demands, and then process the RAW images to perfection for later use. The image to the right of Figure 2-2 shows the settings to capture a large JPEG image with the Fine quality setting and a large RAW image.

5. **After changing a menu option, press Set.**

This commits the change and returns you to the previous menu.

6. **To highlight another option in the current menu, use Multi-controller or the Quick Control dial to select the desired item.**

This highlights the menu option.

7. **To access the menu options, press Set.**

You can now change the menu option. Sometimes you use a combination of the Multi-controller, the Quick Control dial, and the Main dial to make a setting. In most instances, you commit the change by pressing Set, although the Menu button is used on some occasions to apply a setting. An icon appears on each menu, indicating the button to press to apply the change. Some menus let you access help by pressing the Info button.

8. **Press the Multi-controller button right.**

   This displays the Shooting Settings 2 tab. The amount of tabs you have depends on the mode in which you're shooting. If you followed my instructions in Step 2, you see 15 tabs. Note that when you shoot using one of the Basic Zone modes, you have only 11 menu tabs from which to choose. Throughout the rest of the book, I show you how to use options in these tabs to perform various tasks.

9. **Press the Menu button or press the Shutter button halfway to exit the menu.**

   Either operation returns you to Shooting mode. I prefer pressing the Shutter button halfway.

If you've graduated from another Canon camera, or this is your first digital SLR, you may be slightly awed by the fact that you'll have to navigate through 15 menu tabs to find the item you want. Not to worry; Table 2-1 describes the menu tabs and what you can expect to find in each one.

Table 2-1		The Camera Menu Tabs
Icon	*Menu Tab Name*	*Description*
	Shooting Settings 1	Used to specify image format, review time, and similar options.
	Shooting Settings 2	Used to enable Lens Abberation correction, control an external Speedlite, and lock up the mirror.
	Shooting Settings 3	Used to set Exposure compensation, specify ISO settings, set White Balance, specify Color Space, and so on.
	Shooting Settings 4	Used to specify Picture style, enable High ISO noise reduction, Highlight Tone priority, and more.

Icon	Menu Tab Name	Description
	LiveView Settings 1	Used to enable Live View shooting, display a grid during Live View shooting, and similar options. When you create movies with your camera, this menu performs similar functions but is known as Video Settings 1.
	LiveView Settings 2	Used to specify the silent shooting mode and the duration of the metering timer. When you capture video with your camera, this tab is used to set the video size, frame rate, and compression and is known as Video Settings 1.
	Playback Settings 1	Used to protect images, erase images, and similar options.
	Playback Settings 2	Used to resize images, play images as a slide show, and similar options.
	Playback Settings 3	Used to display Highlight alert, change Histogram options, display a playback grid, and more.
	Setup 1	Used to format cards, specify file numbering, and similar options.
	Setup 2	Used to choose LCD brightness option, set date and time, and similar options.
	Setup 3	Used to specify the video system, enable or disable a feature guide, and set WiFi.
	Setup 4	Used to display battery information, add photographer's copyright information to each image, and similar options.
	Custom Functions	Used to select and set custom functions.
	My Menu Settings	Used to create a custom menu with your most frequently used options.

Taking Your First Picture

You can easily get great results with your EOS 6D automatically. In Scene Intelligent Auto mode, all you have to do is compose the picture, achieve focus, and press the Shutter button. The camera literally takes care of everything. You don't have to mess with choosing the shutter speed, aperture, ISO setting, or anything else for that matter. The camera meters the amount of light coming to the camera and makes all the heavy decisions for you.

When you're shooting in Scene Intelligent Auto mode, the camera chooses the actual shutter speed, aperture, and ISO setting, which is determined by the amount of available light. The camera chooses a shutter speed and aperture to ensure a properly exposed image (see the "Understanding Exposure and Focal Length" section later in this chapter). When you're taking pictures in dim lighting or at night, the camera will attempt to choose a shutter speed that ensures a blur-free image (see the "Shutter speed and image sharpness" sidebar later in this chapter). If the shutter speed is too slow, you need to mount the camera on a tripod to ensure a blur-free image.

Depending on the lighting conditions, the camera may have to increase the ISO setting, which makes the camera more sensitive to light. An ISO setting above 800 may result in digital noise in the darker areas of the image. When you shoot in Full Auto mode, the camera also determines the aperture — which, combined with the focal length of the lens you're using, determines how much of the image is in apparent focus from front to back (see the "Understanding Exposure and Focal Length" section of this chapter).

When you unpacked your camera and started exploring the controls, you probably noticed the Mode dial on the top-left side of the camera as you look at it from behind — the same position from which you take pictures. The default setting for this dial is *A+,* which of course means *Scene Intelligent Auto.* These instructions are generic. To take a photograph automatically, follow these steps:

1. **Insert a memory card, attach the desired lens to the camera, and power-on the camera.**

   If you're not familiar with attaching a lens to the camera, check out Chapter 1.

2. **If you're using a lens with image stabilization, move the switch to IS.**

   If you bought the camera as a kit with the 24–105mm lens, you'll find this switch on the left side of the lens with the camera in front of you.

3. **Make sure the lens is set to AF (autofocus).**

   If you're using a Canon lens, you'll find a switch labeled AF on the left side of the lens when the camera is pointed toward your subject.

4. **Rotate the Mode dial to the A+ (Scene Intelligent Auto) setting.**

   It's the green rectangle on the Mode dial (see Figure 2-3).

5. **Look through the viewfinder and compose your scene.**

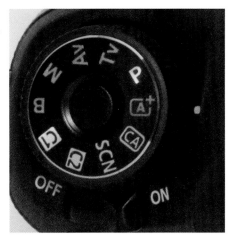

   When you look through the viewfinder, you'll see a lot of black squares, 11 to be exact. These are the *autofocus points,* the points your camera uses to focus. In Scene Intelligent Auto or Creative Auto mode, the focus points are selected automatically, based on the information the camera gathers through the lens. In essence, the camera looks for objects with well-

Figure 2-3: Shooting pictures in Scene Intelligent Auto mode.

   defined edges. You can customize the way the autofocus system works to suit your style of photography when shooting in one of the Creative Modes, something I show you in Chapter 6.

   Make sure your subject is under one of the autofocus squares. If you're photographing a person, make sure the person is in the center of the frame. You can compose the image so that the person isn't centered in the frame. I show you how to do that in the "Focusing On an Off-Center Subject" section later in this chapter.

6. **Press and hold the shutter button halfway.**

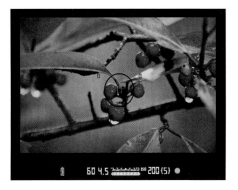

   When your camera achieves focus, a green dot appears on the right side of the viewfinder. If the camera can't achieve focus, the dot flashes. If this occurs, switch to manual focus (see the "Focusing Manually" section later in this chapter). The autofocus points that the camera uses to focus your subject are also illuminated (see Figure 2-4).

Figure 2-4: Taking your first picture.

   If your subject is moving, after the camera achieves focus, your camera automatically switches to another focus mode (AI Servo, which I cover in Chapter 7) and keeps your subject in focus. On the LCD panel on top of the camera and in the viewfinder, you see the shutter speed, aperture, and ISO setting the camera uses for the picture.

7. **Press the Shutter button fully.**

The camera takes the picture.

When the camera records data to the memory card, the access light on the right side of the camera illuminates. Do not turn off your camera while the light is on. If you do, the image isn't recorded to the memory card. Powering off the camera while the light is illuminated may also damage the memory card, the camera, or both.

8. **Review the image on the LCD monitor.**

You can view other information regarding the image on your LCD monitor. You can view exposure information, a histogram, and much more. I show you how to display image information on the LCD monitor in Chapter 4.

In most situations, you get a beautifully exposed image with Scene Intelligent Auto mode. If, however, you're photographing a scene with tricky lighting conditions (or photographing to create a portrait of a person), the image may not be to your liking. If this is the case, Creative Auto mode gives you options for modifying the automatic settings to get an image that suits your taste. I show you how to use Creative Auto mode in the "Shooting Pictures in Creative Auto Mode" section later in this chapter. Or maybe now that you've had a taste of the camera's brilliance, you want to get the most out of your camera. If this is the case, fast-forward to Chapters 6 and 7.

Understanding Exposure and Focal Length

When you take a picture in any of the automatic modes, the camera determines the shutter speed and aperture (see Figure 2-5). The *shutter speed* is the amount of time the shutter remains open. When you use a fast shutter speed, the shutter is open for a short amount of time, which stops action. A slow shutter speed keeps the shutter open for a long time and is needed when you don't have a lot of available light. The *aperture* determines how much light enters the camera. Each aperture equates to an f-stop number.

The f-stop number is a value. A small f-stop number, such as f/2.8, designates a large aperture, which lets a lot of light into the camera. A large f-stop number, such as f/16, is a small aperture that lets a small amount

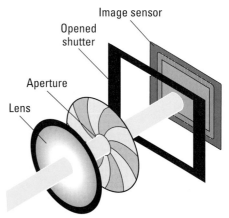

Figure 2-5: The shutter speed and aperture determine the exposure.

of light into the camera. Figure 2-6 shows a comparison of apertures and the amount of light they send to the camera.

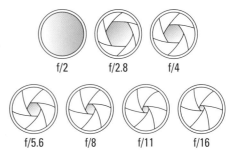

f/2   f/2.8   f/4

f/5.6   f/8   f/11   f/16

The f-stop determines another important factor, the depth of field. The *depth of field* is the amount of the image that's in apparent focus in front of and behind your subject:

Figure 2-6: The aperture opening determines how much light enters the camera.

- ✓ **Shallow depth of field:** A large aperture (small f-stop number) gives you a shallow depth of field, especially when you're shooting the image with a telephoto lens. A telephoto lens has a narrow angle of view, which gets you closer to your subject and results in an even shallower depth of field. Telephoto focal lenses are 70mm and greater. Notice I didn't say 35mm-equivalent. That's only for cameras that don't have full frame sensors. You're shooting with the big guys now. Large apertures and telephoto lenses are ideal for portrait photography.

- ✓ **Large depth of field:** On the other hand, a small aperture (large f-stop number) gives you a very large depth of field, especially when you're using a wide-angle focal length. A wide-angle focal length has a large angle of view. Wide-angle focal lengths have a range from 18mm to 35mm.

As you can see, a large number of factors determine what your image will look like.

The following list explains what action the camera takes when you take pictures in various modes:

- ✓ **Basic Zones:** When you photograph using one of the modes from the Basic Zone, the camera makes most of the decisions for you.

  - • **Scene Intelligent Auto mode:** The camera determines the shutter speed and f-stop based on the lighting conditions and the tonal range from light to dark in the scene that you're photographing.

  - • **Creative Auto mode:** You can apply some settings to blur the background — which, in essence, gives you a shallower depth of field, brightens the image, and so on.

  - • **SCN Mode:** You use this mode in conjunction with menu commands to choose the scene mode that best suits the type of scene you're photographing. Your choices are: Portrait, Landscape, Close-up, Sports, Night Portrait, Handheld Night Scene, and HDR Backlight Control. I show you how to use these picture-taking modes in the "Shooting Pictures in SCN Mode" section later in this chapter.

✔ **Creative Modes:** These include P (Programmed Auto Exposure), Av (Aperture Priority), Tv (Shutter Priority), M (Manual), or B (Bulb). Choosing a creative mode enables you to take complete control by manually setting aperture and/or shutter speed.

- **Aperture Priority mode:** You supply the aperture (f-stop value), and the camera calculates the shutter speed needed for a properly exposed image.

- **Shutter Priority mode:** You supply the shutter speed, and the camera provides the aperture (f-stop value) to create a properly exposed image.

- **Manual:** You choose the shutter speed and aperture to create a perfectly exposed image. When you shoot in manual, the compensation guide tells you when you've achieved the proper exposure for the current lighting conditions.

- **Bulb:** The shutter remains open as long as the shutter button is fully pressed. This zone is used for capturing images at night. This mode is useful when the given lighting conditions and the aperture you choose require a shutter-speed duration in excess of the camera's maximum duration of 30 seconds.

Shutter speed and image sharpness

When you take a picture with the camera cradled in your hands, a certain amount of motion is transmitted to the camera, which is caused by movement made by the camera operator. When you take pictures with a high shutter speed, the shutter isn't open long enough for any operator movement to affect the sharpness of the image. However, when you shoot at a slow shutter speed, the shutter is open long enough for operator movement to be apparent in the image, which shows up as an image that isn't tack-sharp. The clarity of your images depends on how steadily you hold the camera and the shutter speed used to capture the image.

The rule of thumb for handheld photography is to shoot with a shutter speed that's the reciprocal of lens focal length. For example, if you're using a lens with a focal length that measures 50mm, you should use a shutter speed of 1/50 of a second or faster to get a blur-free image. If the camera chooses a slower shutter speed, you need to steady the camera with a tripod. If you use a lens with image stabilization, you can shoot at a slower shutter speed than normal. Even without image stabilization, if you hold the camera very steady, you may be able to shoot at a slower shutter speed than the rule of thumb listed here. The best way to find out how steady you are is to experiment with different shutter speeds on each lens you own. Due to the narrow angle of view, you'll find that operator movement is very apparent when you take pictures with telephoto lenses. The longer the focal length, the more apparent the operator movement.

The decisions the camera makes regarding shutter speed and aperture are determined by lighting conditions. If you're taking pictures in low-light situations or at night, the camera may choose a shutter speed that's too slow to ensure a blur-free picture (see the "Shutter speed and image sharpness" sidebar). If this is the case, you have to mount the camera on a tripod to ensure a blur-free picture. But if you want complete control over the exposure, use one of the creative modes: Programmed Auto Exposure, Aperture Priority, Shutter Priority, Manual, or Bulb, which I outline in detail in Chapter 6.

Focusing On an Off-Center Subject

There are lots of rules for composing photographs, and many of them can be broken. However, one useful rule says that when you're photographing a person, she shouldn't be in the center of the frame. A photograph with your subject to the right or left of center is more interesting than one where she's smack-dab in the center of the frame. You can easily focus on an off-center subject by following these steps:

1. **Compose your scene through the viewfinder.**

   Move the camera until you achieve the desired composition.

2. **Move the camera until the center autofocus point is positioned in the middle of your subject.**

3. **Press the Shutter button halfway.**

   When the camera achieves focus, the green dot on the right side of the viewfinder appears. If the dot is flashing, the camera hasn't focused on your subject.

4. **With the Shutter button held down halfway, move the camera to recompose your picture.**

   By holding down the shutter button halfway, the focus locks on your subject, even as you move the camera.

5. **Press the Shutter button fully.**

   The camera records the image.

Focusing Manually

You can have the greatest camera and lens in the world, but if your images aren't in focus, nobody — including you — will care to look at your pictures. Your EOS 6D has a sophisticated 11-point focus system. In Chapter 7, I show you how to modify the autofocus system to suit particular photography situations.

When you shoot images with the lens set to autofocus (AF on Canon lenses) mode, the camera looks for areas of changing contrast *(edges)* or objects that are under autofocus points, and then uses these areas to focus the scene. However, in low light — or when you're taking a picture of a scene with lots of detail in the foreground and background — the camera may not be able to achieve focus. The green focus-indicator light in the viewfinder flashes when the camera cannot achieve focus, and you may also notice the autofocus motor on the lens is quite active as the camera tries to achieve focus. When you can't achieve focus, you have no choice but to manually focus the lens. Canon lenses and most third-party lenses give you the option of switching to manual focus.

To manually focus the lens, follow these steps:

1. **Move the Focus switch to MF (see Figure 2-7).**

   On most lenses, you'll find this switch on the left side when the camera is facing your subject.

2. **Press the viewfinder to your eye and twist the lens focus ring until your subject is in clear focus.**

   Concentrate on areas with contrast or sharp lines. This makes it easier for you to see when your subject is in focus. Remember to focus on the center of interest in your scene. If you're photographing a person, focus on the eyes. The curve of your subject's eyelid should be in focus in the resulting image; it's also an easy area to focus on.

3. **Take the picture.**

   Switch the lens back to autofocus (AF) when lighting conditions permit the camera to focus automatically. If you switch back to autofocus, and the AF motor still

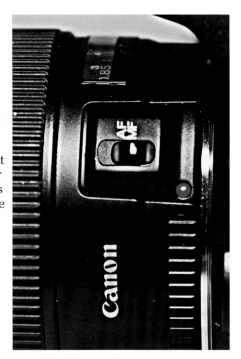

Figure 2-7: Focusing manually.

   racks the lens back and forth but still can't achieve focus, follow Steps 1 and 2 and get the subject in focus as best you can, and then take the picture.

If you're focusing manually in low light, shine a penlight on the focal point of your image, the area that should be in focus. When you're photographing in low light, you should mount the camera on a tripod, which will make it fairly easy to focus on your subject. After you achieve focus, switch off the penlight.

When you mount your camera on a tripod, disable lens image stabilization if the lens is so equipped.

Shooting Pictures in SCN Mode

When you shoot pictures in SCN mode, you choose an option from the Quick Control menu that matches the type of scene you are photographing. In SCN mode, the camera does its best to think like a photographer and choose the proper settings which should result in a good image of the scene you are photographing. For example, when you're photographing a head-and-shoulders portrait of a person with a telephoto lens, the ideal choice is Portrait. When you choose this mode, the camera chooses the largest aperture possible for the given lighting conditions, which yields a shallow depth of field, which means your subject is in focus, but the foreground and background are an out-of-focus blur. Conversely, when you photograph a landscape with a wide-angle lens, you choose Landscape mode. When you choose Landscape mode, the camera chooses the smallest aperture possible for the given light conditions, which gives you an image with a large depth of field; everything is in sharp focus from the foreground to the background. To create images in SCN mode:

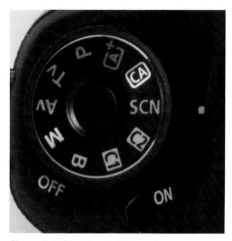

Figure 2-8: Shooting in SCN mode.

1. **Press the Mode Lock button and then select SCN from the Mode Dial (see Figure 2-8.)**

2. **Press the Quick Control button.**

   The Quick Control menu for the SCN mode appears and displays the icons for each SCN mode (see Figure 2-9). After you start shooting with the SCN modes, the last-used mode appears on the Quick Menu. When this happens, press Set to see all of the SCN mode icons on the LCD Monitor.

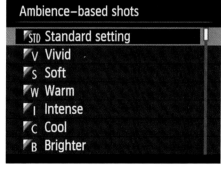

Figure 2-9: Don't make a scene when you use one of the these modes.

3. Use the Multi-controller to select the desired mode.

Each scene mode is discussed in detail in the following sections. When you select a mode, the settings are listed.

When you choose a SCN mode, you can change the settings by highlighting an option with the Multi-controller and then pressing set. But this defeats the purpose of a SCN preset. Use the SCN presets to get familiar with the camera. When you're familiar with all of the controls, then you can branch out and try your hand at some of the Creative Zone modes and choose your own settings. When you graduate to the Creative Zone modes, you're bound to come home with some bad shots, but that's how you learn. Use your camera often. If you're already familiar with photography, you can graduate from the SCN modes relatively quickly. If you're new to photography, the SCN modes help you get a feel for the camera. Ansel Adams didn't create great landscape pictures overnight. He spent years learning his craft. To me the sign of a good or great photographer is one who is a lifelong learner and who is not afraid to experiment with something new.

However, if you do decide to take a walk on the wild side and change some of the settings when using a SCN mode, the first setting you see says Standard setting. This is what Canon calls *ambience*. The second setting you can change in some of the modes says Default Setting, which gives you natural colors under specific types of lighting.

You have the following picture ambience options from which to choose (see Figure 2-10:

- **Standard:** This is the standard option and the colors are not altered digitally by the camera. What you see through the lens is what you get.

- **Vivid:** Enhances the colors to give the image some punch. If you decide to deviate from the Standard setting, try Vivid when you're photographing flowers.

- **Soft:** Gives you an image with nice soft muted colors. Try this option when shooting with the Portrait SCN mode.

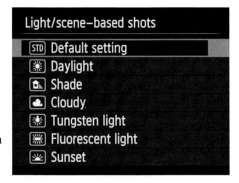

Figure 2-10: Choosing picture ambience.

- **Warm:** Warms the colors in the image. Try this option when photographing on an overcast day to warm up the image. You might also try this setting to warm up a less-than-impressive sunset.

- **Intense:** Gives you strongly saturated colors. Try this option when photographing architecture and graffiti on the sides of buildings or railroad cars.

- **Cool:** Gives colors in the image a bluish tone.

- **Brighter:** Makes the image brighter than the actual scene you're photographing.

- **Darker:** Makes the image darker than the actual scene you're photographing.

- **Monochrome:** Converts the image to black and white (grayscale for you purists).

The other option you can change is the lighting setting. Think of this as white balance. If you take a picture using the Default setting and the whites have a color cast, try changing to one of the following options (see Figure 2-11):

- **Daylight:** Use this option if you're photographing a subject or scene in bright daylight and using one of the Scene modes.

- **Shade:** Use this option if you're photographing a subject or scene in open shade and using one of the Scene modes.

- **Cloudy:** Use this option when you're photographing a subject or scene on a cloudy overcast day and using one of the Scene modes.

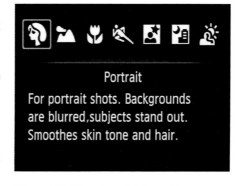

Figure 2-11: Choosing a lighting setting.

- **Tungsten Light:** Use this option when you're photographing a subject or scene in a room illuminated by tungsten light bulbs and using one of the Scene modes.

- **Fluorescent Light:** Use this option when you're photographing a subject or scene in a room illuminated by fluorescent light bulbs and using one of the Scene modes.

- **Sunset:** Use this option when you're photographing a subject or scene in the late afternoon an hour or so before sunset when using one of the Scene modes. I know it seems obvious, but I'll mention it anyway: Make sure the sun is actually out when you use this option. If the sun isn't out and it's close to sunset, switch to Cloudy.

Creating portraits using the Portrait SCN mode

The Portrait SCN mode is used for creating portraits. When you shoot a portrait of a person, you generally use a telephoto lens with a focal length of 80mm or greater. You can, however, create a good portrait using a 50mm lens. Don't use a lens with a focal length shorter than 50mm, because to fill the frame with your subject, you have to get very close to get her in the frame. When you do that, the wide-angle focal length makes the object closest to the camera seem larger than it actually is. When you're creating a portrait, the closest object to the camera is usually the subject's nose. When you shoot a person's portrait, rotate the camera 90 degrees, which gives you an image that is taller than it is wide, which matches your subject. To create a portrait using the Portrait mode:

1. **Press the Mode Lock button and then rotate the Mode dial to SCN.**

2. **Press the Quick Control button.**

   The Quick Control menu for the SCN mode appears. If a SCN mode is displayed, press Set to display all scene mode icons on the LCD Monitor.

3. **Use the Multi-controller to select the Portrait Mode and then press Set.**

   When you shoot in Portrait mode, the default image type is JPEG and the quality is Large with Standard picture ambience, Default lighting, and Continuous Shooting drive mode (see Figure 2-12). These are the settings Canon engineers have deemed optimum for shooting portraits. You can, however, deviate from these standard settings by using the Multi-controller to highlight a setting and then press Set to see the available options, as outlined in the "Shooting Pictures in SCN Mode" section of this chapter.

4. **Press the Shutter button halfway to achieve focus.**

   When you create a portrait of a person, it's better to have your subject on one side of the frame. Alternatively, you can have your subject's body pointed away from the camera and looking at the camera. When you create a portrait of a person, make sure the subject's eyes are in focus. The eyes, after all, are the windows to the soul.

5. **Press the Shutter button fully.**

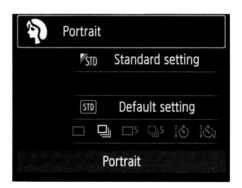

Figure 2-12: Taking pictures in Portrait SCN mode.

The camera starts capturing images of your subject. For this mode, the default drive mode is Continuous, which means the camera will capture images as long as your finger is on the shutter button. This is a great option, especially when you're photographing someone who is comfortable in front of the camera and is able to express a wide range of emotions over a short period of time. This is also great when you're taking candid portraits.

6. **Release the Shutter button to stop taking pictures.**

   After you finish taking pictures of your subject, review the images on the Camera LCD monitor to make sure your subject is in focus, the poses are pleasing, and so on. If you didn't capture the essence of your subject, take some more pictures.

Shooting landscapes using the SCN Landscape mode

There are beautiful landscapes all over this grand country of ours. Even if you live in a major metropolitan area, there is undoubtedly a majestic landscape within easy driving distance of your home. When you photograph landscapes, use a wide angle focal length from 18 to 35 mm. This focal length range enables you to pack a lot of real estate into an image.

1. **Press the Mode Lock button and then rotate the Mode dial to SCN.**

2. **Press the Quick Control button.**

   The Quick Control menu for the SCN mode appears. If another mode is displayed, press Set to display all scene modes on the LCD Monitor.

3. **Use the Multi-controller to select the Landscape mode and then press Set.**

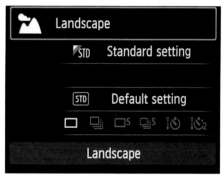

Figure 2-13: Taking pictures in Landscape mode.

   When you shoot in Landscape mode, the default image format is JPEG and the quality is Large. The picture ambience is Standard, Default lighting, and the drive mode is single shot (see Figure 2-13). This mode is optimized for a large depth of field. You can change a setting by highlighting it with the Multi-controller dial, pressing Set, and then choosing the desired setting.

4. **Compose the image and then press the Shutter button halfway to achieve focus.**

5. **Press the Shutter button fully to take the picture.**

   Review the image to make sure the scene is well composed.

When you photograph a vast landscape, make sure you have a large object in the foreground to act as a visual anchor. When you compose the image, place the visual anchor to the left or right of center. The visual anchor is what draws viewers into the image. Without a visual anchor, viewers have no idea where to look or why you were compelled to take the picture.

Shooting images in Close-up mode

If you love nature, or have a wonderful garden, you can use the Close-up SCN mode to get close-up images of flowers and other objects. To make them appear life size or larger, you'll need to use a macro lens. If you don't own a macro lens, you'll get your best results using a telephoto lens. To shoot close-up images:

1. **Press the Mode Lock button and then rotate the Mode dial to SCN.**

2. **Press the Quick Control button.**

   The Quick Control menu for the SCN mode appears and the last used SCN mode is displayed. If you've used a SCN mode previously, press Set to display all of the icons.

3. **Use the Multi-controller to select the Close-up mode and then press Set.**

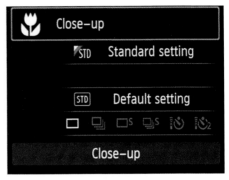

Figure 2-14: Photographing using the Close-up mode.

   When you photograph in Close-up mode, images are saved in the JPEG format with Large image quality, using the Standard picture ambience, Default setting for lighting, and 2-Second delay for the drive mode. See Figure 2-14. You can change a setting by highlighting it with the Multi-controller dial, pressing Set, and then choosing the desired setting.

4. **Compose the picture and then press the Shutter button halfway to achieve focus.**

   When you photograph in Close-up mode, you have a limited depth of field. Make sure your subject is in sharp focus.

5. **Press the Shutter button fully to take the picture.**

   When you photograph subjects like flowers, take several pictures and change your vantage point each time. This will give you a variety of images from which you can choose the best one.

When you photograph flowers, choose a plain solid color background that contrasts well with the color of the flower you're photographing.

When you photograph flowers and other small subjects, use a telephoto lens with a focal length between 80 and 200mm and get as close to your subject as you can and still have it in focus. If you use a zoom telephoto when photographing close-ups, zoom in as close as possible.

Shooting images using Sports mode

If you're photographing a subject such as your son playing soccer or a water-skier, choose Sports mode. When you photograph in this mode, the camera chooses a shutter speed that freezes the action. This mode works well for most action shots. Of course, if you're shooting a racing car coming almost straight at you, the only way to capture the image is to shoot in Shutter Priority mode and pre-focus the camera. To capture images of moving objects:

1. **Press the Mode Lock button and then rotate the Mode dial to SCN.**

2. **Press the Quick Control button.**

   The Quick Control menu for the SCN modes is displayed. If you have photographed with a SCN mode before, the last-used mode is displayed on the Quick Control menu. Press Set to display all of the SCN mode icons.

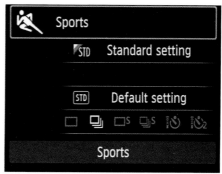

Figure 2-15: Creating images using the Sports SCN mode.

3. **Use the Multi-controller to select the Sports mode and then press Set.**

   When you photograph in Sports mode, images are saved in the JPEG format with the Large Quality setting. This mode uses the Standard setting for picture ambience, Default setting for lighting, and the drive mode is Continuous, which means you capture a sequence of action images as long as your finger is on the Shutter button. (See Figure 2-15.) You can change a setting by highlighting it with the Multi-controller dial, pressing Set, and then choosing the desired setting.

4. **Press the Shutter button halfway to achieve focus.**

   Position the center autofocus point over your subject when you press the Shutter button halfway. You're also shooting in a mode where the camera updates focus as your subject moves closer to or farther from you. At the risk of being redundant, I'll say it again: Your camera will not be able to keep focus on a very fast-moving object like a jet taking off and flying directly at you.

5. **Press the Shutter button fully to begin capturing images.**

   When you shoot in this mode, the camera is in Continuous drive mode, which means the camera will capture images as long as your finger is on the Shutter button. This enables you to capture action sequences of subjects.

6. **Release the Shutter button to stop taking pictures.**

Shoot moving objects with a telephoto lens. This enables you to distance yourself from a potentially dangerous subject like a horse running at full speed. With a telephoto lens, you also end up with a softer background.

Shooting night portraits

When you want to create portraits of subjects at night and use this mode, the shutter stays open long enough to capture detail in the background as well. This means you'll have to mount your camera on a tripod to compensate for the slow shutter speed. You'll also need to use a Canon flash. The burst of light from the flash is what captures a sharp image of your subject. To shoot night portraits:

1. **Press the Mode Lock button and then select SCN from the Mode Dial.**

2. **Press the Quick Control button.**

   The Quick Control menu for the SCN modes is displayed. If you have photographed with an SCN mode before, the last used mode is displayed on the Quick Control menu. Press Set to display all of the SCN mode icons.

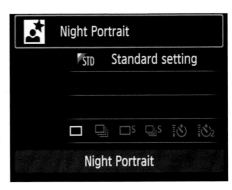

Figure 2-16: Creating images using the Night Portrait mode.

3. **Use the Multi-controller to select the Night Portrait mode and then press Set.**

   When you photograph in this mode, the camera captures images in the JPEG format with Large image quality. This mode uses the Standard setting for picture ambience, and the drive mode is Single Shot. See Figure 2-16. You can change a setting by highlighting it with the Multi-controller dial, pressing Set, and then choosing the desired setting. There is no option to change the lighting setting.

4. **Compose your image and then press the Shutter button halfway to achieve focus.**

When you photograph in this mode, you generally want to show some of the background to give the viewer a sense of the place where the portrait was photographed. Therefore your subject should be on one side of the frame. Make sure you place the center autofocus point over your subject to achieve focus. Then with the shutter button still pressed halfway, move the camera to achieve the desired composition.

5. **Press the Shutter button fully to take the picture.**

Because the shutter will remain open after the flash fires, ask your subject to remain still so the portrait will not be blurred. It's also advisable to use a tripod when photographing with this SCN mode. If you don't have a tripod handy, place your camera on a flat surface and then use the 2-Second Countdown Timer. The two-second delay gives the camera time to stabilize from any vibration that may have occurred when you pressed the Shutter button.

Shooting night scenes while hand holding the camera

If you want to take pictures at night, normally you need a tripod. However, if you've got a steady hand and you've left your tripod at home, you can take pictures at night while holding the camera in your hand. When you photograph using the Handheld Night Scene mode, your EOS 6D combines four shots of different exposures to capture the wide tonal range that is prevalent at night. To take a picture of a night scene while holding the camera by hand:

1. **Press the Mode Lock button and then select SCN from the Mode Dial.**

2. **Press the Quick Control button.**

   The Quick Control menu for the SCN modes appears. If you have photographed with a SCN mode before, the last-used mode is displayed on the Quick Control menu. Press Set to display all of the SCN mode icons.

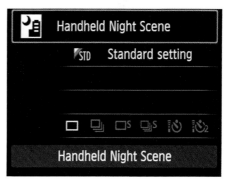

Figure 2-17: Creating images using the Handheld Scene mode.

3. **Use the Multi-controller to select the Handheld Night Scene mode and then press Set.**

Images you create using this mode are saved in the JPEG format with Large quality. This mode uses Standard picture ambience and the Single Shot drive mode. There is no option to change lighting. See Figure 2-17. You can change a setting by highlighting it with the Multi-controller dial, pressing Set, and then choosing the desired setting.

4. **Compose the picture and press the Shutter button halfway to achieve focus.**

5. **Press the Shutter button fully.**

    Your camera takes four pictures and the processor combines them in camera.

 Hold the camera as steady as possible when shooting in this mode. Spread your feet shoulder-width apart and cradle your elbows by your side to be the human equivalent of a tripod. Gently squeeze the shutter button while slowly exhaling.

 Use a dedicated Canon flash unit if you're going to include a person while taking pictures in this mode. The flash will fire on the first shot. Tell your subject to remain still after the flash fires.

Shooting pictures with the HDR Backlight Control SCN mode

Sometimes you want to photograph a scene that has such a wide variance in tonal range, your camera has to compromise and you end up with an image that has detail in the mid-range but lacks detail in the shadow area. You can rectify this problem by using the HDR Backlight Control SCN mode. When you choose this mode, the camera captures three images with different exposures and merges them into one. To create images using the HDR Backlight mode:

1. **Press the Mode Lock button and then select SCN from the Mode Dial.**

 2. **Press the Quick Control button.**

    The Quick Control menu for the SCN modes appears. If you have photographed with a SCN mode before, the last used mode is displayed on the Quick Control menu. Press Set to display all of the SCN mode icons.

 3. **Use the Multi-controller to select the HDR Backlight Control mode and then press Set.**

    Images you create using this mode are saved in the JPEG format with Large quality. The settings on this mode are all automatic (see Figure 2-18).

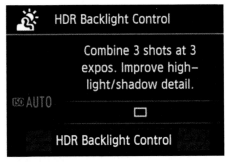

Figure 2-18: Creating images using the Handheld Scene mode.

4. **Compose the picture and press the Shutter button halfway to achieve focus.**

5. **Press the Shutter button fully.**

   Your camera takes three pictures and the processor combines them in camera.

Shooting Pictures in Creative Auto Mode

If you like having control but you're not ready to walk on the wild side and shoot in one of the Creative Modes just yet, Creative Auto mode is right up your alley. When you take pictures in Creative Auto mode, you can control *depth of field* (the amount of the image in front of and behind your subject that's in apparent focus), image brightness, picture style, image format, and shooting mode. When you shoot in Creative Auto mode, all your options display on the camera's LCD monitor. To shoot pictures in Creative Auto mode:

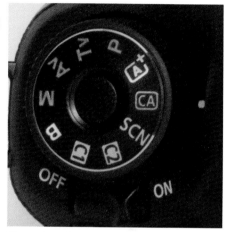
Figure 2-19: Shooting in Creative Auto mode.

1. **Press the Mode Lock button and then select CA from the Mode dial (see Figure 2-19).**

   CA on the Mode dial stands for *Creative Auto mode.* After switching to Creative Auto mode, the camera LCD displays your options.

2. **Press the Quick Control button.**

   This button gives you access to the first set of options: Picture Ambience. The default mode is Standard (see Figure 2-20). However, you can change the mode to suit your taste in the next step.

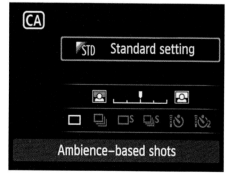
Figure 2-20: A picture's got to have ambience.

3. **Press Set and then rotate the Quick Control dial to choose the desired option.**

The default setting is Standard, but you can choose one of the following:

- **Standard:** This is the standard option and the colors are not altered digitally by the camera. What you see through the lens is what you get.

- **Vivid:** Enhances the colors to give the image some punch. If you decide to deviate from the Standard setting, try Vivid when you're photographing flowers.

- **Soft:** Gives you an image with nice soft muted colors. Try this option when shooting portraits in CA mode.

- **Warm:** Warms the colors in the image. Try this option when photographing on an overcast day to warm up the image. You might also try this setting to warm up a less-than-impressive sunset.

- **Intense:** Gives you strongly saturated colors. Try this option when photographing architecture and graffiti.

- **Cool:** Gives colors in the image a bluish tone.

- **Brighter:** Makes the image brighter than the actual scene you're photographing.

- **Darker:** Makes the image darker than the actual scene you're photographing.

- **Monochrome:** Converts the image to black and white (grayscale for you purists).

4. **After choosing the desired option, press Set.**

   The main menu for the CA shooting mode is displayed.

5. **Use the Multi-controller to highlight the Background section (see Figure 2-21).**

6. **Rotate the Quick Control dial to the right to make the background sharper or to the left to blur it.**

   As you move the dial, the indicator moves to show how much you've sharpened or blurred the background.

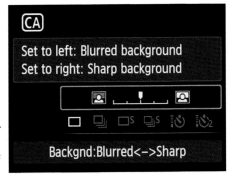

Figure 2-21: Controlling background blur.

7. **After choosing the desired setting, press Set.**

   The main menu for the CA shooting mode is displayed.

8. **Use the Multi-controller button to highlight the Drive section (see Figure 2-22) and then press Set.**

9. **Use the Multi-controller or the Quick Control dial to choose one of the following Drive mode options:**

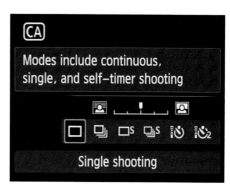

Figure 2-22: Choosing a shooting mode.

- *Single Shooting:* The camera captures a single image each time you press the Shutter button.

- *Single Shooting Silent Mode:* The camera captures a single image, with reduced shutter noise, each time you press the Shutter button.

- *Continuous Shooting:* The camera captures images at a maximum rate of 4.5 fps (frames per second) for as long as you hold down the Shutter button.

- *Continuous Shooting Silent Mode:* The camera captures images at a maximum rate of 4.5 fps (frames per second), with reduced shutter noise, for as long as you hold down the Shutter button.

- *10-Second Countdown Timer:* The camera captures an image ten seconds after you press the Shutter button.

- *2-Second Countdown Timer:* The camera captures an image two seconds after you press the Shutter button.

10. **Press Set.**

    The desired shooting mode is applied and the main CA menu is displayed.

11. **Compose your scene with the viewfinder and then press the Shutter button halfway.**

    The green dot on the right side of the viewfinder appears when you achieve focus.

12. **Press the Shutter button fully to take the picture.**

    The image appears on your LCD monitor almost instantly.

Using the Self-Timer

Your camera has a built-in Self-Timer that you use whenever you want to delay the opening of the shutter. This option is useful when you want to take a self-portrait or you want to be in a picture with other people. The Self-Timer is also handy when you're taking pictures on a tripod, especially when the shot requires a long exposure. The countdown allows time for any camera shake that was caused by pressing the shutter to subside. Your camera has a Self-Timer that counts down from 2 seconds and one that counts down from 10 seconds. To enable the Self-Timer:

1. **Press the Drive button.**

2. **Look at the LCD panel and then turn the Quick Control or Main dial to select either the 2-Second or 10-Second Countdown Timer.**

   The image on the left of Figure 2-23 shows the LCD panel with the 2-Second Timer selected, and the image on the right shows the 10-Second Countdown Timer selected.

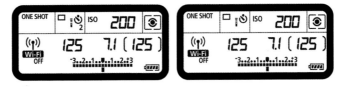

Figure 2-23: Selecting one of the Self-Timer modes.

3. **Compose your scene in the viewfinder.**

   If you're shooting a self-portrait or will be in the picture, mount your camera on a tripod. If you're not looking through the viewfinder when you use the Self-Timer, you'll also have to remove the eyecup and place the eyepiece cover over the viewfinder. This little piece slides into the same slots as the eyecup. The eyepiece cover is somewhere in the box your camera shipped in (that is, unless you realized what the piece is used for and put it in your camera bag right away). The eyepiece cover prevents stray light from changing the exposure.

4. **Press the shutter button halfway to achieve focus.**

   The green light on the right side of the viewfinder shines when focus has been achieved.

5. **Press the shutter button.**

The camera begins to count down. As the camera counts down, you hear a beeping sound and a light on the front of the camera flashes. Two seconds before the end of the countdown, the light stays on and the beeping sounds faster. If you're taking a self-portrait, say "cheese" when the red light is solid.

Triggering the Shutter Remotely

You can trigger the camera shutter remotely using the RC-6 remote controller, which is sold separately. You use the remote controllers in conjunction with the timer. This option is handy when you're creating still-life photos. Instead of walking between the camera and your subject, you can make subtle changes to the composition and then trigger the camera remotely. To trigger your camera remotely:

1. **Mount the camera on a tripod.**

2. **Switch the lens to manual focus and focus on your subject.**

   For more information on manually focusing the camera, see the "Focusing Manually" section earlier in this chapter.

3. **Press the Drive button.**

4. **While looking at the LCD panel, rotate the Quick Control dial to select the desired remote mode.**

   You can trigger the camera remotely and have it count down from 10 or 2 seconds. The left side of Figure 2-24 shows the LCD panel with a 2-second remote, and the right side of the panel shows a 10-second remote.

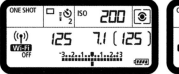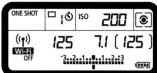

Figure 2-24: Taking a picture with a remote control device.

5. **Compose your scene through the viewfinder and then focus on your subject.**

6. **Point the remote controller at the camera's remote sensor and then press the remote's trigger button.**

   The remote sensor is located near the handgrip on the left side of the camera as you look at it.

   The Self-Timer counts down, the shutter actuates, and the picture is taken.

3

Selecting Image Size and Quality

*Y*our camera captures images with a resolution of 20.2 megapixels, which is humongous, ginormous, or any other adjective you prefer to indicate something that's big. The good news: This gives you a tremendous amount of flexibility. You can print images as large as 23.9 x 15.2 inches. Thinking of the possibilities of decorating your house with your photographs? The bad news: The large size takes up lots of room on your memory card and lots of room on the hard drive that you store your images on. Fortunately, you can specify different sizes by using the camera's menu options if you have memory cards and hard drives with small capacities.

In addition to concerning yourself with image size, you also have the file format you choose to worry about. Your camera can capture images in the RAW or JPEG format, or capture both formats simultaneously. When you capture images in the RAW format, you must process them. Think digital darkroom in a computer, and you get the idea. The RAW format gives you a tremendous amount of flexibility. After you download RAW images to your computer, you process the images with software included with your camera or with third-party software, such as Adobe Lightroom, Adobe Photoshop Elements, Adobe Photoshop, or, if you're a died in the wool Apple user, there's a program called Aperture that can also be used to process RAW images. You can also process images using software that shipped with your camera. I show you how to use the Canon software in Chapters 9 and 10.

If you capture images in the JPEG format, the camera does the processing for you. Think of this as the digital equivalent of a Polaroid image. You get instant gratification but can't do much with the image except crop it and perform minimal image editing. If you capture images in the JPEG format, you also have to think about image quality. The setting you choose determines the image quality and the file size.

If you're new to digital photography, these matters of file format, image size, and quality may seem a tad overwhelming. But hey, don't worry — be happy and have a sip of your favorite beverage. I show you how to specify image size, quality, and a whole lot more in this chapter.

Understanding Image Size and Quality

Your camera can capture large images. The default option captures images at a size that most photographers — except professionals — won't ever need or use. But before you specify sizes, you need to understand the relationship between the image size and the resolution. The default image size your camera can capture measures 5742 x 3648 pixels. If you do the math:

$$5742 \times 3648 = 20{,}946{,}816 \text{ pixels}$$

$$20{,}946{,}816 \div 1{,}000{,}000 = 20.94$$

Round up to get 21 megapixels. Okay, so it didn't round up to 20.2, which is the effective number of pixels the sensor can capture. Maybe Canon uses fuzzy logic to come up with 20.2, or the marketing folks don't like odd numbers, which I think is rather odd.

The default resolution for your camera is 240 pixels per inch (ppi). If you do a little more math, the default image size and resolution equate to an image size of 23.9 x 15.2 inches:

$$5742 \div 240 = 23.9 \text{ inches}$$

$$3648 \div 240 = 15.2 \text{ inches}$$

Please don't try this math at home unless you own a well-lubricated abacus.

Another factor to consider is the final destination of the images. If you're going to edit the images with Canon or third-party software and then print them, you need to factor this into the choices you make when specifying image size and quality. You can get high-quality prints with the 240-ppi default resolution. However, some printers prefer 300 ppi. If you're capturing images that will be displayed on a Web site only, you can get by with a much smaller image and a resolution of 72 or 96 ppi. When you use images on the web, you'll rarely need one with a dimension that's wider than 640 pixels. You can resample images to a higher resolution with third-party software, such as Adobe Photoshop Elements, Adobe Photoshop, or Adobe Photoshop Lightroom.

The default image size is great if you're printing images and have gobs of space on your hard drive and a camera bag full of 16GB memory cards. However, if your storage capacity is at a premium or you're running out of room on your last memory card with no computer readily available to download to, it's important to know how to change image size and quality, a task I show you how to do in the upcoming sections.

Specifying Image Format, Size, and Quality

Your EOS 6D has many options that determine the dimensions, image format, quality, and file size. You can choose from two image formats — JPEG and RAW. You have five different sizes for each image format. If you capture images with the JPEG format, you can also specify image quality. You can capture both formats when you shoot an image, or choose either format.

Your decisions regarding format, image size, and quality determine the crispness of the resulting images, the file size, and the amount of flexibility you have when editing your images. To give you an idea of the difference in file sizes, you'll end up with a file size of 0.3MB when you capture an image using the S3 (Small 3) JPEG format with Fine quality compared to a file size of approximately 23.5MB when you capture an image using the RAW format. I explain the differences between the two formats in an upcoming "JPEG or RAW? Which is right for you?" sidebar. I also give you my take on which options you should choose in the "My recommendations" sidebar later in this chapter. The following sections show you how to choose options from the camera menus.

Choosing the file format, image size, and quality

One of the first decisions you make regarding your images is the file format. You can capture JPEG or RAW images. When you choose the file format, you also specify the image size. If you choose the JPEG format, you specify the quality as well. You even have an option to capture both formats simultaneously. If you're curious about the difference between the formats, check out the "JPEG or RAW? Which is right for you?" sidebar in this chapter. To specify the image format:

1. **Press the Menu button.**

   This displays the last used menu on your LCD monitor.

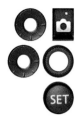

2. **Press the Multi-controller left or right to access the Shooting Settings 1 tab.**

3. **Use the Multi-controller or the Quick Control dial to highlight Image Quality (see the left image in Figure 3-1).**

4. **Press the Set button.**

   Your image format, size, and quality options display (see the right image in Figure 3-1).

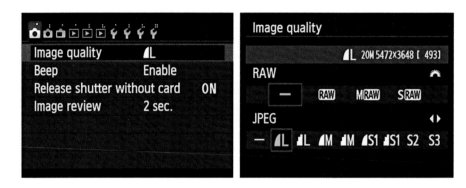

Figure 3-1: Setting Image format, size, and quality options.

5. **Rotate the Main dial to specify a RAW setting.**

   Choose this option to capture RAW images, or if you plan to capture only JPEG images, go to Step 6. If you decide to capture RAW images, your options are RAW (5742 x 3648 pixels), MRAW (4104 x 2736 pixels), or SRAW (2736 x 1824 pixels). When you select an option, the file size, image dimensions in pixels, and the number of images that can be captured on your memory card in the camera display in the upper-right corner of the Quality menu. If you're only going to shoot RAW images, go to Step 7. If you plan on capturing both RAW and JPEG images simultaneously, go to Step 6.

6. **Rotate the Quick Control dial to specify a JPEG setting.**

   Choose this option to capture JPEG images, or perform this step in conjunction with Step 5 to capture RAW images simultaneously when you press the Shutter button. Your options are Large with Fine, Large with Normal, Medium with Fine, Medium with Normal, S1 with Fine, S1 with Normal, S2 with Fine, S2 with Normal, or S3 with Fine. The dimensions, respectively, are 5742 x 3648 pixels, 3648 x 2432 pixels, 2736 x 1824 pixels, 1920 x 1280 pixels, 720 x 480 pixels.

7. **Press Set to apply the change.**

   The selected image information displays next to Quality on the Shooting Settings 1 tab.

JPEG or RAW? Which is right for you?

The answer to this question depends on how serious you are about your photography. Before you decide, let me point out the differences between the two formats. When you capture an image in the JPEG format, the camera processes the image. The camera also compresses the image based on the quality option you specify in the camera menu. You can store more images on a card when you specify a smaller image size and lower image quality. However, you'll notice the difference when you print your images. When you choose the RAW format, you have the ultimate in flexibility. The camera sensor transmits the RAW data to your memory card. Yup. What the sensor captures is what you get. You do have to process RAW images with either the Canon software provided with your camera or with third-party software such as Apple Aperture, Adobe Photoshop Elements, Adobe Photoshop, or Adobe Photoshop Lightroom. The software lets you fine-tune virtually everything about the photo.

Comparing Image Formats and File Sizes

When you capture images with a higher resolution, the file size is bigger and the files take up more room on your memory card. The image format also enters into the equation, and if you choose to capture images with the JPEG format, the image quality is a factor. Photographers also like to know the maximum number of images they can capture when shooting in Continuous (Burst) mode. The number of images depends on the image dimensions and quality, which equates to the file size. When you capture smaller images in the JPEG format that have been compressed, the file size is smaller; therefore the maximum number of images you can capture before the card is filled is greater. Table 3-1 shows you how many images you can fit on a 8GB card for each available format and quality option. The information is based on capturing images with an ISO speed setting of 100. This table is only for reference. Your results will differ based on the subject and ISO speed setting.

Table 3-1		How Many Images Fit on a Card?		
Image Format and Quality	*Megapixels*	*File Size*	*Number of Shots*	*Maximum Burst*
JPEG Large Fine	20	6.0MB	1250	73
JPEG Large Normal	20	3.1MB	2380	2380
JPEG Medium Fine	8.9	3.2MB	2300	2300
JPEG Medium Normal	8.9	1.7MB	4240	4240

(continued)

Table 3-1 *(continued)*

Image Format and Quality	Megapixels	File Size	Number of Shots	Maximum Burst
JPEG S1 Fine	5	2.1MB	3450	3450
JPEG S1 Normal	5	1.1MB	6370	6370
JPEG S2	2.5	1.2MB	6130	6130
JPEG S3	0.3	0.3MB	23070	23070
RAW	20	23.5MB	300	14
MRAW	11	18.5MB	380	8
SRAW	5	13MB	550	12

If you prefer to capture your images in the JPEG format, the quality you choose determines what the final image looks like. If you compare the Normal quality to the Fine quality, you'll notice a difference when you print the image at the largest size possible. The Normal quality image won't be as crisp and sharp as the Fine quality image. The image on the left in Figure 3-2 is an enlargement of an image captured with the JPEG Fine quality. The image on the right in Figure 3-2 was captured with the JPEG Normal quality. The images have been magnified so you can more clearly see the difference in sharpness and detail.

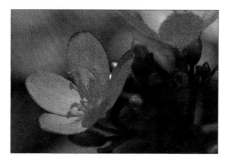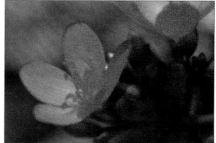

Figure 3-2: Comparing the JPEG Normal and Fine qualities.

My recommendations

When I take a photograph, I think of all possible uses. My first option is to post an image I like to my blog. Eventually I'll make prints of my best images. Some of those prints may be 4 x 6 inches for a small album, I may have the image printed on a 30-x-20-inch canvas to decorate my home, or sell a large image to a client. Therefore I always capture images with the RAW option. This enables me to do anything I want with the image. Yes, they take up a lot of room, but memory cards and hard drives are fairly inexpensive. My backup system is a Drobo, in which I have 7TB worth of drives. I store my backups and older images on it.

Sometimes I photograph events that require me to produce images quickly, yet I still want to edit them to perfection at some point in time. When I run into a scenario like this, I capture RAW and JPEG images simultaneously. If the images that need to be turned around quickly are for the Web, I use the Small JPEG option with Normal quality in addition to the RAW setting. If the images will be printed, say for example in a local newspaper or magazine, I use the Large JPEG option with Fine quality and capture RAW images simultaneously. Both options enable me to give the client a JPEG image almost immediately and then edit RAW images for other outputs at a later date.

If you photograph an event, such as a wedding, you have other options. In this case, I recommend that you use the RAW format for all the standard wedding images, such as exchanging vows and rings, marching down the aisle, and so on. I also recommend you use RAW when shooting the formal shots of the family members with the bride and groom. However, when you're photographing the reception, use RAW for the first dances, and then switch to MRAW or SRAW for the candid shots of the couples at tables and the guests dancing. These photographs are generally ordered as 4-x-6-inch images. Therefore you don't need a full 20-megapixel capture for a high-quality print. Switching to SRAW or MRAW for the less-important shots conserves room on your card.

Managing Image Files

By default, your images are numbered continuously until 9999 and then the file number is reset to 0001. Your images are also stored in a single folder on your memory card. You can, however, create folders in which to store your images and then change the file-numbering method. I show you how in the following sections.

Creating folders

By default, your camera creates the 100Canon folder on your memory card where images are stored. You can, however, create as many folders as you want. A folder can hold a maximum of 9,999 images. When you exceed the maximum allowable images in a folder, a new one is created automatically. You can have a maximum of 999 folders on a card. Organizing your work in folders is a good idea if you work with large memory cards and want to store images from multiple shoots in separate folders. To create a folder:

1. **Press the Menu button.**

2. **Use the Multi-controller button to navigate to the Camera Settings 1 tab.**

   Select Folder is highlighted by default unless you've previously used another menu command.

3. **Use the Multi-controller or the Quick Control dial to highlight Select Folder (see the left image in Figure 3-3).**

4. **Press the Set button.**

   The Select Folder menu appears showing you the current folders on the card and the number of photos in each folder (see the right image in Figure 3-3).

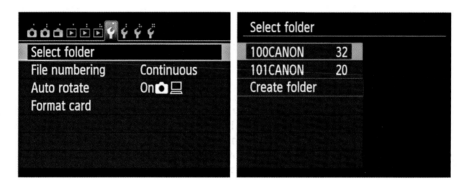

Figure 3-3: Creating a folder.

5. **Rotate the Quick Control dial to highlight Create Folder and press Set.**

   The menu refreshes, and a command to create a folder appears with the next available folder number (see Figure 3-4).

6. **Rotate the Quick Control dial to highlight OK and then press Set.**

   The new folder is created.

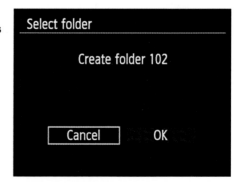

Figure 3-4: Creating a new folder.

Selecting a folder

Folders are convenient when you want to separate images from different photo shoots. When you have more than one folder, you can choose the folder to store your images. To select a folder:

1. **Press the Menu button.**

2. **Use the Multi-controller to navigate to the Camera Settings 1 tab.**

3. **Use the Multi-controller or the Quick Control dial to highlight Select Folder and then press the Set button.**

   The folders you've created display.

4. **Rotate the Quick Control dial to highlight the desired folder and then press Set.**

   The next images you shoot will be stored in that folder.

Choosing a file-numbering method

Your camera automatically names and numbers each image you take. The name isn't all that descriptive, and the numbers are consecutive. Some photographers stay with the default numbering system because it helps keep track of the number of shutter actuations. But your EOS 6D is rated for 100,000 shutter actuations so that's a moot point. To change the file-numbering system:

1. **Press the Menu button.**

   The last used menu command is highlighted.

2. **Use the Multi-controller button to navigate to the Camera Settings 1 tab.**

3. **Use the Multi-controller or the Quick Control dial to highlight File Numbering (see the left side of Figure 3-5) and then press the Set button.**

   A menu appears with your file-numbering options (see the right side of Figure 3-5).

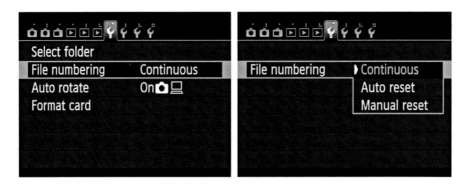

Figure 3-5: Selecting a file-numbering option.

4. **Use the Multi-controller or the Quick Control dial to highlight one of the following options:**

    • *Continuous:* Numbers files in sequence, even when you insert a new card or store images in a different folder. Images are numbered to 9999 and then start over at 0001. When you use this option, start with a newly formatted card each time. If you use multiple cards that already have images on them, you may run into problems with duplicate filenames because file numbering may continue from the last image captured on the card. Duplicating filenames isn't a good thing if you're storing all your images in the same folder.

    • *Auto Reset:* Numbers the first image with 0001 each time you insert the card in the camera or when images are stored in a new folder. This option works well if you store images from each shoot in their own folder when you download them to your computer, or as I strongly suggest, rename the images when you download them to your computer.

    • *Manual Reset:* Creates a new folder and resets the numbering to 0001 after you press the Set button. After manually resetting file numbering, the numbering system reverts to the last option you specified, whether Continuous or Auto Reset.

5. **After highlighting the desired option, press Set to commit the change.**

    The file-numbering option remains in effect until you change it with this menu command.

Using the LCD Monitor

*D*igital photography is all about instant gratification. You snap a picture, and it appears on your LCD monitor almost instantaneously. This gives you a chance to see whether you captured the image you envisioned, or you've got an overexposed, out-of-focus dud on your card. But your LCD monitor can do much more than just display your picture. You can get all sorts of useful information, such as the shutter speed, aperture, and other pertinent information about the image. You can even display a spiffy graph known as a *histogram* that shows the distribution of pixels from shadows (the darkest tones) to highlights (the brightest tones).

The information you can display on the camera LCD monitor gives you the opportunity to examine each image and make sure you got it right in the camera. Photographers should always do their best to get it right in the camera and rely as little as possible on programs like Adobe Photoshop to correct exposure problems and other issues that could have been avoided when taking the picture. After all, Adobe Photoshop is a noun, not a verb. So instead of taking the picture and saying you'll Photoshop it, rely on the information your camera supplies to determine whether you got the exposure right. Programs like Adobe Photoshop are designed to enhance images, not fix them.

In this chapter, I show you how to use your LCD monitor to review images, display image information, and much more. I also show you how to erase, rotate, and protect images.

Displaying Image Information

When you take a picture, you see it almost immediately on your LCD monitor. When you want the big picture, you view the image and nothing else. The large image lets you evaluate things like composition and image sharpness, which enables you to decide whether the image is worth keeping. However, if you can deal with a smaller image, you can view all sorts of information about the image that can tell you whether you nailed the shot. If you're shooting in one of the Basic Zone automatic modes, examining this information helps you become a better photographer. If you're an astute student, and remember some of the settings the camera uses in the automatic modes, you can venture forth and use one of the Creative modes like Aperture Priority when depth of field is a priority, or Shutter Priority when you want to freeze action.

Getting camera information about an image you're previewing on the camera LCD monitor is easy. All you need to do is press the Info button. Each time you press the button, the display changes to reveal different information. The image size changes depending on the information shown.

Each time you press the Info button a different set of information appears, as shown in Figure 4-1. The default display shows the image (in the upper-left corner of Figure 4-1). Press the Info button again to add the file format and the image number out of the total number of images recorded on the card to date (at upper right). Press the Info button again to display a histogram with the image, the shooting mode, and other information such as the metering mode, the color profile, and the date and time (at lower left). Press the Info button yet again to display a histogram for each color channel (lower right).

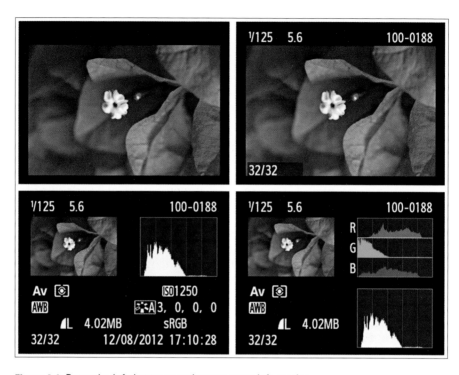

Figure 4-1: Press the Info button to review exposure information.

Using the Histogram

Even though your EOS 6D is a very capable camera, it can get it wrong when you're shooting under difficult lighting conditions. That's why your camera lets you display a histogram (see Figure 4-2) alongside the image on your camera LCD monitor. A *histogram* is a wonderful thing: It's a graph — well actually it looks more like a mountain — that shows the distribution of pixels from shadows to highlights. Study the histogram to decide whether the camera — or you, if you manually exposed the image — properly exposed the image. The histogram can tell you whether

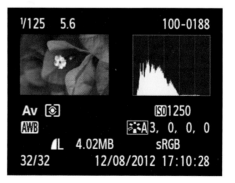

Figure 4-2: Deciphering a histogram.

the image was underexposed or overexposed. Notice the flat area on the right side of Figure 4-2. You might think this would indicate that the image was underexposed. Had I relied solely on the histogram, that would have been my conclusion. However, the brightness of the image on the LCD monitor matched the scene before me so I moved on to the next shot instead of fiddling with exposure compensation and taking another picture. Your camera can display a single histogram or display a histogram for the red, green, and blue channels compared with the brightness histogram (see Figure 4-3).

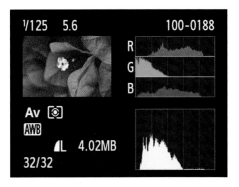

Figure 4-3: Displaying a histogram for each color channel.

A peak in the histogram shows a lot of pixels for a brightness level. A valley, however, shows fewer pixels at that brightness range. Where the graph hits the floor of the histogram, you have no data for that brightness range.

When analyzing a histogram, look for sharp peaks at either end of the scale. If you have a sharp peak on the shadow (or left) side of the histogram, the image is underexposed. Also, if the graph is on the floor of the histogram in the highlight (or right) side, the image is underexposed. However, if a large spike is right up against the highlight (right) side of the histogram, the image is overexposed and a lot of the details in the image highlights have been blown out to pure white. You can correct for overexposure and underexposure to a degree in your image-editing program, but it's always best to get it right in the camera. If you analyze a histogram and notice that the image is overexposed or underexposed, you can use your camera's exposure compensation feature to rectify the problem. For more information on exposure compensation, see Chapter 6.

The histogram is a tool. Use it wisely. When you're analyzing a scene that doesn't have any bright highlights, you may end up with a histogram that's relatively flat on the right side. When that happens, judge whether the image on the camera LCD monitor looks like the actual scene. If you rely on the histogram when you see a flat area in the highlights and add exposure compensation, you may make the image brighter than the scene actually was.

If the image you're photographing has a wide dynamic range from dark shadows to bright highlights, your camera does its best to deliver a pleasing image. If, however, you notice that there are shadow areas and highlights with no details, it's time to use the HDR feature of your camera, which I show you in Chapter 12.

Previewing Your Images

In addition to displaying information with your images, you can display multiple images on the monitor, zoom in to study the image in greater detail, or zoom out. This flexibility makes it easier for you to select a single image from thumbnails, to study the image up close to make sure the camera focused properly, and to ensure that you have a blur-free image.

To preview images on the camera LCD monitor:

1. **Click the Playback button to preview an image.**

   The last image photographed or reviewed displays on the monitor (see Figure 4-4). You can change the information displayed with the image or video by pressing the Info button, as I outline in the "Displaying Image Information" section earlier in this chapter. A movie is designated by an old-fashioned movie-camera icon with the duration of the movie shown above the icon. For more information on playing movies, refer to Chapter 5.

2. **Rotate the Quick Control dial or use the Multi-controller to navigate from one image to another.**

3. **Rotate the Main dial to the right to jump ahead 10 images, or to the left to jump back 10 images (see Figure 4-5).**

4. **Press the Index/Magnify button and rotate the Main dial to the right to zoom in on the image.**

   As you rotate the Main dial, you zoom in on the image (see Figure 4-6).

5. **Use the Multi-controller to navigate within the image.**

   As you navigate within the image, you see a small rectangle in the lower right corner of the image. Inside the rectangle is a solid square to show you the location in the image that you're exploring.

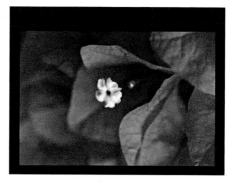

Figure 4-4: Displaying a single image.

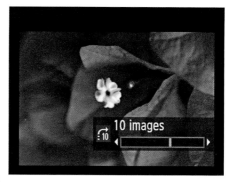

Figure 4-5: Rotate the Main dial to jump ahead 10 images, or jump back 10 images.

6. **Continue rotating the Main dial to the left to zoom all the way out and then rotate the dial one more time to display four thumbnails on the LCD monitor (see the left image in Figure 4-7).**

   Use the Multi-controller or Quick Control dial to navigate from one thumbnail to another.

7. **Rotate the Main dial left once more to display nine thumbnails (see the right image in Figure 4-7).**

   Use the Multi-controller or Quick Control dial to navigate from one thumbnail to another.

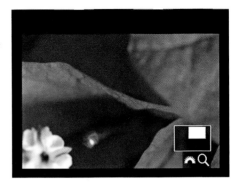

Figure 4-6: Zoom in on the image.

8. **Press the Set button to fill the monitor with the selected image.**

   If the image was shot with the camera held vertically, the image doesn't fill the screen unless you enable the menu option to rotate images (see the section, "Rotating Images," later in this chapter).

9. **Press the Index/Magnify/Reduce button to return to standard image viewing mode with a single image filling the LCD monitor.**

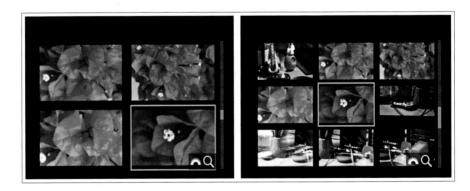

Figure 4-7: View images as thumbnails.

There are options when reviewing images to rate them. Rating images is all well and good, but the place to rate images is in an image-editing program, not when you're out shooting. You can also resize images to save space on a memory card. The place to resize images is in your image-editing program. If you find the need to resize images in camera, buy extra memory cards. Your time is valuable and memory cards are cheap. Use your time wisely to photograph images, but don't get sucked into using technology you don't really need.

Modifying Image Review Time

You can modify the amount of time the image displays on the LCD monitor after the camera writes it to your memory card. You can set the preview time from 2 to 8 seconds or display the image until you turn off the camera. To modify the image review time:

1. **Press the Menu button.**

2. **Press the Multi-controller button right or left to navigate to the Shooting Settings 1 tab.**

3. **Use the Multi-controller or the Quick Control dial to highlight Image Review (see the left image in Figure 4-8).**

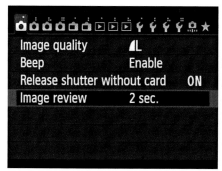
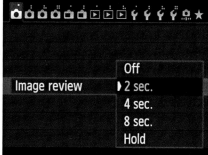

Figure 4-8: Changing image review time.

4. **Press the Set button.**

The Review Time menu appears showing the options for image review (see the right image in Figure 4-8). The Hold option displays the image until you press the shutter button halfway, navigate to another image, or power off the camera.

When you increase image review time, you decrease battery life.

5. **Use the Multi-controller or Quick Control dial to highlight the desired option and then press Set.**

The new review options take effect the next time you take a picture.

Notice that there is an option to Release the Shutter without Card option on the Shooting Settings 1 tab. I recommend that you disable this setting. Of course you should always check to make sure you never leave home without a card in the camera, but what happens if someone else in the family uses your precious camera and downloads a card to her computer and forgets to put it back in and format it. That's right, you can trigger the shutter without a card in the camera. There is a warning displayed on the LCD monitor when you shoot without a card, but not in the viewfinder. Imagine your disappointment when you thought you captured a bunch of images of Rex catching the Frisbee only to find out you don't have a card in the camera. I recommend you disable this option. When you do disable this option and try to take a picture without a card in the camera, "Card" flashes in the viewfinder.

Changing Monitor Brightness

Camera LCD monitors have come a long way, baby. The monitor on your EOS 6D offers a brilliant display with lots of pixels; the better to see images with, my dear reader. However, at times the monitor isn't bright enough; for example, when the setting sun is shining brightly waiting for "Sister Moon" (thank you, Sting). You can get some help by shading the monitor with your hand or the brim of a baseball cap. You can also get some assistance from the camera by changing the monitor brightness. You can increase or decrease the default brightness of your LCD monitor manually.

To change the brightness of the LCD monitor:

 1. Press the Menu button and then use the Multi-controller to navigate to the Camera Settings 2 tab (see the left image in Figure 4-9).

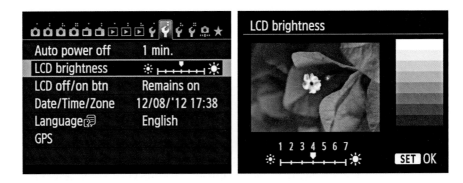

Figure 4-9: LCD brightness options.

2. Use the Multi-controller or the Quick Control dial to highlight LCD Brightness and then press the Set button.

The LCD Brightness menu displays (see the right image in Figure 4-9). In most instances, the default option (setting number 4) is perfect. You can, however, increase or decrease the relative brightness of your monitor to suit your vision and taste.

3. Rotate the Quick Control dial to increase or decrease brightness.

Use this option if the default brightness of the LCD display is too dark or too bright. As you rotate the dial, the image thumbnail gets brighter or darker. If you prefer to use the Multi-controller, you can press right to increase monitor brightness or left to decrease monitor brightness.

4. When the image is the ideal brightness for the current conditions, press Set.

Your changes are applied.

Making the monitor brighter does sap more juice from your battery, so unless you have a spare battery, increase monitor brightness at your discretion.

The LCD monitor on this camera does not automatically adjust for brightness. When you change brightness, the setting holds, even when you power off the camera. Reset the brightness to its default level when the ambient light becomes brighter, or when you power off the camera.

Deleting Images

When you review an image, you decide whether it's a keeper. If while reviewing an image, you don't like the image for any reason, you can delete it. However, deleting images needs to be done with extreme caution because the task can't be undone. After you delete an image from your card, it's gone forever.

To delete a single image:

1. Press the Playback button to display the last image reviewed, and then rotate the Quick Control dial to navigate to review the images you've photographed.

Each time you rotate the dial, you display a different image. Sometimes you'll just know that an image is a clunker as soon as it appears on the LCD monitor, which is usually what happens to me. Unless I'm really pressed for time, I examine each image immediately after I shoot it.

You can also review the images as thumbnails and delete an image, as outlined previously in this chapter. If you decide this is faster, I recommend you press the Set button to fill the monitor with the image and review it carefully before you decide to delete it.

2. **Press the Erase button.**

   The Erase menu appears at the bottom of your LCD monitor (see Figure 4-10). At the risk of being redundant, deleting an image can't be undone. At this stage, you still have the chance to stop this action by highlighting Cancel and then pressing Set.

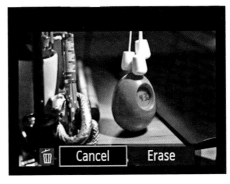

Figure 4-10: Delete images with extreme caution.

3. **Use the Multi-controller or the Quick Control dial to highlight Erase and press the Set button.**

   The image is deleted.

You can also mark multiple images for deletion. This is similar to deleting a bunch of images in an image-editing program. My opinion: Images should be reviewed on a computer in which case you have a bigger screen and it's easier to examine images in detail. Deleting in the camera should be used only for obvious clunkers, such as out-of-focus images, or when you photographed a moving target like a bird in flight and cut off half its body. But some may find deleting multiple images useful, and you can do so with your EOS 6D. To delete multiple images:

1. **Press the Menu button.**

   The last-used camera menu displays on the camera LCD monitor.

2. **Use the Multi-controller to highlight the Playback Settings 1 tab.**

3. **Use the Multi-controller or the Quick Control dial to highlight Erase Images (see the left image in Figure 4-11), and then press the Set button.**

   The options for erasing images display on the camera LCD monitor.

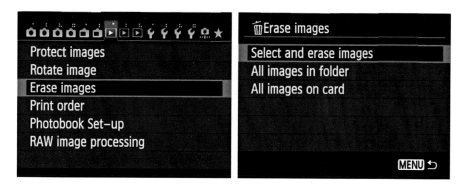

Figure 4-11: Erasing images.

4. Use the Multi-controller or the Quick Control dial to highlight Select and Erase Images (see the right image in Figure 4-11).

5. Press Set.

A single image displays (see the left image in Figure 4-12) on the camera LCD monitor unless you're viewing multiple thumbnails while reviewing. If you are reviewing single images and prefer to view thumbnails while marking images for deletion, press the Index/Magnify button and then rotate the Main dial left until three thumbnails appear on the LCD monitor.

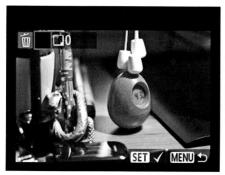 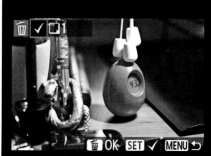

Figure 4-12: Marking images for deletion.

6. Press Set to mark an image for deletion.

After you mark an image for deletion, a check mark appears (see the right image in Figure 4-12).

If you're viewing three images as thumbnails, rotate the Quick Control dial to highlight an image and then press Set to mark it for deletion. Alternatively, you can use the Multi-controller to navigate between images and then press Set to mark an image for deletion. After you mark a thumbnail for deletion, a check mark appears above it. I suggest you view one image at a time when deleting images. The thumbnails are too small to give you enough information to determine whether an image needs to be deleted.

If you accidentally select an image for deletion that you don't want to delete, press Set to deselect the image.

If you're viewing thumbnails and want to see the bigger picture before you mark an image for deletion, press the Index/Magnify button to display a single image on the monitor. Rotate the Main dial to zoom in and then use the Multi-controller button to pan to different parts of the image.

7. **Review other images and mark the duds for deletion.**

   A check mark appears on the display when you mark an image for deletion. The total number of images you've marked for deletion appears to the right of the word *Set* in the LCD monitor.

8. **Press the Erase button to delete the images.**

   The Erase Images menu displays (see Figure 4-13). At this stage, you still have the chance to back out if you navigate to the Cancel button and press Set.

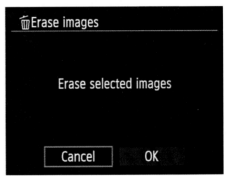

Figure 4-13: Deleting selected images.

9. **Use the Multi-controller or the Quick Control dial to highlight OK and then press Set.**

   Faster than a bullet from a gun, the images are toast.

Your camera also has menu options to erase all images in a folder or on the card. This type of heavy lifting needs to be done with your computer and not in the camera because erasing images uses battery power. I always review my images after I download them to my computer and do wholesale deletion there. My computer has a bigger monitor in better light and, most important, I'm seated in a comfortable chair. After all the heavy work is done on the computer, format the camera card and then you're ready to shoot up a storm.

If you do a lot of work away from your main computer and need to download cards after a day of shooting, consider investing in one of the small laptop computers. You can install your image-editing software on the laptop computer, download images from a card, and then do some preliminary winnowing and editing.

Rotating Images

Many photographers — me included — rotate the camera 90 degrees when taking a picture of an object that's taller than it is wide. When these images are displayed on the camera LCD monitor, you must rotate the camera 90 degrees to view them in the correct orientation. Auto-rotation is enabled by default; however, when the camera auto-rotates an image on the LCD monitor, it's very small. Some photographers prefer not to rotate images so they can see the big picture on the camera LCD monitor. You can change the options as follows:

1. **Press the Menu button and then use the Quick Control dial to highlight the Camera Settings 1 tab.**

2. **Use the Multi-controller or the Quick Control dial to highlight Auto Rotate (see the left side of Figure 4-14) and then press the Set button.**

   The Auto Rotate options display (see the right side of Figure 4-14).

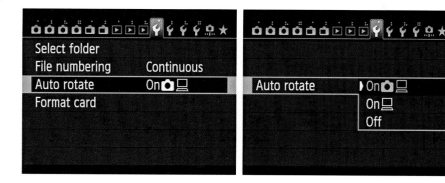

Figure 4-14: Auto-rotating images.

3. Rotate the Quick Control dial to highlight one of the following options:

- *LCD Monitor and computer:* The default setting rotates the image automatically on the camera monitor and when downloaded to the computer.

- *LCD Monitor only:* Rotates the image automatically on the computer monitor, but not on the camera. Use this option if you prefer to view a bigger image on your camera LCD monitor. Note that you will have to rotate the camera manually to view the image in its proper orientation.

- *Off:* Images are not rotated.

4. Press Set.

Your desired rotation option is now applied to all images taken from this point forward. If you choose to rotate the image when downloaded to your computer and it doesn't rotate, that means your software can't automatically rotate images from this command. If the camera is pointed up or down when you take a picture, an image photographed with the camera rotated 90 degrees may not rotate automatically.

There is also a menu command on the Playback menu to rotate individual images. But let's face it folks, if you have time to stop and rotate individual images on a card, you're photographing either a person, place, or thing that is drop dead boring to you. If this is the case, don't muck about in the camera menu; find something, someplace, or someone that gets your photography mojo into high gear. Life is too short to navigate through a million menu commands.

Protecting Images

When you photograph a person, place, or thing, you're freezing a moment in time, a moment that may never happen again. Therefore you need to be very careful when you delete images from a card because when deleted, an image is lost forever. That's why I recommend doing the majority of your *winnowing* (photographer-speak for separating the duds from the keepers) in an image-editing program. However, if you decide to delete lots of your images with camera erase options, you can protect any image to prevent accidental deletion. **Note:** This also protects the image in Canon's image-editing software. This option, however, doesn't protect the image when you format the card. To protect an image:

1. **Press the Menu button and use the Multi-controller to navigate to the Playback Settings 1 tab.**

   Protect Images is the first menu option (see Figure 4-15).

2. **Press the Set button.**

   The Protect Images menu appears (see the left image in Figure 4-16).

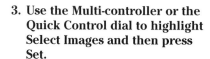

3. **Use the Multi-controller or the Quick Control dial to highlight Select Images and then press Set.**

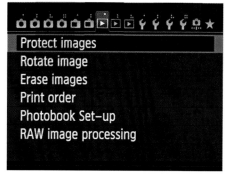

Figure 4-15: The image protection program begins here.

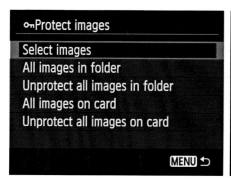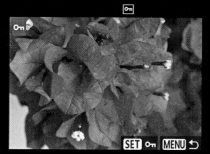

Figure 4-16: Selecting images for protection.

4. **Use the Multi-controller or the Quick Control dial to select an image you want to protect and then press Set.**

   The image is protected and can't be deleted. A lock icon appears on the screen when an image is protected (see the right image in Figure 4-16). Press Set again to unprotect a protected image.

You can also protect images while viewing them as thumbnails. Press the Index/Magnify button and then rotate the Main dial left until you see four thumbnail images. Rotate the dial left once more to view nine thumbnail images. Rotate the Quick Control dial to navigate to the next set of thumbnails and then use the multi-controller button to navigate to an individual thumbnail. Press Set to protect the highlighted image.

5. **Repeat Step 4 to protect additional images.**

6. **Press the Menu button to return to the main menu.**

   The images you've marked enter into the Pixel Protection Program.

Third-party software is available that can rescue images that were deleted accidentally or were lost when a card became corrupt. In fact, SanDisk includes rescue software with some of its cards. If you do accidentally delete a keeper, you have to use the software immediately.

You can also protect a folder or images as follows:

1. **Press the Menu button and use the Multi-controller to navigate to the Playback Settings 1 tab.**

   Protect Images is the first menu option.

2. **Use the Multi-controller or Quick Control dial to highlight Protect Images and then press Set.**

   The Protect Images menu is displayed.

3. **Use the Multi-controller or Quick Control dial to select All images in folder and then press Set.**

   All folders on the card are displayed as well as the number of images in each folder (see the left image in Figure 4-17).

4. **Rotate the Quick Control dial, or use the Multi-controller to highlight the folder you want to protect and then press Set.**

   A dialog box appears, asking you to confirm that you want to protect the folder of images (see the right image in Figure 4-17).

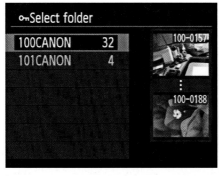
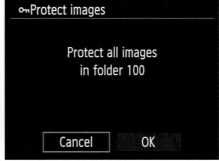

Figure 4-17: Protecting images in a folder.

5. **Use the Multi-controller or the Quick Control dial to highlight OK and then press Set.**

   The images in the folder are protected and cannot be inadvertently deleted. They will only be deleted when you reformat the card.

To unprotect images in a folder:

1. **Press the Menu button and use the Multi-controller to navigate to the Playback Settings 1 tab.**

   Protect Images is the first menu option.

2. **Use the Multi-controller or the Quick Control dial to highlight Protect Images and then press Set.**

   The Protect Images menu is displayed.

3. **Use the Multi-controller or the Quick Control dial to select Unprotect all images in folder and then press Set.**

   All folders on the card are displayed. Image thumbnails are displayed to the right of the selected folder. If the images in that folder are protected, a key symbol appears on each thumbnail (see the left image in Figure 4-18).

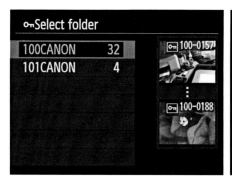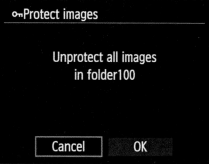

Figure 4-18: A folder of images is about to leave the image protection program.

4. **Use the Quick Control dial or Multi-controller to navigate to the folder of images you want to unprotect and then press Set.**

   A dialog box appears, asking you to confirm the fact that you want to unprotect all images in the selected folder (see the right image in Figure 4-18).

5. Use the Quick Control dial or Multi-controller to select OK.

If you decide not to unprotect the images, accept the default option of Cancel and press Set.

6. Press Set.

The folder of images is unprotected.

There are two more commands on the Protect Images menu:

✔ **All images on card:** Highlight this command and press Set to protect all images on the card.

✔ **Unprotect all images on card:** Highlight this command and press Set to unprotect all images on the card.

Using the Quick Control Screen

A good idea is to know what all the dials and buttons on your camera do. However, at times in the heat of battle you need to make one or more changes quickly, as when you want to change image size, enable the 10-second Self-Timer when shooting in Full Auto mode, or change multiple options quickly when shooting with one of the Creative shooting modes. So if you're in a New York state of mind and want to change camera settings in a New York minute, follow these steps:

1. Press the Shutter button halfway.

This action returns you to shooting mode if you've been reviewing images. If you're in the desired shooting mode, go to Step 3.

2. Press the Mode dial lock and rotate the Mode dial to the desired shooting mode.

Now you're cooking with gas.

3. Press the Quick Control button.

The Quick Control menu appears on your LCD monitor. The display varies depending on which mode you've selected from the Mode dial. Figure 4-19 shows the Quick Control screen when taking pictures in Aperture Priority mode.

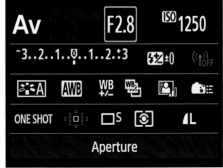

Figure 4-19: Changing shooting options with the Quick Control screen.

4. Press the Multi-controller button right or left to navigate between shooting options, and then rotate the Quick Control dial to change the setting.

Notice that as you select a shooting option, a dialog box appears underneath to tell you about the option you've selected. Figure 4-20 shows the screen that appears for changing ISO speed with the Quick Control screen. As you rotate the Quick Control dial, the setting changes. I discuss in detail the settings you can change with the Quick Control screen in Chapters 6 and 7.

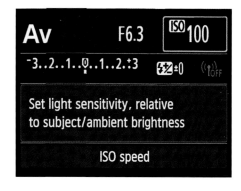

Figure 4-20: Accessing an option for a setting from the Quick Control screen.

As you move through selections on the Quick Control screen, you notice a text tip appears that tells you about what the setting you're about to change does for the pictures you're about to take. This information is useful. However, when you feel that you're an old hand at photography and the text tip is redundant and annoying, you can navigate to the Camera Setup 3 tab, choose the Feature Guide menu control, and then disable it.

5. **Repeat Step 4 for any other setting you want to modify.**

6. **Press the shutter button halfway to exit the Quick Control menu and begin taking pictures with the new settings.**

Now that was quick and easy, wasn't it?

Viewing Images as a Slide Show

If you're the type of photographer who likes to razzle and dazzle yourself and your friends by viewing images you've just shot by putting them on the camera LCD monitor — also known as *chimping* because photographers sometimes make noises like chimpanzees in a zoo when they see a cool image — you'll love viewing images on the camera LCD monitor as a slide show. To view images as a slide show:

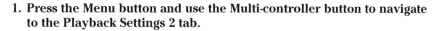

1. **Press the Menu button and use the Multi-controller button to navigate to the Playback Settings 2 tab.**

2. **Use the Multi-controller or the Quick Control dial to highlight Slide Show (see the left image in Figure 4-21) and then press the Set button.**

The Slide Show menu appears (see the right image in Figure 4-21). The default slide show displays all images with a 1-second delay, and the show loops until you exit the slide show. To accept the default slide-show options, fast-forward to Step 6.

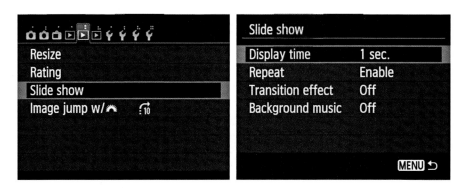

Figure 4-21: Slide-show settings — popcorn optional.

3. To select a different viewing option, use the Multi-controller or the Quick Control dial to highlight All Images and then press Set.

Two arrows appear indicating that you have options.

4. Rotate the Quick Control dial to scroll through the options.

The options vary depending on what you've captured on the card and whether you've put images into a different folder. If you have multiple folders, they appear on this menu. Rotate the Quick Control dial to select the desired photos. If you have movies on the card, you can view movies on the camera monitor. You can also view stills in the slide show only, view images by date, or view images you've rated.

5. After choosing an option, press Set.

The images or movies display as a slide show after you set up the slide show.

6. Use the Multi-controller or the Quick Control dial to highlight Set Up and then press Set.

The menu changes to display the playback options (see the left image in Figure 4-22).

7. Highlight Display Time and press Set.

The menu changes to show the options for the duration of each slide (see the right image in Figure 4-22).

8. Use the Multi-controller or the Quick Control dial to select a Display time option and then press Set.

The previous slide-show menu displays.

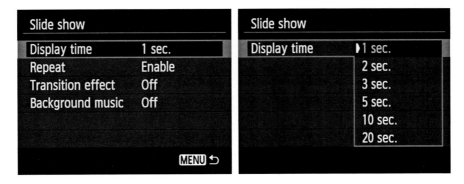

Figure 4-22: Setting playback options for the slide show.

9. Use the Multi-controller or the Quick Control dial to highlight Repeat and press Set.

The Repeat options display (see the left image in Figure 4-23). The default Enable option repeats the slide show until you press the Shutter button halfway or press the Menu button. The Disable option plays the slide show once. After pressing Set the previous screen displays.

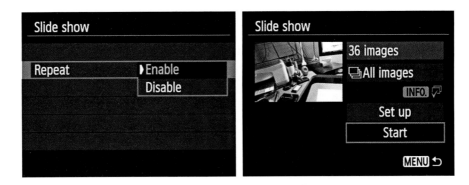

Figure 4-23: Finalizing slide show options.

10. Use the Multi-controller or the Quick Control dial to highlight Transition effect and press Set.

The Transition effect options are displays. Most of the transition effects will have little effect on a slide show on your LCD monitor. I invite you to investigate these options if you decide to show your slide shows on your TV set.

11. Select the desired Transition Effect and press Set.

The previous slide-show menu displays.

12. Use the Multi-controller or the Quick Control dial to highlight Background Music and then press set.

You can get music files from the EOS Utilities disk, but as a serious photographer, I need to put my two cents' worth in here: Why would you want to take up room on your memory card with music files?

13. Select the desired music file and press Set.

Hmmm... If you were photographing Bike Week at Daytona Beach, you could have "Born to Be Wild" on your memory card. But I digress and assume you are a serious photographer as well. I'm also quite sure that Steppenwolf has not licensed the song to Canon.

14. Press Menu to return to the main Slide Show menu, use the Multi-controller or the Quick Control dial to highlight Start, and press Set (see the right image in Figure 4-23).

The slide show begins.

15. Press Set to pause the slide show.

Use this option to examine a single image. You can't magnify an image while in slide show mode. When the slide show is paused, you can rotate the Main dial or Quick Control dial to view a different image. You can press the Info button to show a different display with the image. Pressing Set also pauses a movie that's part of the slide show.

16. Press Set to continue the slide show.

When you're tired of watching the slide show or your battery starts running low (auto-power-off is disabled when you view a slide show), press the Shutter button halfway to return to picture-taking mode. Alternatively, you can press the Menu button to specify different slide-show options or to view images in a different folder.

Viewing Images on a TV Set

You have a digital camera capable of capturing colorful images with an impressive resolution of 20.2 megapixels. Your television set is a grand device on which to display your images. You can display still images or a slide show on your TV screen. And if you have a high-definition (HD) television set, you can knock your socks off — and for that matter, the socks of your friends and anybody else within viewing distance — by viewing your precious images onscreen. Video also looks awesome on a television set.

To view your images on a regular TV set:

1. **Open the AV slot on the side of your camera (see Figure 4-24).**

2. **Insert the AV cable supplied with your camera into the A/V Out/Digital terminal.**

   The Canon logo needs to face the back of the camera for proper insertion.

3. **Connect the other end of the AV cable to your TV set.**

   The plugs are color-coded. Connect the red and white plugs to the Audio In ports and the yellow plug to the Video In port on your TV set. Refer to your television manual to choose video as the input source.

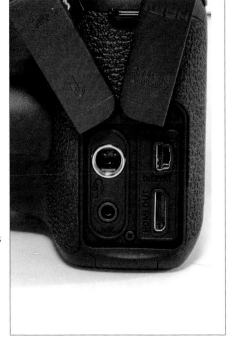

Figure 4-24: Accessing your camera's AV slot.

4. **Press the Playback button.**

   An image displays on your television set.

5. **Use the Multi-controller or the Quick Control dial to view the next image.**

   You can also set up a slide show, as I outline in the section, "Viewing Images as a Slide Show," earlier in this chapter.

To view images on an HD television set:

1. **Open the AV slot on the side of your camera (see Figure 4-24).**

2. **Connect the HDMI cable HTC-100 (sold separately) to the HDMI Out terminal on your camera.**

   The HDMI mini logo needs to face the front of the camera for proper insertion.

3. **Connect the HDMI mini cable to your TV set and then press the Playback button.**

   An image displays on your television set. Images are adjusted for optimal viewing on an HD television set. If your set can't display the captured images, unplug the HDMI cable from the camera and TV set; then connect the AV cable, as I outline in the preceding steps.

4. **Use the Multi-controller or the Quick Control dial to view the next image.**

   You can also set up a slide show, as I outline in the "Viewing Images as a Slide Show" section earlier in this chapter. In fact, if you're viewing single images and decide you want to view them as a slide show, press the Menu button to display the camera menu on your TV screen and then follow the steps in that section.

Part II
Going Beyond Point-and-Shoot Photography

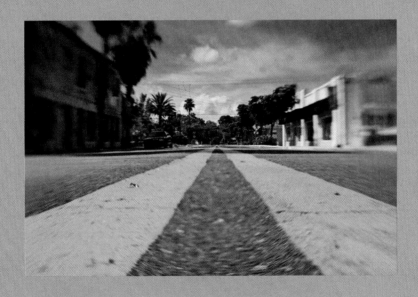

Check out the article "How to Use the Zone System with Your EOS 6D" online at www.dummies.com/extras/canoneos6d.

In this part . . .

- ✔ Find out how to use some of the very cool features of your Canon EOS 6D. Gain the ability to shoot photographs outside of Scene Intelligent Automode and take full advantage of the high power technology that Canon is very proud of.

- ✔ Get familiar with Live View and compose your images through the LCD monitor. Discover how to capture movies in Live View mode, as well as how to utilize all the Live View features.

- ✔ Explore how to use the creative shooting modes to photograph action, wildlife, people, pets, places, and things.

- ✔ Check out the article "How to Use the Zone System with Your EOS 6D" online at www.dummies.com/extras/canoneos6d.

5

Shooting Pictures and Movies with Live View

In This Chapter

▶ Exploring Live View menu options and photography

▶ Shooting and focusing in Live View mode

▶ Using the Quick Control menu

▶ Recording and previewing movies

▶ Getting some tips for movie shooting

*P*hotographers who own point-and-shoot cameras use the LCD monitor to compose their pictures, which has some definite advantages. For instance, you can place the camera close to the ground and compose an image through the monitor, or hold the camera over your head to do the same. Digital SLR (single-lens reflex) owners didn't have this option until the Live View mode began popping up on digital SLR cameras. And fortunately for you, your EOS 6D has this option. Live View mode has lots of benefits when creating images, including what you see is what you get. However, Live View mode has a few disadvantages as well. You hold the camera in front of you at arm's length, which, unless you work out at the gym five days a week, can be a bit tiring. Many people use tripods when shooting images and movies using Live View mode.

In addition to taking great pictures in Live View mode, you can also capture high-definition (HD) movies. You can specify the size of the movie and the frame rate. So if you're ready to go live, read on. In this chapter, I show you how to take pictures, capture movies, and more in the upcoming sections. Live View shooting is enabled by default. Figure 5-1 shows the Live View Menus. If you should ever decide to disable Live View shooting, use the Multi-controller or Quick Control dial to highlight Live View and choose Disable.

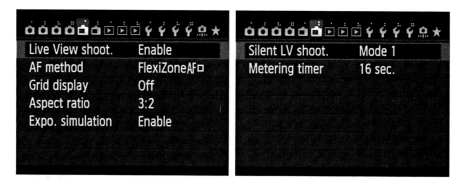

Figure 5-1: Live View at 5:00.

Taking Pictures with Live View

Live View is the bee's knees when it comes to picture taking. You have a much larger view of your subject and you can compose pictures holding the camera low to the ground — which beats crawling on your belly — or over your head. To take pictures in Live View mode:

1. **Press the Start/Stop button.**

   What's in the lens's field of view appears on the camera monitor.

2. **Press the shutter button halfway to focus the scene (see Figure 5-2).**

   When you shoot in Live View, the camera uses the default FlexiZone-Single focusing mode, which gives you a single auto-focus point in the center of the LCD monitor. You can use the Multi-controller to move the AF point when you use the default FlexiZone-Single focusing mode. When the camera achieves focus, the autofocus point turns green.

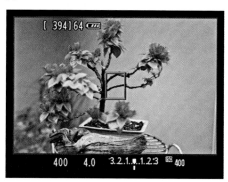

Figure 5-2: Focusing in Live View mode.

The default autofocus mode works great when shooting in Live View mode, but you have other options, as I show you in the "Focusing with Live View" section of this chapter.

To display the electronic level while shooting pictures in Live View mode, press the Info button to cycle through the information displays until you see the level.

3. **Press the Shutter button fully to take the picture.**

   The LCD monitor displays the image almost immediately. After the designated image-review time, the monitor returns to Live View mode.

4. **Press the Start/Stop button to exit Live View mode.**

   The camera automatically exits Live View mode after the time designated by auto power off (see Chapter 1).

When you shoot in Live View mode, you hold the camera in front of you. Therefore, you can't hold the camera as steadily as you can when shooting through the viewfinder. Using a lens with image stabilization helps, but if you don't have one, shoot at a higher shutter speed than you normally would. For example, if you're taking pictures in Live View mode with a lens with a focal length of 85mm, use a shutter speed of 1/125 of a second or faster. Otherwise mount the camera on a tripod.

Shooting images in Live View mode takes a toll on battery life. You'll get anywhere from 210 to 230 images on a fully charged battery, depending upon the ambient temperature and the amount of images taken with flash.

When you shoot in Live View mode in hot conditions or in direct sunlight, the internal temperature of the camera increases. A white warning icon appears when the internal temperature of the camera is near the danger point, and a red warning light appears when the temperature is at the danger point. Press the Start/Stop button to stop Live View when you see this warning and let the camera cool down before taking any more pictures.

When shooting in Live View mode, don't point the camera directly at the sun. Because the mirror is locked up during Live View, exposure to the sun can damage internal components of the camera.

Displaying shooting information

Shooting information is important to many photographers. When you compose a picture in standard shooting mode, you have a lot of information at your disposal in the viewfinder and on the LCD panel. You can also display information when shooting in Live View mode by pressing the Info button. Each time you press the button, the screen changes. The default screen shows the autofocus (AF) points without shooting information. Press the Info button once to display the screen, as shown in Figure 5-3.

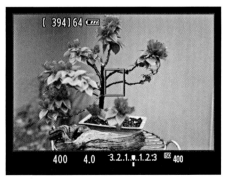

Figure 5-3: Displaying exposure information while shooting in Live View mode.

The first level of information displays the exposure compensation scale, shots remaining on the memory card, the ISO speed setting, and the battery status. Press the Shutter button halfway, and the AF point will turn green when the camera has achieved focus and the shutter speed and aperture display. If you choose the Quick autofocus mode, the 11 points you normally see when shooting through the viewfinder are displayed. The points that are used to achieve focus are highlighted in red when you press the shutter button halfway.

To view additional information, press the Info button again. The second level of information (see Figure 5-4) displays all the information from the preceding screen with these additions: the Live View AF mode, the image format, exposure simulation, Auto Lighting Optimizer mode, picture style, and white balance. You see additional information if you've enabled features such as flash exposure bracketing, automatic exposure bracketing, and so on.

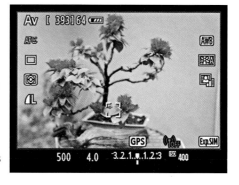

Figure 5-4: Displaying more information.

If you accept the default option of Exposure Simulation, press the button again and a histogram appears (see Figure 5-5). You can use this information to increase or decrease the exposure with exposure compensation.

Focusing with Live View

When you shoot in Live View mode, you have three focusing options. Two options are used for taking photographs of landscapes and objects,

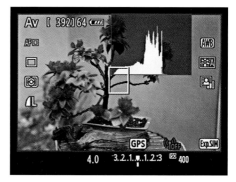

Figure 5-5: Displaying the histogram.

and the other focusing mode is used to detect faces. To specify the autofocus (AF) mode:

1. **Press the Menu button.**

2. **Use the Multi-controller button to navigate to the Live View Shooting Settings 1 tab.**

3. **Use the Multi-controller or the Quick Control dial to highlight AF Method (see the left image in Figure 5-6) and then press the Set button.**

   The Live View AF Method options display on the camera LCD monitor (see the right image in Figure 5-6).

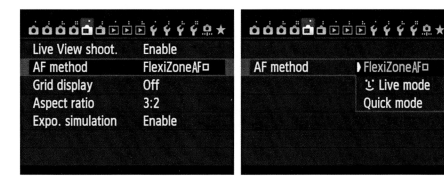

Figure 5-6: Choosing a Live View AF mode.

4. **Use Multi-controller or the Quick Control dial to highlight one of the following options:**

   • *FlexZoneAF:* When you choose this mode, the camera uses the sensor to achieve focus. You have a single autofocus point in the center of the LCD monitor. If the autofocus point is not over the part of the scene or subject you're photographing that must be in focus, you can use the Multi-controller to move the autofocus point to the desired position. When you use this mode, it may take longer for the camera to achieve focus than when using the Quick mode.

   • *Live Mode (Face Detection):* Uses the sensor to focus but detects faces.

   • *Quick Mode:* Uses the camera AF sensor to focus the image. As the name implies, this mode is quicker than using the camera sensor. The Live View image momentarily blacks out while the camera achieves focus. You also have all 11 autofocus points to work with.

5. **Press Set.**

   The selected focusing mode is used whenever you shoot images with Live View.

After working with the camera, I find that Quick Mode does the best job of focusing. Occasionally the Live View modes have problems achieving focus. If you prefer to use one of the Live View focus modes, you find the camera has a difficult time focusing, and you have a lens that lets you focus manually when in autofocus mode, twist the focus ring until the scene is close to being in focus and then the Live View focusing should snap the scene into focus.

To focus the camera while using Live Mode focusing:

1. **Press the Start/Stop button to enable Live View shooting.**

   An autofocus (AF) point appears in the center of the image.

2. **(Optional) Use the Multi-controller button to move the AF point.**

   Move the AF point over the part of the image that you want the camera to focus.

3. **Press the shutter button halfway.**

   When the camera achieves focus, the AF point turns green and the camera beeps.

4. **Press the shutter button fully.**

   The camera takes the picture.

To focus the camera with Live Mode (Face Detection) focusing:

1. **Press the Start/Stop button to enable Live View shooting.**

   An AF point appears in the center of the image.

2. **Press the shutter button halfway.**

   The camera sensor detects faces in front of the lens by placing a rectangular AF frame over it. When the camera achieves focus, the frame turns green and the camera beeps. If the camera detects multiple faces, an AF frame with a right- and left-pointing arrow appears. Use the Multi-controller button to drag the AF frame over the person who's the center of interest and who should be in focus.

3. **Press the shutter button fully.**

   The camera takes the picture.

To focus with Quick Mode focusing:

1. **Press the Start/Stop button to enable Live View shooting.**

   An autofocus frame point appears in the center of the image.

2. Press the shutter button halfway.

The AF points for the autofocus point mode you specify for standard shooting appear on the camera LCD monitor. A white frame appears over the AF points. The point(s) used to achieve focus turns green.

3. (Optional) Use the Multi-controller button to move the white autofocus frame.

4. Press the shutter button fully.

The camera takes the picture.

If the camera has a difficult time achieving focus in Live View mode, switch your lens to manual focus, and then press the Index/Magnify button to display a small frame in the center of the image. You can then use the Multi-controller to move the frame over the part of the subject or scene that you're photographing that needs to be in sharp focus. Press the Index Magnify button again to magnify the area in the frame 5 times. Press the button one more time to magnify the area 10 times. You can then easily focus manually on the magnified portion of the scene.

Using the Quick Control menu to shoot pictures in Live View mode

When you shoot in Live View mode, you can quickly change the Auto Lighting Optimizer and the image quality through the Quick Control menu. If you're using the Quick Live View autofocus (AF) mode, you can change the AF points as well. To change Live View shooting options with the Quick Control menu:

1. Press the Start/Stop button to enable Live View shooting and then press the Quick Control button.

The Quick Control menu appears on the LCD monitor (see Figure 5-7).

2. Use the Multi-controller button to navigate to and highlight an option.

The option icon becomes orange. In Figure 5-7, the AF Method is highlighted. The current option is AutoFlex Single Point, as noted on the bottom of the screen.

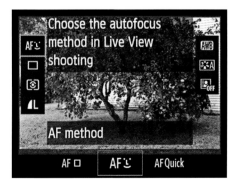

Figure 5-7: Using the Live View picture-taking Quick Control menu.

3. **Use the Multi-controller or the Quick Control dial to change the option setting.**

   As you rotate the Quick Control dial, you see different icons on the screen. With the exception of the AF points at the bottom of the screen, you see text that describes what the icon represents. For example, if you're changing image quality, you see the format and size displayed.

4. **Use the Multi-controller button and the Quick Control dial to change other settings as needed and then press the shutter button halfway.**

   You're ready to start shooting with your new settings.

Displaying a grid in Live View mode

When shooting in Live View mode, you can display a grid on the LCD monitor. This grid is useful when aligning objects that are supposed to be horizontal or vertical. You can also use the grid when composing your images (see Chapter 7). You have three grids from which to choose: a 3 x 3 grid, a 6 x 4 grid, or a 3 x 3 grid with diagonal lines. To display a grid on the camera LCD monitor when shooting in Live View mode:

1. **Press the Menu button.**

   The previously used menu appears.

2. **Use the Multi-controller or Quick Control dial to navigate to the Live View Shooting Settings 1 tab.**

3. **Use the Multi-controller or the Quick Control dial to highlight Grid Display (see the left image in Figure 5-8) and then press the Set button.**

   The Grid Display options display (see the right image in Figure 5-8).

Live View shoot.	Enable
AF method	FlexiZoneAF□
Grid display	Off
Aspect ratio	3:2
Expo. simulation	Enable

Grid display	▸ Off
	3x3 ╫
	6x4 ▦
	3x3+diag ✳

Figure 5-8: Enabling the Live View grid.

4. **Use the Multi-controller or the Quick Control dial to highlight the desired grid.**

    In my opinion, the first grid, with nine squares, is the most useful. This is identical to the Rule of Thirds (see Chapter 8) photographers use when composing images.

5. **Press Set.**

    The selected grid displays in the monitor when you shoot in Live View mode.

Exploring Other Useful Live View Options

In the previous sections of this chapter, I discuss menu commands that enable Live View shooting, choose a Live View autofocus mode, and display a grid over the LCD monitor while shooting in Live View mode. You may find other Live View menu options and one custom function (that displays a cropping grid) useful. To take a look at the other options, follow these steps:

1. **Press the Menu button.**

    The previously used menu displays.

2. **Use the Multi-controller to navigate to the Live View Shooting Settings 1 tab (see the left image in Figure 5-9).**

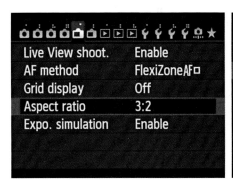 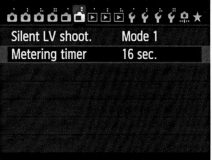

Live View shoot.	Enable
AF method	FlexiZoneAF◻
Grid display	Off
Aspect ratio	3:2
Expo. simulation	Enable

| Silent LV shoot. | Mode 1 |
| Metering timer | 16 sec. |

Figure 5-9: Taking pictures with Live View.

3. **Use the Multi-controller or the Quick Control dial to review these commands:**

- *Expo. Simulation:* This option is enabled by default and displays a histogram with one of the shooting information displays. When this command is enabled, Exp.SIM appears on the LCD monitor when you enable Live View. Press the Info button until you see the histogram. Use the histogram to make sure the image is exposed properly. You can also disable this option, or you can choose an option that changes the brightness of the monitor to simulate what the actual picture will look like when you press the Depth of Field preview button.

- *Aspect Ratio:* With this option, you can change the Aspect ratio of the image in camera. I don't find this option especially useful. I suggest you stick with the default 3:2 aspect ratio, which is the aspect ratio of the sensor. This enables you to create images with all of the pixels the sensor is capable of capturing. You can always crop the image to a different aspect ratio in your favorite image-editing application.

 4. **Use the Multi-controller to navigate to the Live View Shooting Settings 2 tab (see the right image in Figure 5-9).**

   That's right. Live View is so cool they gave it two menu tabs.

5. **Use the Multi-controller or Quick Control dial to explore the following settings:**

   - *Silent LV Shoot:* You have three options from which to choose. Mode 1 is considerably quieter than normal Live View shooting. When you choose this option, you can shoot continuously. If you choose Continuous Drive mode, you can capture images at 4.1 fps (frames per second). Mode 2 takes one shot when you press the shutter. Camera operation is suspended as long as the shutter button is pressed. When you release the shutter button, camera operation resumes. This mode is quieter than Mode 1. Your third option is to disable silent shooting.

   - *Metering Timer:* This option enables you to change the amount of time exposure settings are displayed on the LCD monitor. The default setting of 16 seconds gives you plenty of time to examine the histogram and change exposure compensation, but you can decrease the display time to 5 seconds, or increase it to as long as 30 minutes.

Making Movies with Your Camera

With your EOS 6D, you can create high-definition (HD) video. Your camera records video in Apple's QuickTime MOV format. You can specify the size of the movies you capture and the frame rate. In the following sections, I show you how to capture video and other movie-shooting tasks with your camera.

Recording movies

Recording movies on your EOS 6D is easy. Flip a switch and push a button and you're recording. And you see the whole movie unfold on the camera LCD monitor. When you've recorded your fill, push the button again to stop recording. You can preview the movie on the camera LCD monitor to decide whether you want to keep it. When recording movies in a shooting mode other than M (Manual), the camera automatically determines the aperture, shutter speed, and ISO speed based on the current ambient lighting conditions. Monaural sound is recorded with your movie unless you disable sound or insert a stereo microphone into the microphone in-port on the side of the camera. To record a movie:

1. **Flip the Live View/Movie Shooting switch to the left.**

   The switch stops at the red icon that looks like a movie camera. The scene in front of your lens displays on the LCD monitor. With all the shooting information displayed, the remaining recording time displays next to the video size and frame rate information.

2. **Choose the desired shooting mode.**

   I suggest you use Aperture Priority mode to record video. With Aperture Priority mode, you can control how much of the scene you're record-ing is in focus by aperture choice. Choose a small aperture (large f-stop value) when you want a large depth of field. A small aperture with a wide-angle lens is the perfect recipe for recording a video of a beautiful landscape like the Grand Canyon. Choose a large aperture (small f-stop value) when you're recording a video of a person. In conjunction with a medium telephoto lens with a focal length of 80 or 105 mm, your subject will be in focus, but the foreground and background will be out of focus.

3. **Press the Shutter button halfway to achieve focus.**

   When you record movies, you use one of the Live View autofocus modes that I discuss in the "Focusing with Live View" section earlier in this chapter. If the camera can't achieve focus, switch the lens to manual focus and twist the focusing ring until your subject snaps into focus.

   You can also achieve focus with the AF-On button.

   You can lock exposure to a specific part of the scene you're recording by moving the center autofocus point over the spot that you want to lock focus and then pressing the AE Lock button.

4. **Press the Start/Stop button.**

   A red dot appears in the upper-right corner of the LCD monitor when you're recording (see Figure 5-10), and the elapsed time appears in the center of the frame near the top. A semi-transparent frame appears around the edge of the Live View image. The area inside the frame is what the camera records. Maximum recording time for a 16GB card at the maximum video dimensions is 1 hour and 4 minutes. The maximum amount of time for which you can continuously record video is 29 minutes and 59 seconds. If you record a video that reaches maximum duration, the camera will automatically shut off. Your camera cannot record videos with a file size larger than 4GB.

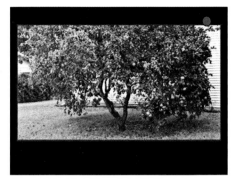

Figure 5-10: Quiet, numbskulls. You're making a movie here.

However, if you do reach that magic number, your camera will automatically create a new file so you can record without interruption.

 To display the electronic level while shooting video in Live View mode, press the Info button to cycle through the information displays until you see the level.

5. Press the Start/Stop button.

Recording stops and the red dot disappears.

Using manual exposure when recording a movie

You can manually expose your movies to gain complete control. When you manually expose a movie, you can set the shutter speed, aperture, and ISO speed rating. This is useful when you want to control the depth of field in a movie. For example, when you're recording a video of a scenic vista, a small aperture gives you a greater depth of field. When you manually expose a movie, use the exposure compensation scale at the bottom of the LCD monitor as a meter. To manually expose a movie:

 1. Flip the Live View/Movie Shooting switch to the left.

Live View video recording is enabled.

 2. Press the Info button until you see the exposure compensation scale at the bottom middle of the Live View display.

Use this scale to get the correct exposure.

3. Rotate the Mode dial to M.

You can manually set exposure in this mode.

4. Point the camera toward the scene you're going to record.

5. **Rotate the Main dial to set the shutter speed and then rotate the Quick Control dial to set the aperture.**

   While setting the shutter speed and aperture, look at the exposure compensation scale. A flashing bar appears below the scale when the exposure isn't perfect. If the bar is to the left of center, you need to increase exposure; if it's to the right, you need to decrease exposure. When the indicator bar is aligned perfectly with the center of the scale, the exposure is perfect for the lighting condition. The aperture you choose determines the depth of field. If you're recording a talking head video, you can choose a large aperture (small f-stop value) and your subject will be in focus, but the background will be out of focus. If you're recording a video of a stunning landscape using a wide-angle focal length, choose a small aperture with an f-stop value between f/8.0 and f/13.

6. **Press the ISO button and then rotate the Quick Control dial to set the desired ISO speed setting (see Figure 5-11).**

   Choose the lowest possible speed for the lighting conditions while maintaining shutter speed that is 1/50 of a second. This shutter speed is deemed ideal for video recording by many videographers due to the fact that it is almost double the standard video frame rate of 24 fps (frames per second), which results in smooth video

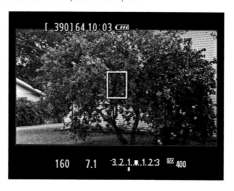

Figure 5-11: Manually setting the shutter speed and aperture for video recording.

   with good transitions between frames. If you shoot video at 30 fps, choose an ISO that will give you a shutter speed of 1/60 of a second. In Figure 5-12 the exposure indicator shows that the scene is still slightly underexposed. A slightly higher ISO setting is needed to properly expose the scene and achieve the desired shutter speed of 1/60 of a second.

7. **Press the Start/Stop button to start recording video and then press it again to stop recording.**

   When you're finished recording, make sure you choose a different shooting mode or manually set exposure for the next scene you're going to record.

When you're recording video the camera will not refocus as you pan the camera, nor will it set exposure automatically. If you're recording video of a scene that has objects that are varying distances from the camera, either use a small aperture, which ensures a large depth of field, or focus manually on the important objects that you want to be in clear focus. If you're recording video and will be panning from dark to light, meter the darkest spot in the scene and record the aperture, and then meter the lightest part of the scene and record the aperture. Split the difference and you'll be able to capture a good video.

Displaying video shooting information

When recording video, you can display a lot of shooting information, a little information, or no information. You can display the aperture and shutter speed, battery information, exposure compensation scale, autofocus mode, and much more, depending on which information screen you display. To display information when recording movies:

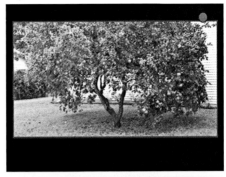

1. **Flip the Live View/Movie Shooting switch to the left.**

   Live View movie recording is enabled.

2. **Press the Info button.**

   A shooting information screen is displayed.

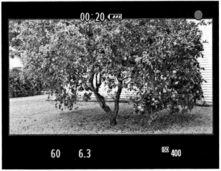

3. **Press the Info button repeatedly to display different shooting information.**

The first shooting information screen (the top image in Figure 5-12) displays the focus frame. This is perfect for when you're going commando and want to see every subtle nuance of the scene you're recording. The second shooting screen (middle image) displays the battery information, aperture, ISO speed rating, and the exposure compensation scale. The final screen adds the camera mode and any other shooting commands you may be using to capture your video (bottom image).

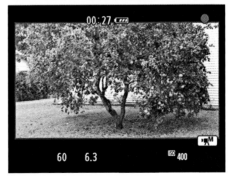

Figure 5-12: Displaying shooting information.

Changing video dimensions and frame rate

Your camera can capture high-definition video with dimensions of up to 1920 x 1080 and a frame rate up to 60 fps. You can modify the video dimensions and frame rate to suit your intended destination. To change video dimensions and frame rate:

1. **Flip the Live View/Movie Shooting switch to the left.**

   You can change video menu options only when video recording is enabled.

2. **Press the Menu button.**

   The last used menu displays. When you capture video, the Live View Shooting tabs become video shooting tabs (see Figure 5-13). The first Video Shooting tab is identical to the first Live View shooting tab previously discussed.

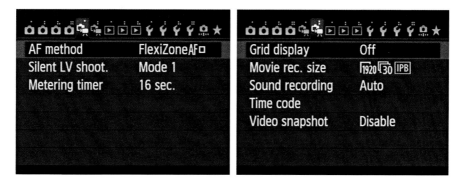

Figure 5-13: Menus for video settings.

3. **Use the Multi-controller button to navigate to the Video Shooting 2 tab.**

   Your Live View video recording options display.

4. **Use the Multi-controller or the Quick Control dial to highlight Movie Rec. Size (see the left image in Figure 5-14) and then press the Set button.**

   The video dimension and frame rate options display (see the right image in Figure 5-14). Yikes. I know what you're thinking. It looks all Greek. Well it looked Greek to me too until the great Fredrico Fettuccini spelled it all out with garlic breath and a hint of Chianti. One of the settings you can choose from is: [1920] [30] [IPB]. The first option is the dimension, the second is the frame rate, and the third option is the type of compression applied to the video. Here's what all the symbols stand for:

   Movie Dimensions:

   - *1920*: This stands for 1920 x 1080, which is the dimension of the video in pixels. It's full HD (High Definition), the real deal, Lucille.

   - *1080*: This stands for 1080 x 720, which is the dimension of this option in pixels. It's HD video as well.

   - *640*: This stands for 640 x 480, the dimension of the video in pixels. This is standard-definition video.

Frame Rate:

- *30:* 30 frames per second. Use this frame rate for NTSC video, which is shown in North American countries.

- *60:* 60 frames per second. This frame rate can also be used for NTSC video.

- *25:* 25 frames per second. Use this frame rate for PAL video, which is used in Europe.

- *50:* 50 frames per second. This frame rate is also used for PAL video.

- *24:* 24 frames per second. This frame rate is used for movies. You can also use it for any type of video you record. This was the same frame rate used when video was actually captured on film. The resulting video has a slightly different look, which is reminiscent of video on the big screen.

Compression:

- *IPB:* Compresses several frames at once, which results in a smaller file size meaning you can fit more video on a card.

- *ALL-I:* Compresses one frame at a time. This form of compression results in a larger file size, but is better suited for editing due to the fact that you've got more information with which to work.

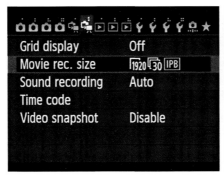 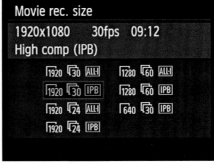

Figure 5-14: Changing video dimensions and frame rate.

5. **Use the Multi-controller or the Quick Control dial to select the desired video dimension, frame rate, and compression format.**

6. **Press Set.**

    You're ready to record video with the specified dimension and frame rate.

For more information about digital video, check out *Digital SLR Video and Filmmaking For Dummies* by John Carucci.

Changing audio recording options

When you record video with your EOS 6D, you record audio as well. You can change the record level, disable audio, and enable a wind filter and a sound attenuator. And you thought those little holes in the front of the camera were just a dinky microphone. To beef up the audio in your movies:

1. **Flip the Live View/Movie Shooting switch to the left.**

   You can change video menu options only when video recording is enabled.

2. **Press the Menu button.**

   The last used menu appears.

3. **Use the Multi-controller to navigate to the Video Settings 2 tab.**

4. **Use the Multi-controller or the Quick Control dial to navigate to Sound Recording (see the left image in Figure 5-15) and then press Set.**

   The Sound Recording options appear (see the right image in Figure 5-15).

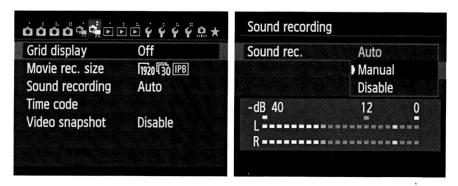

Figure 5-15: Changing the sound recording option.

5. **Use the Multi-controller or Quick Control dial to highlight Manual and then press Set.**

   The Manual recording menu appears. This menu gives you a right and left meter, which you use to accurately set the recording level. The meters record the highest decibel rating and hold it for three seconds.

6. **While looking at the peak-level meter, rotate the Main dial until the loudest sound recorded is –12 on the scale.**

   If the sound exceeds 0, the sound will be clipped (distorted).

7. Press Menu to apply the changes.

The recording level is optimum for the scene you are recording. You'll have to reset the levels when you record a scene in a louder or quieter environment.

 You can also enable a wind filter which will eliminate some wind noise when you're recording video in windy conditions, and a sound attenuator, which is useful for suppressing loud sounds when recording.

Using the Quick Control menu to shoot video in Live View mode

When you shoot video in Live View mode, you can quickly change the movie dimensions, frame rate, and much more through the Quick Control menu. To change Live View shooting options with the Quick Control menu:

 1. Press the Start/Stop button to enable Live View shooting, rotate the Live View button to video, and then press the Quick Control button.

The Quick Control menu appears on the LCD monitor (see Figure 5-16).

 2. Use the Multi-controller button to navigate to and highlight an option.

The option icon becomes orange. In Figure 5-16, the option to change the video dimensions and frame rate is highlighted.

 3. Use the Multi-controller or the Quick Control dial to change the option setting.

As you rotate the Quick Control dial, you see different icons on the screen.

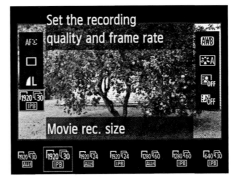
Figure 5-16: Using the Live View video Quick Control menu.

4. Use the Multi-controller button and the Quick Control dial to change other settings as needed, and then press the Shutter button halfway.

You're ready to start capturing video with your new settings.

Taking a still picture while recording a movie

You can take a picture while recording a movie. This option is handy when you're making a recording and something interesting happens that you want to save as a still picture. The still image uses the exposure information displayed in the Live View shooting information. The image is the format and quality you specify with the camera menu. To take a still picture while recording a video:

1. **Begin recording a movie.**

2. **Press the Shutter button when you see something you want to record as a still image.**

   The Live View turns black while the camera takes the picture. You may notice a glitch at that point in the video unless you're using a fast SD card.

Previewing Movies on the Camera LCD Monitor

You can preview movies in all their glory on the camera LCD monitor. When you preview a movie, buttons appear that let you play the movie at full speed or in slow motion, pause the movie, preview it frame by frame, and navigate to the first or last frame. You can also edit movies in the camera, which I show you how to do in Chapter 11. To preview a movie on the camera LCD monitor:

1. **Press the Playback button to navigate to the desired movie.**

   You can preview images and movies as single images or thumbnails. A movie is designated by an old-fashioned movie camera icon when you view single images or with a filmstrip border when you view them as thumbnails.

2. **Press the Set button.**

   Buttons appear beneath the movie (see Figure 5-17).

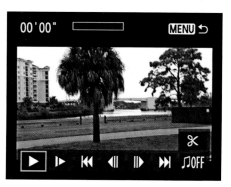

Figure 5-17: Please pass the popcorn.

3. **Use the Multi-controller the Quick Control dial to select an option.**

   Choose one of the following options (from left to right in Figure 5-17):

   - *Exit:* Exits movie playing mode.
   - *Play:* Plays the movie at full speed.
   - *Slow Motion:* Plays the movie in slow motion.
   - *First Frame:* Rewinds the movie to the first frame.
   - *Previous Frame:* Rewinds the movie to the previous frame.
   - *Next Frame:* Fast-forwards to the next frame.
   - *Last Frame:* Fast-forwards to the last frame.
   - *Edit:* Edits the movie.
   - *Background Music:* Gives you the option to play background music when you preview the video on your camera. You add background music to the card from the EOS Utility disk.

4. **Press Set to perform the option you choose in Step 3.**

Tips for Movie Shooting

Your camera captures awesome video. I've used my EOS 6D to capture some beautiful video from the nearby beaches. I'll send a copy of the video to my relatives who live north of the Mason-Dixon line in January to show them how the other half lives. I've also seen some awesome videos on the web that were shot with this camera. Here are a few movie-shooting tips:

- For the best results, consider purchasing a high-speed memory card that writes data at a speed of 33MB per second.
- Don't point the camera directly at the sun when shooting video, which can damage the camera sensor.
- Mount the camera on a tripod; it's hard to hold a camera steady for a long time while recording video. If your tripod has a pan head, you're in business.
- Pan slowly. If you pan too fast, your video looks very amateurish.

✔ If you plan on doing a lot of video recording with your camera, consider purchasing a device that steadies the camera (such as SteadiCam) while you move. You can find these at your favorite camera retailer that also sells video equipment.

You can also find lots of DIY devices that will steady your camera while you move. Do a Google search for "homemade steadicam," and you'll find quite a few resources with instructions on how to build your own. Some of them are quite good.

✔ Remember to push the Start/Stop button when you're finished recording. Otherwise you get several minutes of very choppy video as you move to the next scene. Worst-case scenario, you capture video of your feet shuffling on the sidewalk.

6

Getting the Most from Your Camera

In This Chapter

▶ Clarifying metering

▶ Using the Creative shooting modes

▶ Using exposure compensation

▶ Locking your focus

▶ Choosing a Drive mode

▶ Working with and clearing custom functions

Your camera has a plethora of features that are designed to enable you to capture stunning images. You can shoot images continuously at a rate of 4.5 frames per second, which is great for action photography. Your camera also has modes that take you way beyond point-and-shoot photography. When you take photographs with either Aperture Priority (Av) or Shutter Priority (Tv) mode, you supply one part of the exposure equation and your EOS 6D supplies the other part. Plus you can do all sorts of things to hedge your bet and make sure you get stellar photos from your camera. You can use exposure compensation when you need to tweak the exposure the camera meters. You can also bracket exposure and tweak the white balance.

If you're a geek photographer like me who likes complete control over every aspect of your photography, you'll love the features I show you in this chapter.

Understanding Metering

Your camera's metering device examines the scene and determines which shutter speed and f-stop combination will yield a properly exposed image. The camera can choose a fast shutter speed and large aperture, or a slow shutter speed and small aperture.

When you take pictures in Scene Intelligent Auto or Creative Auto mode, the camera makes both decisions for you. But you're much smarter than the processor inside your camera. If you take control of the reins and supply one piece of the puzzle, the camera will supply the rest. When you're taking certain types of pictures, it makes sense to determine which f-stop will be best for what you're photographing. In other scenarios, it makes more sense to choose the shutter speed and let the camera determine the f-stop. In the upcoming sections, I show you how to use the Creative shooting modes your camera has to offer. In Chapter 8, I show you how to use these modes for specific picture-taking situations.

Using Your Camera's Creative Exposure Modes

You bought an EOS 6D because you're a creative photographer. The SCN, Scene Intelligent Auto, and Creative Auto shooting modes are useful when you're getting used to the camera. But after you know where the controls are, branch out and use shooting modes in which you control the manner in which your images are exposed. In the upcoming sections, I show you how to expose images with the creative shooting modes: P (Programmed Auto Exposure), Av (Aperture Priority), Tv (Shutter Priority), M (Manual), and B (Bulb).

The following list describes each mode in detail:

- **Programmed Auto Exposure mode (P):** This mode is like stepping out of the kids' pool into the shallow end of the deep pool. The camera still determines what shutter speed and aperture will yield a perfectly exposed image, but you can change the values to suit the type of scene you're photographing.

- **Aperture Priority mode (Av):** When you switch to this mode, you supply the f-stop value (aperture) and the camera determines what shutter speed will result in a perfectly exposed image.

- **Shutter Priority mode (Tv):** In this mode, you determine the shutter speed and the camera meter does the math to determine what f-stop value (aperture) is needed to create a pixel-perfect image.

  ✔ **Manual mode (M):** When you decide to shoot in this mode, you supply the shutter speed and f-stop, but the camera does give you some help in determining whether the combination you provide will yield a perfectly exposed image.

  ✔ **Bulb mode (B):** If you've been a photographer for any length of time, you know that the Bulb mode enables you to shoot *time exposures,* which means the shutter can stay open longer than the slowest shutter speed provided by the camera, which is 30 seconds.

But before you can determine which mode is best for you, you need to understand how exposure works, which is the topic of the next section.

Understanding how exposure works in the camera

Your EOS 6D exposes images in the same way as film cameras did. Light enters the camera through the lens and is recorded on the sensor. The amount of time the shutter is open and the amount of light entering the camera determines whether the resulting image is too dark, too bright, or properly exposed.

The duration of the exposure is the *shutter speed.* Your camera has a shutter speed range from as long as 30 seconds in duration to as fast as 1/4000 of a second. A fast shutter speed stops action, and a slow shutter speed leaves the shutter open for a long time to record images in low-light situations.

The *aperture* is the opening in the lens that lets light into the camera when the shutter opens. You can change the aperture diameter to let a lot, or a small amount, of light into the camera. The *f-stop value* determines the size of the aperture. A low f-stop value (large aperture) lets a lot of light into the camera, and a high f-stop value (small aperture) lets a small amount of light into the camera. Depending on the lens you're using, the f-stop range can be from f/1.8, which sends huge gobs of light into the camera, to f/32, which lets a minuscule splash of light into the camera. The f-stop also determines the depth of field, a concept I explain in the "Controlling depth of field" section later in this chapter.

The duration of the exposure (shutter speed) and aperture (f-stop value) combination determines the exposure. For each lighting scenario you encounter, several different combinations render a perfectly exposed photograph. You use different combinations for different types of photography. The camera's metering device examines the scene and determines which shutter speed and f-stop combination will yield a properly exposed image. The camera can choose a fast shutter speed and large aperture, or a slow shutter speed and small aperture.

Using Programmed Auto Exposure mode

When you take pictures with the Programmed Auto Exposure mode, the camera determines the shutter speed and aperture (f-stop value) that yields a properly exposed image for the lighting conditions. Even though this sounds identical to Scene Intelligent Auto mode, with this mode you can change the AF (autofocus) mode, Drive mode, ISO speed, picture style, and more. You can also change the shutter speed and aperture to suit the scene you're photographing. To take pictures in Programmed Auto Exposure mode:

1. **Press the Mode Dial lock and Rotate the Mode dial to P (see Figure 6-1).**

2. **Press the ISO button and then rotate the Main dial to change the ISO speed to the desired setting.**

   Higher ISO speeds make the camera sensor more sensitive to light, which is ideal when you're photographing in dim light or at night. For more information on changing ISO speed, see Chapter 7.

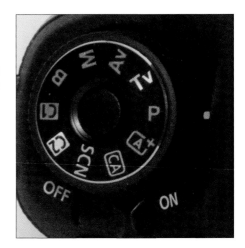

3. **Press the Shutter button halfway to achieve focus.**

Figure 6-1: Rotating the Mode dial to P.

   The green dot on the right side of the viewfinder appears when the camera achieves focus. If the dot is flashing, the camera can't achieve focus and you must manually focus the camera.

4. **Check the shutter speed and aperture.**

   You can use the viewfinder or LCD panel (see Figure 6-2) to check the shutter speed and aperture. If you notice a shutter speed of 4000 and the minimum aperture for the lens blinking, the image will be overexposed. If you notice a shutter speed of 30 seconds and the maximum aperture for the lens blinking, the image will be underexposed.

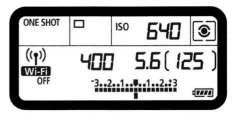

Figure 6-2: Check the shutter speed and aperture.

5. **Press the Shutter button fully to take the picture.**

   The image displays almost immediately on your LCD monitor.

You can shift the exposure and choose a different shutter speed and aperture combination. Use this option when you want to shoot with a faster shutter speed to freeze action or a different aperture to control depth of field. To shift the Programmed Auto Exposure:

1. **Follow Steps 1–3 of the preceding instructions; then press the Shutter button halfway.**

   The camera achieves focus.

2. **Rotate the Main dial.**

   As you rotate the dial, you see different shutter speed and aperture combinations in the viewfinder and LCD panel (see Figure 6-3). If you notice that the shutter speed is too slow for a blur-free picture, you have to put the camera on a tripod or increase the ISO speed setting.

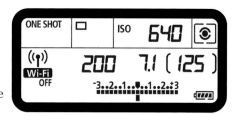
Figure 6-3: You can shift programmed exposure.

3. **When you see the desired combination of shutter speed and aperture, press the Shutter button fully to take the picture.**

   The image appears almost immediately on your LCD monitor.

Using Aperture Priority mode

If you like to photograph landscapes, Aperture Priority mode is right up your alley. When you take pictures with Aperture Priority mode, you choose the desired f-stop and the camera supplies the proper shutter speed to achieve a properly exposed image. A large aperture (small f-stop value) lets a lot of light into the camera, and a small aperture (large f-stop value) lets a small amount of light into the camera. The benefit of shooting in Aperture Priority mode is that you have complete control over the depth of field (see the "Controlling depth of field" section later in this chapter). You also have access to all the other options, such as setting the ISO speed, choosing a picture style, changing the AF mode or Drive mode, and so on. To take pictures with Aperture Priority mode:

1. **Press the Mode Dial lock and rotate the Mode dial to Av (Aperture value) (see Figure 6-4).**

2. **Press the ISO button and then rotate the Main dial to change the ISO speed to the desired setting.**

   When choosing an ISO speed, choose the slowest speed for the available lighting conditions. For more information on changing ISO speed, see Chapter 7.

3. **Rotate the Main dial to select the desired f-stop.**

   As you change the aperture, the camera calculates the proper shutter speed to achieve a properly exposed image. The change appears in the LCD panel and the viewfinder. As you rotate the dial, monitor the shutter speed in the viewfinder (see Figure 6-5). If you notice that the shutter speed is too slow for a blur-free picture, you have to put the camera on a tripod or increase the ISO speed setting. If you see the minimum shutter speed (30 seconds) blinking, the image will be underexposed with the selected f-stop. If you see the maximum shutter speed (1/4000 second) blinking, the image will be overexposed with the selected f-stop. The scenario in Figure 6-5 would limit the photographer who wants to take a picture hand holding the camera to a 50mm lens.

4. **Press the Shutter button halfway to achieve focus.**

   A green dot appears in the viewfinder when the camera achieves focus.

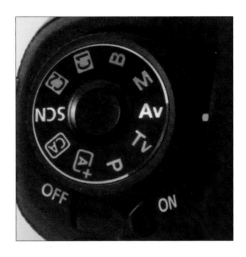

Figure 6-4: Rotating the Mode dial to Av.

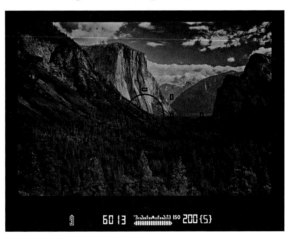

Figure 6-5: Make sure the shutter speed is fast enough for a blur-free picture.

5. Press the Shutter button fully to take the picture.

The image appears on your LCD monitor almost immediately.

Controlling depth of field

Depth of field determines how much of your image looks sharp and is in apparent focus in front of and behind your subject. When you're taking pictures of landscapes on a bright sunny day, you want a depth of field that produces an image in which you can see the details for miles and miles and miles . . . . Other times, you want to have a very shallow depth of field in which your subject is in sharp focus but the foreground and background are a pleasant out-of-focus blur. A shallow depth of field is ideal when you're shooting a portrait.

You control the depth of field in an image by selecting the f-stop in Aperture Priority (Av) mode and letting the camera do the math to determine what shutter speed will yield a properly exposed image. You get a limited depth of field when using a small f-stop value (large aperture), which lets a lot of light into the camera. A fast lens:

- ✔ Has an f-stop value of 2.8 or smaller
- ✔ Gives you the capability to shoot in low-light conditions
- ✔ Gives you a wonderfully shallow depth of field

When shooting at a lens's smallest f-stop value, you're letting the most light into the camera, which is known as shooting *wide open.* The lens you use also determines how large the depth of field will be for a given f-stop. At the same f-stop, a wide-angle lens has a greater depth of field than a telephoto lens. When you're photographing a landscape, the ideal recipe is a wide-angle lens and a small aperture (large f-stop value). When you're shooting a portrait of someone, you want a shallow depth of field. Therefore a telephoto lens with a focal length that is the 35mm equivalent of 85mm with a large aperture (small f-stop value) is the ideal solution.

Figure 6-6 shows two pictures of the same subject. The first image was shot with an exposure of 1/640 second at f/1.8, and the second image was shot with an exposure of 1/80 second at f/10. In both cases, I focused on the subject. Notice how much more of the image shot at f/10 is in focus. The detail of the flowers in the second shot distracts the viewer's attention from the subject. The first image has a shallow depth of field that draws the viewer's attention to the subject.

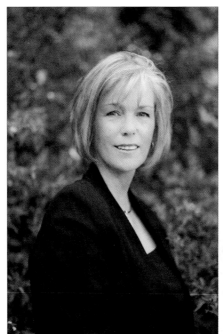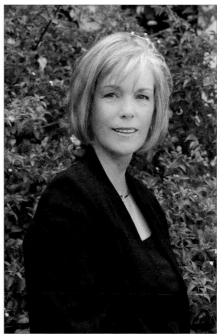

Figure 6-6: The f-stop you choose determines the depth of field.

Using depth-of-field preview

When you compose a scene through your viewfinder, the camera aperture is wide open, which means you have no idea how much depth of field you'll have in the resulting image. You can preview the depth of field for a selected f-stop by pressing a button on your camera. To preview depth of field:

1. **Compose the picture and choose the desired f-stop in Aperture Priority (Av) mode.**

   See the section, "Using Aperture Priority mode," earlier in this chapter if you need help.

2. **Press the Shutter button halfway to achieve focus.**

   A green dot shines solid on the right side of the viewfinder when the camera focuses on your subject.

3. **Press the Depth-of-Field Preview button (see Figure 6-7).**

The button is conveniently located on the right front side of the camera when your camera is pointed toward your subject. You can easily locate the button by feel. I cradle the lens with my left hand when shooting. To find the Depth-of-Field Preview button, I move my fourth finger back until I feel the button on the camera body. When you press the button, the image in the viewfinder may become dim, especially when you're using a small aperture (large f-stop number) that doesn't let a lot of light into the camera. Don't worry; the camera chooses the proper shutter speed to compensate for the f-stop you select.

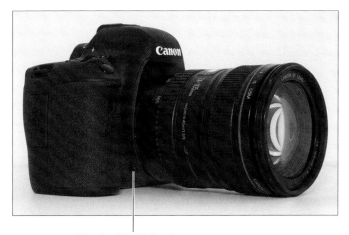

Depth-of-Field Preview

Figure 6-7: The Depth-of-Field Preview button.

When you use depth-of-field preview, pay attention to how much of the image is in apparent focus in front of and behind your subject. To see what the depth of field looks like with different f-stops:

a. *Select what you think is the optimal f-stop for the scene you're photographing.*

b. *Press the shutter button halfway to achieve focus, press the Depth-of-Field Preview button as I outline earlier, and then rotate the Main dial to choose different f-stop values.*

As long as you hold down the Depth-of-Field Preview button while you're choosing different f-stops, you can see the effect each f-stop has on the depth of field.

Using Shutter Priority mode

When your goal is to accentuate an object's motion, choose Shutter Priority (Tv) mode. When you take pictures in Shutter Priority mode, you choose the shutter speed and the camera supplies the proper f-stop value to properly expose the scene. Your camera has a shutter-speed range from 30 seconds to 1/4000 of a second. When you choose a slow shutter speed, the shutter is open for a long time. When you choose a fast shutter speed, the shutter is open for a short duration and you can freeze action. To take pictures in Shutter Priority mode:

1. **Press the Mode Lock button, and rotate the Mode dial to Tv (Time Value) (see Figure 6-8).**

2. **Rotate the Main dial to choose the desired shutter speed.**

   As you change the shutter speed, the camera determines the proper f-stop to achieve a properly exposed image. If you notice that the shutter speed is too slow for a blur-free picture, you have to put the camera on a tripod or increase the ISO speed setting. If you see the minimum aperture (largest f-stop value) for the lens blinking, the image will be underexposed with the

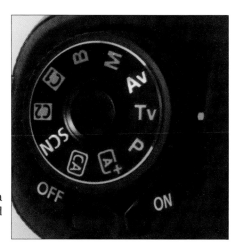

Figure 6-8: Rotating the Mode dial to Tv.

   selected shutter speed. If you see the maximum aperture (smallest f-stop number) blinking, the image will be overexposed with the selected shutter speed. If you choose a shutter speed that's too slow for a blur-free picture, mount the camera on a tripod or choose a higher ISO speed setting.

3. **Press the ISO button and then rotate the Main dial to change the ISO speed to the desired setting.**

   Choose an ISO setting that enables you to achieve the desired shutter speed. For more information on changing ISO speed, see Chapter 7.

4. **Rotate the Main dial to choose the desired shutter speed.**

As you rotate the dial, the shutter speed value changes on the LCD panel and in the viewfinder. I rarely look at the LCD panel when changing shutter speed or aperture. I like to see my subject while I make the changes.

5. **Press the Shutter button halfway to achieve focus.**

   A green dot appears in the right side of the viewfinder. If the dot is flashing, the camera can't achieve focus. If this occurs, switch the lens to manual focus and twist the focusing barrel until your subject snaps into focus. Figure 6-9 shows the viewfinder when working in Shutter Priority mode.

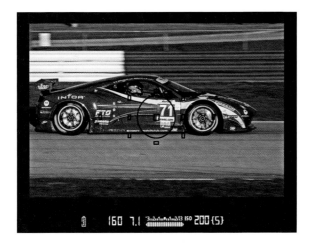

Figure 6-9: Adjusting the shutter speed.

6. **Press the shutter button fully to take the picture.**

   Shutter Priority mode is the way to go whenever you need to stop action or show the grace of an athlete in motion. You'd use Shutter Priority mode in lots of scenarios. Figure 6-10 shows the effects you can achieve with different shutter speeds. The image on the left was photographed with a slow shutter speed, and the image on the right was photographed with a fast shutter speed to freeze the action. For more information on using Shutter Priority mode when photographing action, check out Chapter 8.

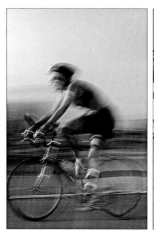 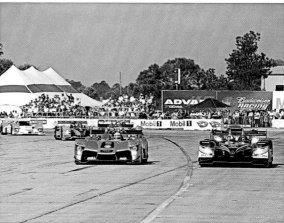

Figure 6-10: A tale of two shutter speeds.

Manually exposing images

You can also manually expose your images. When you choose this option, you supply the f-stop value and the shutter speed. You can choose from several combinations to properly expose the image for the lighting conditions. Your camera meter gives you some assistance to select the right f-stop and shutter speed combination to properly expose the image. If you fast-forwarded to this section and don't understand how your camera determines shutter speed and exposure, check out the "Understanding how exposure works in the camera" section earlier in this chapter. To manually expose your images:

1. **Press the Mode Lock button and rotate the Mode dial to M (see Figure 6-11) and then rotate the Main dial to set the shutter speed.**

   The shutter speed determines how long the shutter stays open. A slow shutter speed is perfect for a scene with low light. A fast shutter speed freezes action. As you change the shutter speed, review the exposure indicator in the LCD panel, or if you have the shutter button pressed halfway, in the viewfinder. When the exposure is correct for the

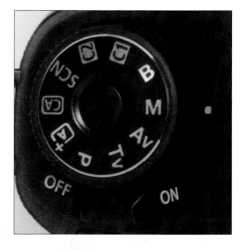

Figure 6-11: Manually exposing the image.

lighting conditions, the exposure level mark aligns with the center of the scale. If the exposure level mark is to the right of center, the image will be overexposed (see Figure 6-12); if to the left of center, the image will be underexposed. Of course, you're in control. You may want to intentionally overexpose or

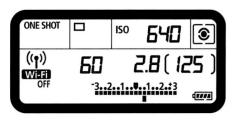

Figure 6-12: Monitor the exposure in the LCD panel.

underexpose for special effects. For example, if you slightly underexpose the image, the colors will be more saturated.

2. **Rotate the Quick Control dial to set the f-stop value.**

   If moving the Quick Control dial does not change the f-stop value, make sure the Lock slider is to the left. The f-stop value determines how much light enters the camera. A small f-stop value, such as f/2.8, lets a lot of light into the camera and also gives a shallow depth of field. A large f-stop value lets a small amount of light into the camera and gives you a large depth of field. As you change the f-stop value, review the exposure indicator in the LCD panel, or if you have the shutter button pressed halfway, in the viewfinder. When the exposure is correct for the lighting conditions, the exposure-level mark aligns with the center of the scale. If the exposure-level mark is to the right of center, the image will be overexposed; if to the left of center, the image will be underexposed.

3. **Press the Shutter button halfway to achieve focus.**

   A green dot appears in the viewfinder when the camera has achieved focus. If the dot is flashing, the camera can't achieve focus and you must focus manually.

4. **Press the Shutter button fully to take the picture.**

Shooting time exposures

When you switch to Bulb mode, the shutter stays open as long as you press the shutter button. If you've ever seen night pictures in which you can actually see trails from stars that follow the curvature of the earth, you've seen a photograph that was taken with the Bulb mode. The photographer left the shutter open for a long period of time, and the earth rotated while the photograph was taken. These types of images are known as *time exposures* because the image was exposed over a long period of time. To shoot time exposures:

1. **Mount the camera on a tripod.**

   The lens will be open for a long time. The slightest movement will show up as a blur in the final image. Unless you want the image blurred for a creative effect, you need to stabilize the camera on a tripod.

2. **Rotate the Mode dial to B (see Figure 6-13).**

   B means Bulb mode. Back in the old days of film cameras, photographers would open the shutter with a pneumatic device that looked like a bulb. The shutter opened when the photographer squeezed the device and remained open until the photographer released his grip.

3. **Rotate the Quick Control dial or the Main dial to set the f-stop value.**

   A small f-stop value such as f/2.8 (large aperture) lets a lot of light into the camera and gives a shallow depth of field. A large f-stop value (small aperture), such as f/16, lets a small amount of light into the camera and gives a large depth of field. You also need to leave the shutter open longer when using a large f-stop value, which in most instances is desirable. However, a longer exposure can add digital noise to the image. When you have an exposure that leaves the shutter open for several seconds, or perhaps minutes, use an ISO speed setting of 100 to minimize digital noise.

4. **Connect a remote switch to the camera.**

   If you hold the shutter button open with your finger, you'll transmit vibrations to the camera, which yields a blurry image. A remote switch, such as the Canon RS-80N3, or a remote timer and switch, such as the Canon TC-80N3, triggers the shutter remotely and no vibration is transmitted to the camera. Both plug into a port on the side of your camera (see Figure 6-14).

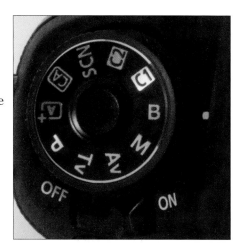

Figure 6-13: Rotate the Mode dial to B to select Bulb mode.

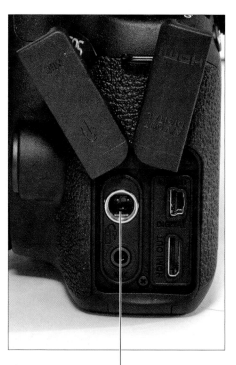

Insert remote switch here

Figure 6-14: Attach a Canon remote switch.

5. **Press the button on the remote switch to open the shutter.**

   The shutter remains open as long as you hold the button. The time is noted in the LCD panel.

6. **Release the button on the remote switch to close the shutter.**

7. **Review the image on your LCD monitor.**

   I find it useful to take one picture, note the time the lens remained open, and examine the image carefully on the LCD monitor. If I'm not pleased, I take another shot, leaving the lens open longer if the test image is underexposed or for a shorter duration if the test image is overexposed.

Time exposures can be a lot of fun. You can use them to record artistic depictions of headlight patterns on a curved stretch of road (see Figure 6-15) or capture the motion of the ocean at night. The possibilities are limited only by your imagination.

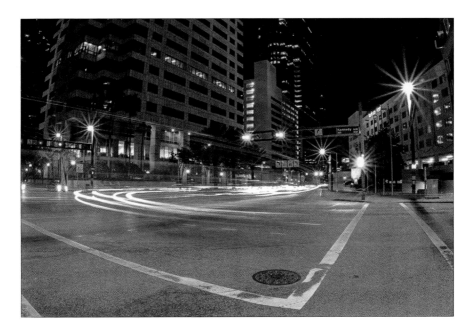

Figure 6-15: A time exposure that records headlight trails at night.

Modifying Camera Exposure

Your camera has a built-in metering device that automatically determines the proper shutter speed and aperture to create a perfectly exposed image for most lighting scenarios. However, at times, you need to modify the exposure to suit the current lighting conditions. Modify camera exposure for individual shots, or hedge your bets and create several exposures of each shot. You can also lock focus and exposure to a specific location in the scene you're photographing. I show you how to achieve these tasks in the upcoming sections.

Using exposure compensation

When your camera gets the exposure right, it's a wonderful thing. At times, however, the camera doesn't get it right. When you review an image on the camera LCD monitor and it's not exposed to suit your taste, you can compensate manually by increasing or decreasing exposure. To manually compensate camera exposure:

1. **Choose P, Av, or Tv from the Mode dial (see Figure 6-16).**

   Exposure compensation is available only when you take pictures with Programmed Auto Exposure, Aperture Priority, or Shutter Priority mode.

2. **Rotate the Quick Control dial while holding the Shutter button halfway.**

   Rotate the dial counterclockwise to decrease exposure or clockwise to increase exposure. As you rotate the dial, you see the exposure indicator in the viewfinder and LCD panel move, which shows you the amount of exposure compensation you're applying (see Figure 6-17). In this figure, the exposure is decreased by 2/3 of a stop.

   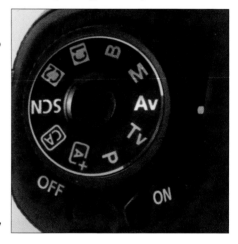

   Figure 6-16: Use exposure compensation with these shooting modes.

3. **Press the shutter button fully to take the picture.**

4. **To cancel exposure compensation, press the shutter button halfway and rotate the Quick Control dial until the exposure indicator is in the center of the exposure-compensation scale.**

   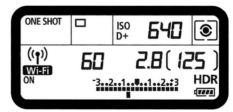

   Figure 6-17: Using exposure compensation.

You see the exposure-compensation scale in the viewfinder and on the LCD panel.

Exposure compensation stays in effect even after you power off the camera. You can inadvertently add exposure compensation by accidentally rotating the Quick Control dial when you have the shutter button pressed halfway. You can safeguard against this by keeping the Lock switch (below the Quick Control dial) in the locked position when you don't need to use the Quick Control dial.

Bracketing exposure

When you're photographing an important event, properly exposed images are a must. Many photographers get lazy and don't feel they need to get it right in the camera when they have programs like Adobe Photoshop or Adobe Photoshop Lightroom. However, you get much better results when you process an image that's been exposed correctly. Professional photographers bracket their exposures when they photograph important events or places they may never visit again. When you bracket an exposure, you take three pictures: one with the exposure as metered by the camera, one with exposure that's been decreased, and one with exposure that's been increased. You can bracket up to plus or minus 3 EV (exposure value) in ⅓ EV increments. To bracket your exposures:

1. **Press the Menu button.**

   The previously used menu displays.

2. **Use the Multi-controller or Quick Control dial to navigate to the Shooting Settings 3 tab and then rotate the Quick Control dial to highlight Expo.Comp./AEB (automatic exposure bracketing).**

   See the left image in Figure 6-18.

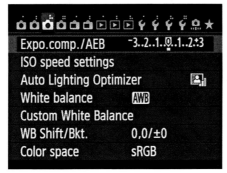
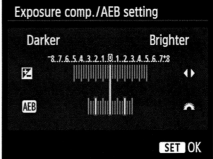

Figure 6-18: Setting automatic exposure bracketing.

3. Press the Set button.

The Exposure Comp./AEB Setting menu appears.

4. Rotate the Main dial to set the amount of bracketing.

When you rotate the dial, a new scale appears below the exposure compensation scale and a line appears on each side of the center of the scale (see the right image in Figure 6-18). Each mark indicates 1/3 f-stop correction.

5. (Optional) Rotate the Quick Control dial to apply exposure compensation to the settings determined by the camera meter.

This step is optional if you're comfortable with the way the camera has been setting exposure. You can use exposure compensation to increase or decrease the exposure metered by the camera. When you add exposure compensation to the mix, the automatic exposure bracketing (AEB) marks move as well. In other words, the exposure will be increased and decreased relative to the compensated exposure.

6. Press Set.

The settings are applied. The Expo.Comp./AEB menu option shows the amount of bracketing and exposure compensation you've applied. The AEB icon appears in the viewfinder and LCD panel (see Figure 6-19).

AEB icon

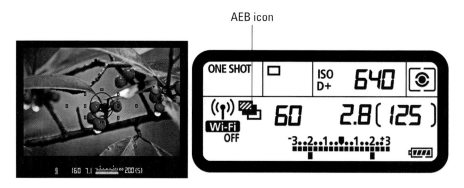

Figure 6-19: These icons appear after you set AEB.

7. Press the AF-Drive button and rotate the Quick Control dial to choose one of the Continuous Drive modes.

The Continuous Drive icon appears on the LCD panel.

8. **Press the Shutter button halfway to achieve focus and then press the Shutter button fully.**

   When you press the Shutter button, the camera creates three images: one with standard exposure, one with decreased exposure, and one with increased exposure. To cancel AEB, turn off the camera. When you power up the camera again, remember to change the Drive mode to one of the single-shot Drive modes.

Locking exposure

You can also lock exposure on a specific part of the frame, which is handy when you want a specific part of the frame exposed correctly. For example, recently I was photographing a beautiful sunset. The camera meter averaged the exposure for the scene, and the image ended up with blown-out highlights around the sun and clouds that weren't as dark and colorful as I saw them. To compensate for this, I locked exposure on the blue sky, and the picture turned out perfect. To lock exposure:

1. **Look through the viewfinder and move the camera until the center of the viewfinder is over the area to which you want to lock exposure.**

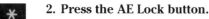

2. **Press the AE Lock button.**

   The autoexposure lock icon appears in the viewfinder (see Figure 6-20).

3. **Move the camera to achieve the desired composition.**

   For example, you may want to lock exposure on some clouds, but compose your image so the clouds are near the top of the frame. You do so by locking exposure on the cloud that you want to be perfectly exposed and then moving the camera to frame the scene just the way you want it in the viewfinder.

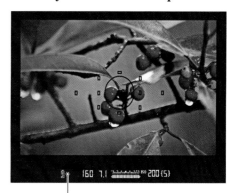

Autoexposure lock icon

Figure 6-20: This icon notifies that exposure lock is enabled.

4. **Press the Shutter button halfway to achieve focus.**

   A green dot in the viewfinder tells you that the camera has achieved focus. You also see black rectangles that designate the areas on which the camera has focused.

5. **Press the Shutter button fully to take the picture.**

   After you take the picture Exposure Lock is disabled until the next time you press the Exposure Lock button.

Locking Focus

You can choose from two ways to lock focus on an object that isn't in the center of the frame: the shutter button or the AF-On button. This option comes in handy when your center of interest isn't in the center of the frame.

To lock focus with the shutter button:

1. **While looking through the viewfinder, move your camera until the center of the viewfinder is over the subject that you want the camera to lock focus on.**

2. **Press the Shutter button halfway.**

   Make sure that a black autofocus square appears over your subject. When I'm photographing people who aren't in the center of the frame, I switch to a single autofocus point that's in the center of the frame and center the single autofocus point over my subject before locking focus. For more information on selecting and modifying autofocus points, see Chapter 7. When the camera achieves focus, a green dot appears in the viewfinder.

3. **While holding the Shutter button halfway, recompose your picture.**

4. **Press the Shutter button fully to take the picture.**

You can also lock focus with the AF-On button on the back right-hand side of your camera near the top. This is a little easier because you don't have to hold the Shutter button halfway while composing your picture. To lock focus with the AF-On button:

1. **Look through the viewfinder and move the camera until the center of the viewfinder is over the subject that you want the camera to lock focus on.**

2. **Press the AF-On button.**

   Red autofocus squares appear momentarily in the viewfinder over the subjects that the camera will lock focus on. The squares turn black after the camera achieves focus. Make sure the autofocus points that display are over the object that you want the camera to lock focus on. I find it useful to switch to a single autofocus point in the center of the frame when I'm photographing a person or subject that isn't in the center.

3. Move the camera to recompose the picture and then press the Shutter button fully.

An image appears almost instantaneously on the camera LCD monitor. Review the image to make sure the camera locked focus on the desired object.

Choosing a Drive Mode

Your camera can capture multiple images when you press the Shutter button. Your camera's Continuous Drive mode can capture images at the rate of 4.5 frames per second. If you're taking pictures at a place where you don't want to be heard, you can employ a Silent Drive mode capturing one shot at a time, and you also have a Silent mode for capturing continuous images. The Silent modes are not completely silent, but they are considerably quieter than the standard Single Shot and Continuous Drive modes. To specify the Drive mode, follow these steps:

1. Choose desired shooting mode.

In many of the automatic modes, the drive mode is chosen for you, but you can override the drive mode with the push of a button, or by using the Quick Command menu. However, the drive mode in most of the SCN modes should not be changed as the default drive mode was chosen by Canon engineers and professional photographers as the optimum drive mode.

2. Press the Drive button.

3. Rotate the Main dial while looking at the LCD panel and then choose one of the following:

- *Single Shot:* You capture one picture each time you press the shutter button. (See the left image in Figure 6-21.)

- *Continuous Shooting:* You can capture up to 4.5 fps when you press and hold the shutter button. (See the right image in Figure 6-21.)

- *Single Shot Silent Shooting:* You capture one image each time you press the shutter button, and the mechanical noise of the shutter is considerably less than the standard single shot mode. (See the left image in Figure 6-22.)

- *Silent Continuous Shooting:* You can capture up to 4.5 fps when you press and hold the shutter button, and the mechanical noise of the shutter is considerably less than the standard continuous shooting mode. (See the right image in Figure 6-22.)

- *2-Second Self-Timer/Remote Control:* Starts the 2-Second Self-Timer when you press the shutter button or trigger the shutter with a remote control unit. (See the left image in Figure 6-23.)

- *10-Second Self-Timer/Remote Control:* Starts the 10-Second Self-Timer when you press the shutter button or trigger the shutter with a remote control unit. A light in front of the camera beeps and blinks while counting down. At the 2-second mark, the light stays on and the beeping is faster. (See the right image in Figure 6-23.)

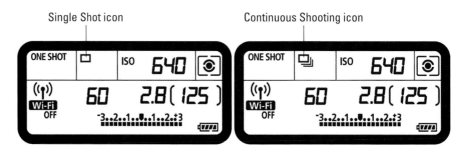

Figure 6-21: Single Shot and Continuous Drive modes.

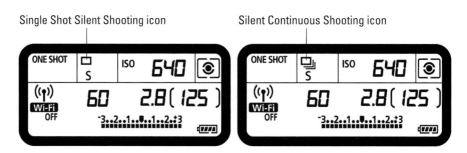

Figure 6-22: The Silent Drive modes.

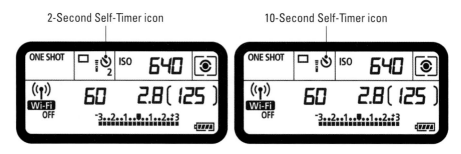

Figure 6-23: 2-Second Self-Timer and 10-Second Self-Timer Drive modes.

4. Take some pictures.

The Drive mode you select stays in effect until you change it. If you power off the camera, the Drive mode still stays in effect. Switch back to Single Shot mode when you no longer need to capture images continuously.

The 2-Second Self-Timer is ideal when you're photographing with the camera mounted to a tripod. The two-second delay gives the camera a chance to stabilize from any vibration that occurred when you pressed the Shutter button.

The Continuous Drive mode's capture rate will be slower than 4.5 frames per second when the battery is near the end of its life or when you choose a shutter speed slower than 1/1500 of a second.

Exploring Useful Image Menu Commands

There are lots of menu commands, more than you'll ever use. But the Canon engineers wanted to cover just about every possible scenario for photographers who own an EOS 6D. In the following sections, I show you some menu commands that may be useful in specific picture taking scenarios.

Enabling Long Exposure Noise Reduction

If you shoot long time exposures at night in secluded places, you'll capture some wonderful images of the stars in the sky, and if you live in a real remote area, or capture your images in an area with little or no ambient light, you'll see galaxies like the Milky Way in your images. However, when you use the B (Bulb) mode to leave the shutter open for several minutes, or in some cases several hours, your images will be noisy. If the previous scenario sounds familiar, you can eliminate some of the noise with Long Exposure Noise Reduction as follows:

1. Press the Menu button.

The previously used menu displays.

2. Use the Multi-controller to navigate to the Shooting Settings 4 menu tab.

3. Use the Multi-controller or Quick Control dial to highlight Long exp. noise reduction (see the left image in Figure 6-24) and then press Set.

The Long Exposure Noise Reduction options are displayed (see the right image in Figure 6-24).

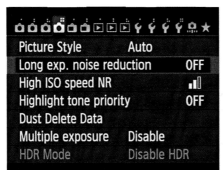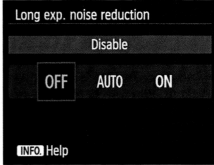

Figure 6-24: Enabling Long Exposure Noise Reduction.

4. Use the Multi-controller or Quick Control dial to highlight one of the following:

- **Disable:** The default option disables long exposure noise reduction.

- **Auto:** Applies long exposure noise reduction with exposures longer than one second when typical long exposure noise is detected.

- **On:** Applies long exposure to every image with an exposure longer than one second. This option may also reduce noise that the Auto option cannot detect.

5. Press Set.

The desired option is applied.

Long exposure noise reduction increases the time it takes for the camera to process each image. If you do occasionally create long time exposures, either choose the Auto option, or choose the On option before the photo shoot, and then change to Disable when the photo shoot is completed.

Enabling High ISO Speed Noise Reduction

The Canon engineers know that using high ISO settings will increase image noise, which is why they have added a feature to your camera that applies noise reduction to all images and is biased to apply more noise reduction to images captured with a high ISO. If you do a lot of shooting in low light with high ISO settings, you can modify the amount of noise reduction applied to images captured at high ISO settings as follows:

1. **Press the Menu button.**

   The previously used menu displays.

2. **Use the Multi-controller button to navigate to the Shooting Settings 4 tab.**

3. **Use the Multi-controller or Quick Control dial to highlight High ISO speed NR (see the left image in Figure 6-25).**

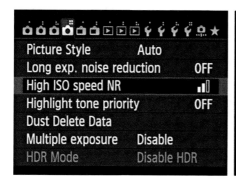
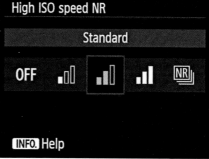

Figure 6-25: Enable High ISO Speed Noise Reduction.

4. **Press Set.**

   The High ISO Speed NR options are displayed (see the right image in Figure 6-25).

5. **Use the Multi-controller or Quick Control dial to choose one of the following options:**

   - **Off:** Noise reduction is not applied to any image.

   - **Low:** A low amount of noise reduction is applied to all images.

   - **Standard:** The default option applies noise reduction to all images.

   - **High:** Applies a stronger amount of noise reduction to all images.

   - **Multi-shot Noise Reduction:** This option captures four images and combines them in camera to create a noise free image.

6. **Press Set to apply the change.**

I haven't performed extensive tests on these options. Change this setting at your discretion and with however many grains of salt you choose.

If you choose Multi-shot Noise Reduction, your camera will capture four images every time you press the shutter button, regardless of the ISO setting you use, and the combined image will be in the JPEG format. I advise you to only use this setting if you're photographing in extreme low light at an ISO higher than 1600. Due to the fact the camera is combining multiple images, I suggest you use a tripod to get the sharpest image when using this option.

Enable Highlight Tone Priority

If you photograph lots of images in bright light and detail in highlight areas is important to you, consider trying the Highlight Tone Priority menu command. This option ensures that images with a lot of bright highlights will have highlight details. The con for this menu command is that you may find increased noise in shadow areas. When you use this option, the lowest ISO setting available is 200. To use Highlight Tone Priority:

1. Press the Menu button.

The previously used menu displays.

2. Use the Multi-controller to navigate to the Shooting Settings 4 tab.

3. Use the Multi-controller or Quick Control dial to select Highlight Tone Priority (see the left side of Figure 6-26) and then press Set.

The Highlight Tone Priority options are displayed (see the right side of Figure 6-26).

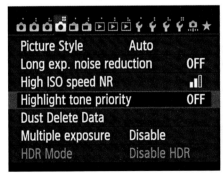
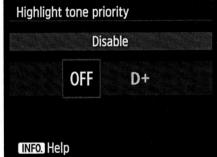

Figure 6-26: Enabling Highlight Tone Priority.

4. Use the Multi-controller or Quick Control dial to highlight D+ and then press Set.

Highlight Tone Priority is enabled. When you enable Highlight Tone Priority, you see a D+ in the LCD panel and in the viewfinder.

Enabling Highlight Alert

If you don't want to use Highlight Priority to ensure that highlights in images are not blown out, you can enable an option to show blown out highlights as a blinking overlay on images you review. When you see the blinking highlights, affectionately known as "Blinkies," use Exposure Compensation to banish the dreaded "Blinkies" to infinity and beyond. To enable Highlight Alert:

1. Press the Menu button.

The previously used menu displays.

2. Use the Multi-controller to navigate to the Playback Settings 3 tab.

3. Use the Multi-controller or Quick Control dial to highlight the Highlight Alert Option (see the left side of Figure 6-27) and then press Set.

The Highlight Alert options are displayed.

Highlight alert	Disable
AF point disp.	Disable
Playback grid	Off
Histogram disp	Brightness
Movie play count	Rec time
Magnificatn (apx)	2x
Ctrl over HDMI	Disable

Highlight alert	▶Disable
	Enable

Figure 6-27: Blinkies for fun and profit.

4. Use the Multi-controller or Quick Control dial to highlight Enable and then press Set.

Blinkies are enabled.

Using Custom Functions

Your camera has almost as many custom functions as there are Smiths in the New York City phone book. Well almost. At any rate, I find some custom functions extremely useful. In fact, I've already covered a couple custom functions in earlier chapters. Unfortunately, I'd have to buy my project editor a year's supply of his favorite beverage if I covered every custom function. In the upcoming sections, I cover the custom functions I think are most important. I leave it to you, dear reader, to explore the other custom functions when the weather's not conducive to photography. But then again, when the weather's bad, you may prefer to try some still-life photography on common household items instead of exploring custom functions.

Exploring Exposure custom functions

You can choose from six custom functions to modify exposure. I cover one — C.Fn I: Exposure — in Chapter 7. Other functions enable you to change exposure or ISO increments, but the default settings are usually fine. One useful custom function is *Safety Shift.* When you shoot in Aperture Priority or Shutter Priority mode, you can choose to shift the shutter speed and aperture, or the ISO if the lighting changes dramatically and the subject gets considerably brighter or darker. When you shoot in Programmed Exposure mode (P), your only option is to shift the ISO speed. Here's how to enable it:

1. **Press the Menu button.**

   The previously used menu displays.

2. **Use the Multi-controller button to navigate to the Custom Functions tab.**

   C.Fn I: Exposure is first on the hit parade (see the left side of Figure 6-28) and is selected unless you've dabbled with another custom function previously.

3. **If C.Fn I: Exposure is not highlighted, use the Multi-controller or the Quick Control dial to highlight the option and then press the Set button.**

   The Exposure custom functions display.

4. **Press the Multi-controller button until 6 appears in the window on the right side of the dialog and then press Set.**

   The default Safety Shift option displays (see the right side of Figure 6-28). The default option is to Disable Safety Shift.

5. **Use the Multi-controller or the Quick Control dial to highlight the desired option.**

   The text of the option you choose changes to blue. Choose Shutter Speed/Aperture to shift the shutter speed and/or aperture when lighting conditions change dramatically, or choose ISO speed to shift the ISO to a setting that will maintain a normal shutter speed and aperture when lighting conditions change dramatically.

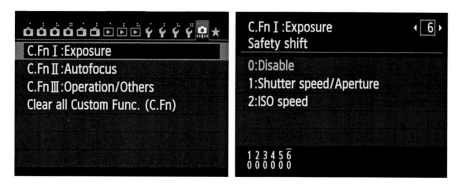

Figure 6-28: The Safety Shift options.

6. Press Set to apply the change.

There are other custom functions that may be useful for the type of photography you do, or for the way you photograph. I invite you to explore the other custom functions to see which ones may be useful to you.

Clearing Custom Functions

Enabling custom functions and customizing your camera can be quite useful. However, sometimes you get carried away and go over the top. Other times you've experimented with a bunch of custom functions and decide they no longer suit your style of photography. You can wipe out all the custom functions and any changes you've applied to camera buttons by doing the following:

1. Press the Menu button.

The previously used menu displays.

2. Use the Multi-controller button to navigate to the Custom Functions tab.

The last-used Custom Functions option is highlighted.

3. Rotate the Quick Control dial to highlight the Custom Functions tab.

The last-used Custom Functions option is highlighted.

4. Rotate the Quick Control dial to highlight Clear All Custom Func. (C.Fn) (see the left side of Figure 6-29) and then press the Set button.

A dialog box appears asking you to confirm clearing all custom functions (see the right side of Figure 6-29).

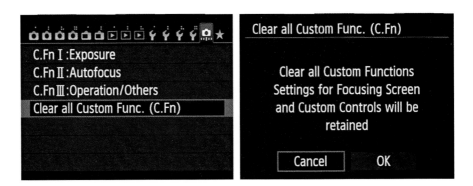

Figure 6-29: Clearing all custom functions.

5. Rotate the Quick Control dial to highlight OK and press Set.

Any custom function you've enabled has been cleared.

Using Advanced Camera Features

*Y*our camera has lots of great features that enable you to create great pictures. When you shoot in one of the creative modes, you can modify lots of things. If the light is a bit dim and you don't feel like flashing your subject, you can increase the ISO speed setting. You can also change the way the camera meters the scene before you. You also have lots of options when you insert a supported flash unit in the camera's hot shoe. In short, the sky's the limit when you employ the advanced features of your camera.

To bring you up to speed on all the advanced features you can use, read the sections in this chapter in which I show you how to harness all the cool features.

Viewing Battery Information

Your camera provides gobs of useful information about pictures and camera settings. You also have a *smart battery* powering your EOS 6D. For instance, you can access information about how much charge is left in your battery, how many shutter actuations have occurred since you last charged it, and the battery's condition. View the battery information on your LCD monitor. To check your battery's condition:

1. **Press the Menu button.**

   The last-used menu displays.

2. **Use the Multi-controller to navigate to the Camera Settings 4 tab (see the left image in Figure 7-1).**

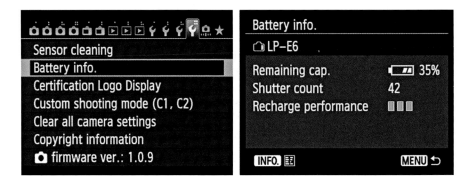

Figure 7-1: Displaying battery information.

3. **Use the Multi-controller or the Quick Control dial to highlight Battery Info and then press the Set.**

   The following battery information displays (see the right image in Figure 7-1):

   - *Model:* Displays the battery model or household power source being used to power the camera.

   - *Remaining Cap.:* Displays the remaining power capacity in 1-percent increments.

   - *Shutter Count:* Displays the number of shutter actuations for the current battery. When a recharged battery is inserted, the count resets to zero.

   - *Recharge Performance:* Displays the recharge performance. Three green squares indicate excellent recharging performance, two green squares indicate the recharging performance is slightly degraded, and one red square indicates poor performance. When you see one red square, it's time to think about replacing the battery.

4. Press the Shutter button halfway.

You're ready to take pictures.

Using the Auto Lighting Optimizer

If you capture images in JPEG mode, you can invoke a menu command that gives you better-looking images when you're shooting in dark conditions. Instead of getting a shot with too much contrast, you end up with a brighter shot. This option may add *digital noise* to the image. Digital noise comes in two flavors:

- **Color:** Shows up as specks of color.
- **Luminance:** Shows up as random gray clumps.

Digital noise is most prevalent in areas of solid color, such as the dark shadow areas in your image. If you shoot images in the RAW format, you can adjust image brightness after you download images to your computer with Canon's Digital Photo Professional. When you use one of the Basic Zone shooting modes, this option is set to Standard. To enable the Auto Lighting Optimizer:

1. Press the Menu button.

The previously used menu displays.

2. Use the Multi-controller button to navigate to the Shooting Settings 3 tab.

3. Use the Multi-controller or the Quick Control dial to highlight Auto Lighting Optimizer (see the left image in Figure 7-2) and then press Set.

The Auto Lighting Optimizer menu displays (see the right image in Figure 7-2).

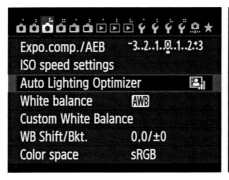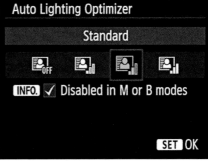

Figure 7-2: Selecting the Auto Lighting Optimizer.

4. **Use the Multi-controller or the Quick Control dial to highlight one of the following options:**

   • *Standard:* The default option adjusts the lighting to create a picture that brightens backlit subjects.

   • *Low:* This option adds a minimal amount of brightness to a backlit subject.

   • *High:* This option adds a considerable amount of brightness to a backlit subject.

   • *Disable:* Brightness and contrast are not corrected when photographing backlit subjects.

   When you pause the Quick Control dial over an option, it turns blue and the name displays above the icons.

5. **Press Info to disable this option when you photograph using M or B modes.**

   When you photograph in M or B modes, you control the exposure and normally won't need to use the Auto Lighting Optimizer.

6. **Press Set.**

   The change is applied, and you return to the Shooting Settings 3 tab.

7. **Press the Shutter button halfway to return to take pictures.**

   The Auto Lighting Optimizer setting you choose remains in effect until you select a different option. In some cases, digital noise may be apparent when the Auto Lighting Optimizer is used.

This menu command is disabled when you enable Highlight tone priority.

This menu command is disabled when you use multiple exposure shooting or HDR shooting. When HDR or multiple-exposure shooting is cancelled, the Auto Lighting Optimizer returns to the default Standard setting.

Correcting Lens Peripheral Illumination

Some lenses have a problem with light falloff toward the edge of the frame. If you've ever taken a picture and noticed that the edges of the image were dark, you've experienced this phenomenon firsthand. The amount of light falloff depends on the lens you're using. You can, however, go a long way toward correcting this problem with a camera menu command. This feature is available only for Canon lenses. The peripheral illumination data is stored in the camera's database. Another problem with lenses is chromatic aberration, which is color fringing around the edges of subjects. You can cure both. To enable lens peripheral illumination:

1. **Press the Menu button.**

   The previously used menu displays on the camera LCD monitor.

2. **Use the Multi-controller to navigate to the Shooting Settings 2 tab.**

3. **Use the Multi-controller or the Quick Control dial to highlight Lens Aberration Correction (see the left image in Figure 7-3) and then press the Set button.**

   Note that both problems are corrected by default (see the right image in Figure 7-3). Don't use this command with a third-party lens due to the fact that third-party lenses are not in the camera's database. If you have a Canon lens attached to the camera and data for the lens is in the camera's database, this information is noted in the dialog box. If a third-party lens is attached to the camera, a message appears telling you correction data isn't available.

4. **Press the Menu button to exit the menu command.**

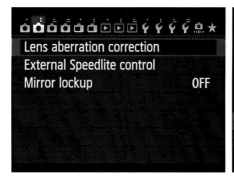
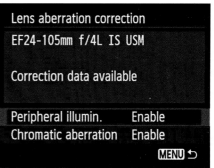

Figure 7-3: Enabling Lens Aberration Correction.

Choosing a Metering Mode

When you press the Shutter button halfway, your camera meters the scene you photograph to determine the optimal exposure settings. The default metering mode (Evaluative) works well for most lighting conditions. When you shoot in Scene Intelligent Auto or Creative Auto mode, the Evaluative metering mode is used by default. To change the metering mode to suit different lighting and picture-taking situations:

1. Press the Metering Mode button on the top of your camera.

This button is in front of the LCD panel and to the right when you point the camera toward your subject.

2. Rotate the Main dial or Quick Control dial to choose one of the following metering options:

- *Evaluative:* This is the default mode for your camera. You can use this mode for most of your work, including backlit scenes. The camera divides the scene into several zones and evaluates the brightness of the scene, direct light, and backlighting, factoring these variables to create the correct exposure for your subject.

- *Partial:* This mode meters a small area in the center of the scene. This option is useful when the background is much brighter than your subject. A perfect example of this is a beach scene at sunset when you're pointing the camera toward the sun and your subject is in front of you.

- *Center-Weighted Average:* This metering mode meters the entire scene, but gives more importance to the subject in the center. Use this mode when one part of your scene is significantly brighter than the rest; for example, when the sun is in the picture. If your bright light source is near the center of the scene, this mode prevents the image from being overexposed.

- *Spot:* This mode meters a small area in the center of the scene. Use this mode when your subject is in the center and is significantly brighter than the rest of your scene. Your camera also has the option to spot-meter where the autofocus frame is. Simply move the autofocus frame to your subject and you can accurately spot-meter a subject that isn't in the center of the frame.

Choosing the Autofocus Mode

Your camera focuses automatically on objects that intersect autofocus points. You have three autofocus modes on your camera. One is ideally suited for still objects, and another is ideally suited for objects that are moving. You have yet a third Autofocus mode, which is Chameleon; you use it for still objects that may move. To choose an Autofocus mode:

1. Press the AF-Drive button on top of your camera and directly in front of the LCD panel.

Figure 7-4 shows the LCD panel as it appears when you're using One-Shot mode.

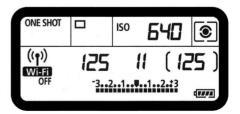

Figure 7-4: Photographing in One-Shot AF mode.

2. **Rotate the Main dial while viewing the LCD panel to select one of the following autofocus modes:**

- *One-Shot:* Use this Autofocus mode for objects that don't move. It's ideally suited for shooting portraits and landscapes.

- *AI Focus:* Use this Autofocus mode for objects that are stationary but may begin to move. The camera locks focus using One-Shot but switches to AI Servo if the subject starts moving. This option is ideally suited for macro photography of objects like flowers on a windy day. Figure 7-5 shows the LCD panel when you're shooting in AI Focus mode.

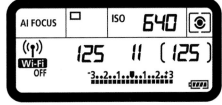

Figure 7-5: Photographing in AI Focus mode.

- *AI Servo:* Use this auto focus mode for objects in motion. After the camera locks focus on the object, the camera updates the focus as the subject moves. This mode is ideally suited for objects that are moving toward or away from you. Figure 7-6 shows the LCD panel when you're shooting in AI Servo mode.

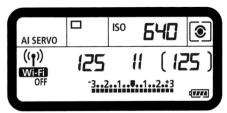

Figure 7-6: Photographing in AI Servo mode.

None of the Autofocus modes are effective on fast-moving objects, such as racecars or airplanes. To capture blur-free shots of objects like these that move toward or away from you, switch the lens to manual focus and then focus on a spot your subject will cross. Press the Shutter button shortly before your subject reaches the point on which you have focused. The amount of time varies, depending on how fast your subject is moving.

Changing the Autofocus Point

By default, your camera displays 11 autofocus points. The camera focuses on subjects that intersect autofocus points. The default number of autofocus points works fine for most picture-taking situations. However, at times, it makes sense to switch to a single autofocus point that you align with a single object, such as the edge of a building. This option is useful when you want to focus selectively on a single subject in a scene that has other objects that the camera may lock focus on. To change the autofocus point:

1. **Press the AF Point Selection button in the upper right corner on the back of your camera as you point the camera toward the scene or subject you are photographing.**

2. **While looking at the viewfinder, or at the LCD monitor, move the Multi-controller to switch from multiple autofocus points to a single auto-focus point.**

   This indicates the other possible points on which you can focus from.

3. **Press the Multi-controller button to navigate to the desired autofocus point.**

   You can navigate to any of the autofocus targets (the small red squares) to designate the point from which the camera will focus. Figure 7-7 shows one of the side autofocus points selected. The camera focuses on an object under that autofocus point.

4. **Press the Shutter button halfway.**

   You're ready to take pictures with a single autofocus point. The autofocus point is the default autofocus point until you

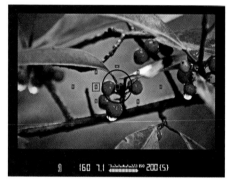

Figure 7-7: Choosing an autofocus point.

use the AF Point Selection button to designate another autofocus point.

Choosing a Picture Style

When you photograph a scene or image, your camera sensor captures the colors and subtle nuances of shadow and light to create a faithful rendition of the scene. At times, however, you want a different type of picture. For example, when you're photographing a landscape, you want vivid blues and greens in the image. You can choose from a variety of picture styles and create up to three custom picture styles. When you take pictures in Scene Intelligent Auto mode, this option isn't available. To choose a picture style:

1. **Press the Menu button.**

   The last menu command you used is displayed.

2. **Use the Multi-controller to navigate to Shooting tab 4.**

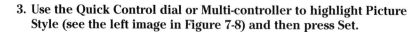

3. **Use the Quick Control dial or Multi-controller to highlight Picture Style (see the left image in Figure 7-8) and then press Set.**

The Picture Style options appear on your LCD monitor (see the right image in Figure 7-8). Auto is the default option, which means the camera adjusts the colors based on the scene you are photographing.

4. **Use the Multi-controller or the Quick Control dial to choose one of the following styles:**

   - *Standard:* The default style captures crisp, sharp images and is suitable for most photography situations.

   - *Portrait:* This style renders a soft image with flattering skin tones. This style is ideally suited for portraits of women and children.

   - *Landscape:* This style renders an image with vivid blues and greens. Landscape is ideally suited for — you guessed it — landscapes. I love truth in advertising.

   - *Neutral:* This style renders an image with no in-camera enhancement and is ideally suited for photographers who will be editing and enhancing their images with a computer image-editing application, such as Adobe Photoshop or Adobe Photoshop Lightroom. The resulting image has natural colors.

   - *Faithful:* This is another style ideally suited for photographers who like to edit their images with a computer image-editing application. When you photograph a subject in daylight with a color temperature of 5200K, the camera automatically adjusts the image color to match the color of your subject.

   - *Monochrome:* This style creates a black-and-white image. If you use this style and choose JPEG as the file format, you can't convert the image to color with your computer. If you use this style when using the JPEG format, make sure you switch back to one of the other picture styles when you want to capture images with color again.

   - *User-Created Styles:* These slots are for styles you've created. I show you how to create custom picture styles in Chapter 11.

Picture Style	Auto
Long exp. noise reduction	OFF
High ISO speed NR	▪▫
Highlight tone priority	OFF
Dust Delete Data	
Multiple exposure	Disable
HDR Mode	Disable HDR

Picture Style		
A Auto	3, 0, 0, 0	
S Standard	3, 0, 0, 0	
P Portrait	2, 0, 0, 0	
L Landscape	4, 0, 0, 0	
N Neutral	0, 0, 0, 0	
F Faithful	0, 0, 0, 0	
INFO. Detail set.		SET OK

Figure 7-8: Choosing a Picture Style option.

Figure 7-9 shows a comparison of the different picture styles.

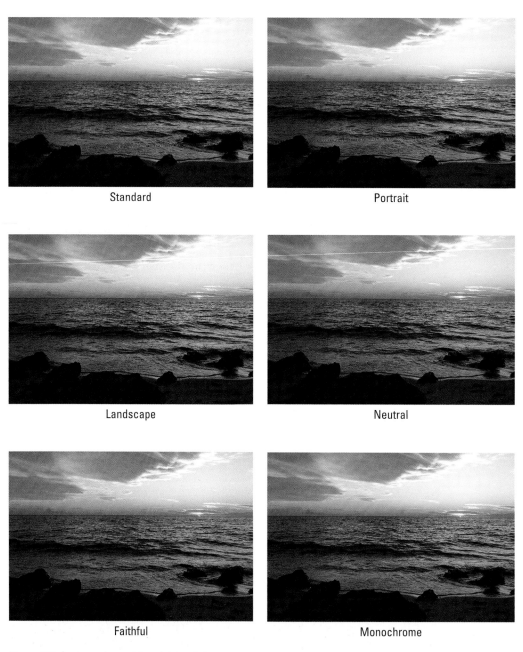

Figure 7-9: A comparison of the picture styles.

Specifying the Color Space

Several color spaces are used in photography and image-editing applications. The *color space* determines the range of colors you have to work with. The default color space (sRGB) in your camera is ideal if you're not editing your images in an application like Adobe Photoshop or Adobe Photoshop Lightroom. However, if you do edit your images in an image-editing application and want the widest range of colors (also known as *gamut*) with which to work, you can specify the Adobe RGB color space. To specify the color space that your camera records images with, follow these steps:

1. **Press the Menu button.**

   The last-used menu displays.

2. **Use the Multi-controller button to navigate to the Shooting Settings 3 tab (see the left image in Figure 7-10).**

3. **Use the Multi-controller or the Quick Control dial to highlight Color Space and then press the Set button.**

   The Color Space menu displays (see the right image in Figure 7-10).

4. **Use the Multi-controller or the Quick Control dial to highlight one of the following and then press the Set button again:**

   - *sRGB:* The default color space is ideal if you don't edit your images or do minimal editing.

   - *Adobe RGB:* Use this color space if you're editing your images in an application, such as Adobe Photoshop or Adobe Photoshop Lightroom.

5. **Press the Shutter button halfway.**

   You exit the menu and are ready to shoot pictures with your desired color space.

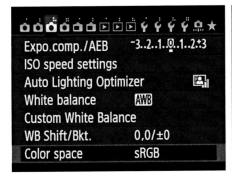
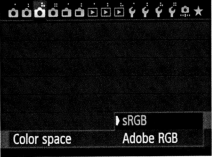

Figure 7-10: Choosing a color space.

After you edit images that were created with the Adobe RGB color space, you must convert them to sRGB in your image-editing application before printing them or displaying them on the web. For more information, see a *For Dummies* book about the software application you're using to edit your work.

Setting White Balance

The human eye can see the color white without a colorcast no matter what type of light the white object is illuminated with. Your digital camera can't compensate for different lighting scenarios; it uses *white balance* in order for white to appear as white in the captured image. Without white balance, images photographed with fluorescent light have a green colorcast and images photographed with tungsten light sources have a yellow/orange colorcast. Yup, your subject would be "green around the gills," or have some other ghastly colorcast, depending on the light sources used to illuminate the scene.

The default White Balance setting AWB (not to be confused with the old music group "Average White Band") automatically sets the white balance. If however, you notice that your images have a colorcast when letting the camera automatically set the white balance, you can choose a White Balance setting to suit the light in the scene you're photographing. You can also change white balance when you want to create an image with some special effects. If you shoot images with the RAW format and inadvertently choose the wrong White Balance setting or your camera doesn't get it right, you can change the White Balance setting in an application like Adobe Photoshop, Adobe Photoshop Lightroom, or Canon's Digital Photo Professional. To set white balance:

1. **Press the Menu button.**

   The last used menu displays.

2. **Use the Multi-controller to navigate to the Shooting Settings 3 tab.**

3. **Use the Multi-controller or Quick Control dial to highlight White Balance (see the left image in Figure 7-11) and then press Set.**

   The White Balance menu appears on the LCD monitor.

4. **Rotate the Quick Control dial while looking at your LCD panel (see the right image in Figure 7-11) and choose one of the following White Balance options:**

   - *Auto White Balance:* The camera automatically sets the white balance based on the lighting conditions.

   - *Daylight:* Use this option when photographing subjects on a bright, sunny day.

   - *Shade:* Use this option when photographing subjects in shaded conditions.

   - *Cloudy:* Use this option when photographing subjects on a cloudy day.

   - *Tungsten:* Use this option when photographing subjects illuminated by tungsten light.

   - *White Fluorescent:* Use this option when photographing subjects illuminated by fluorescent lights.

   - *Flash:* Use this option when photographing subjects with an auxiliary flash unit.

   - *Custom:* Use when creating a custom white balance. See the "Creating a Custom White Balance" section later in this chapter.

   - *K:* Use when a color temperature has been specified with a menu command. (See the next section, "Specifying Color Temperature.")

5. **Press Set.**

   The White Balance option you choose is used to balance white colors in the scenes you photograph until you choose another setting.

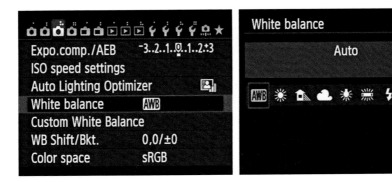

Figure 7-11: Choosing a White Balance option.

Specifying Color Temperature

If you use studio lighting, you can set the color temperature to the same temperature as the light emitted from your strobes. Color temperature is measured on the Kelvin scale. You can easily set the color temperature for the camera white balance to match the color temperature of your studio lights with a menu command. To specify a color temperature:

1. **Press the Menu button.**

2. **Use the Multi-controller to navigate to the Shooting Settings 3 tab.**

3. **Use the Multi-controller or the Quick Control dial to highlight White Balance (see the left image in Figure 7-12) and then press the Set button.**

   The White Balance menu appears on the LCD monitor.

4. **Rotate the Quick Control dial to highlight K and then rotate the Main dial to specify the color temperature (see the right image in Figure 7-12).**

   Choose the same color temperature as the lights you're using to illuminate your subject. Most studio lights are set to 5500 degrees Kelvin. Refer to the manual that came with your lighting system for the definitive answer.

5. **Press set to apply the change.**

   Your camera will balance white colors based on the color temperature you specify in Step 4 until you change the white balance setting.

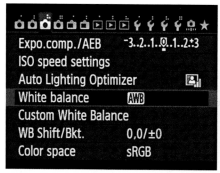
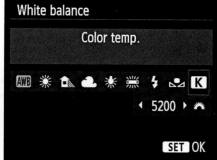

Figure 7-12: Specifying the color temperature.

Creating a Custom White Balance

When you photograph a scene that's illuminated with several different light sources, your camera may have a hard time figuring out how to set the white balance. And if the camera has a hard time, chances are you can't use one of the presets to accurately set the white balance. You can, however, set a custom white balance by following these steps:

1. **Photograph a white object.**

   Photograph the object under the light source that will be used to illuminate your scene. Photograph something that's pure white, such as a sheet of paper without lines. You won't get accurate results if you photograph something that's off-white. You'll also get better results if you use the Neutral picture style. If you use the Monochrome picture style, you can't obtain a white balance reading.

   Note: Some papers contain optical brighteners. If you use one of those to set your white balance, your images may be a little warmer (more reddish-orange in color) than normal.

   You can purchase an 18-percent gray card from your favorite camera retailer and use this in place of a white object in Step 1. The 18-percent gray card gives you extremely accurate results.

2. **Press the Menu button.**

   The last used menu command is displayed.

3. **Use the Multi-controller to navigate to the Shooting Settings 3 tab and then use the Multi-controller or the Quick Control dial to highlight Custom White Balance (see the left image in Figure 7-13).**

4. **Press the Set button.**

   The image you just photographed displays onscreen (see the right image in Figure 7-13).

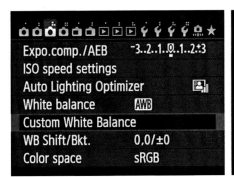

Figure 7-13: Setting a custom white balance.

A dialog box appears asking you to confirm that you want to use the image to set the white balance (see the left image in Figure 7-14).

5. **Use the Multi-controller or the Quick Control dial to highlight OK and press Set.**

The camera calculates the color temperature for the light source. After the camera completes the calculation, a dialog box appears, asking you whether you want to assign the color temperature derived from the calculation to the Custom White Balance setting (see the right image in Figure 7-14).

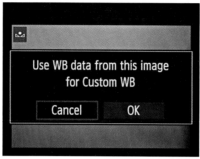
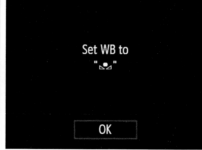

Figure 7-14: Finalizing the custom white balance.

6. **Use the Multi-controller or the Quick Control dial to select OK and then press Set.**

7. **When the menu reappears, use the Quick Control dial or Multi-controller to highlight White Balance and then press Set.**

The white balance options appear.

8. **Use the Multi-controller or the Quick Control dial to highlight Custom (see Figure 7-15).**

9. **Press Set.**

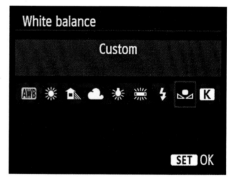

Figure 7-15: Creating a custom white balance.

Your custom white balance determines the image's white balance until you select a different White Balance option.

The custom white balance remains in effect and is used whenever you select the Custom White Balance option. You can register only one custom white balance. When you encounter a different lighting scenario that requires a custom white balance, repeat these steps.

Setting the ISO Speed

The ISO speed determines how sensitive your camera sensor is to light. When you specify a high ISO speed, you can capture images when photographing in dark conditions. When you specify a high ISO speed, you run the risk of adding digital noise to your images. When you specify a higher ISO speed, you also extend the range of the camera flash. To change the ISO speed:

1. **Press the ISO button.**

   It's the third button in from the right side of the camera when you point it at the subject or scene you're going to photograph. Note that the button is indented and has a raised dimple in the middle so you can locate the button by feel.

2. **Rotate the Main dial to specify the ISO setting while viewing the LCD panel to see the settings as you rotate the dial.**

   The default ISO for the camera is A (Automatic), which means the camera chooses the ISO based on the lighting conditions. When you decide to manually set the ISO, you can choose an ISO setting from 100 to 25600. Figure 7-16 shows the LCD panel after setting the ISO to 640.

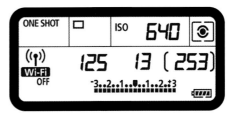

Figure 7-16: Choosing the ISO setting.

When you exceed ISO 1600, you will see digital noise in your image. If you continually shoot at high ISO settings, consider investing in noise reduction software. I use DFine 2.0 by Nik Software (www.niksoftware.com). I've used it to good effect on images I've photographed at ISO settings as high as 128000.

Expanding the ISO Range

You can extend the ISO range of your camera to give you a range from ISO 50 to ISO 102400. The high end will enable you to photographs fireflies in the dead of night. Kidding. But seriously, the extended ISO range will definitely enable you to capture images in very dim lighting conditions, but there is a payback in the form of some pretty gnarly digital noise. On the low end of the spectrum, ISO 50, you'll be able to shoot at slower shutter speeds, which is a definite bonus when you photograph beautiful waterfalls. To extend the ISO range of your camera:

1. **Press the Menu button.**

   The last-used menu command is displayed.

2. **Use the Multi-controller to navigate to the Shooting Settings 3 tab and then use the Multi-controller or the Quick Control dial to highlight ISO Speed Settings (see the left image in Figure 7-17).**

3. **Press Set.**

   The ISO Speed Settings options are displayed (see the right image in Figure 7-17). Note that you can manually set the ISO using the first menu command. I question the wisdom of that command when you can quickly set the ISO using a button and dial as shown in the previous section. (Perhaps that command exists for gluttons for punishment who have used menu-concentric cameras in the past. You know who you are.)

4. **Use the Multi-controller or Quick Control dial to highlight ISO Speed Range and then press Set.**

   The Minimum ISO setting box is highlighted.

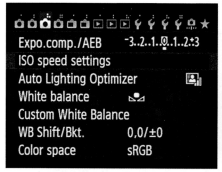

Figure 7-17: Adjusting ISO settings.

5. **Press Set.**

   An arrow appears above and below the current minimum setting. That's right, if you wanted to, you could increase the minimum setting, although I recommend against it. You always get the best-quality images shooting with the lowest possible ISO setting.

6. **Use the Multi-controller to select 50.**

   A dialog box appears, showing you that the ISO setting of 50 will appear as L when you select it. You're also warned that the low ISO setting will be bumped to 100 when you capture video (see the left image in Figure 7-18).

7. **Press Set.**

   The change is applied. If you only want to change the minimum ISO setting go to Step 10.

8. **Use the Multi-controller right to highlight the current maximum ISO setting and then press Set.**

   An arrow appears above and below the current maximum ISO setting. If you're not happy with the results you're getting at the current maximum ISO settings, press the Multi-controller down to select a lower maximum ISO setting.

9. **To increase the maximum ISO setting, press the top of the Multi-controller once to select H1(102400) and a second time to select H2(512400). After highlighting the desired setting, press Set.**

   The change is applied (see the right image in Figure 7-18).

10. **Use the Multi-controller highlight OK and then press Set.**

   The changes are applied and the ISO settings you have to work with have been extended.

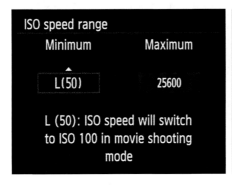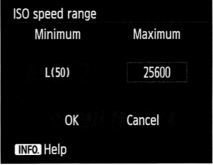

Figure 7-18: Expanding the ISO range.

In addition to expanding the ISO range, you can specify the Auto ISO Range by choosing that command from the ISO menu. If you use Auto ISO, you may find it useful to specify the minimum and maximum ISO that can be used when you let the camera automatically choose the ISO setting. The manner in which you set the Auto ISO Range is identical to the way you expand the ISO settings as outlined in the previous steps.

Another option you may find useful is setting the minimum shutter speed that will be used when Auto ISO is in effect. This prevents using an ISO that would result in a slow shutter speed, potentially causing a blurred picture. This option is set to Auto by default, however, you can modify it by choosing Min Shutter Spd under the ISO Speed Settings menu.

Using White Balance Compensation

If you find that images photographed with a custom white balance have a colorcast, you can apply compensation to remove that colorcast. This is pretty advanced stuff, so unless you know a lot about color correction, color temperatures, and so on, stick to AWB (Auto White Balance) and do any necessary color correction in your favorite image-editing application. You can only use White Balance Compensation when shooting in the following modes: Programmed Auto, Shutter Priority, Aperture Priority, Manual, and Bulb. So if you're dying to know what it's all about, follow these steps:

1. **Press the Menu button.**

   The previously used menu displays on the camera LCD monitor.

2. **Use the Multi-controller to navigate to the Shooting Settings 3 tab.**

3. **Use the Multi-controller or the Quick Control dial to highlight WB Shift/BKT (see the left image in Figure 7-19) and then press the Set button.**

   The White Balance Correction dialog box appears (see the right image in Figure 7-19). Notice there are four letters: one at the center top (*G* for green), one at the center bottom (*M* for magenta), one at the left center (*B* for blue), and one at the right center (*A* for amber).

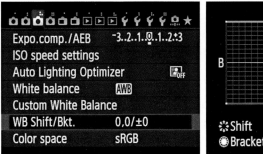
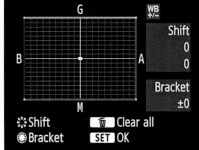

Figure 7-19: Applying a custom white balance.

4. Use the Multi-controller to move the dot.

You can move the dot toward one color and then move it up or down to shift the white balance toward a combination of amber and green. When you're adjusting white balance, you have the use of all Multi-controller arrows, which means you can precisely move the dot to exactly where you want to. When you move the dot, the color shift is designated in the dialog box (see Figure 7-20). In this case, the white balance has been shifted two levels toward amber and two levels toward magenta.

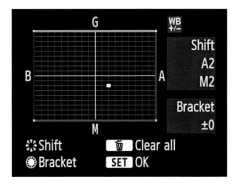

Figure 7-20: Applying a color shift to a custom white balance.

5. Rotate the Quick Control dial to the right to bracket Green and Magenta, or left to bracket Blue and Amber (see the left image in Figure 7-21) and then press Set.

Your changes are applied and the shift is noted next to the WB Shift/BKT menu command (see the left image in Figure 7-21).

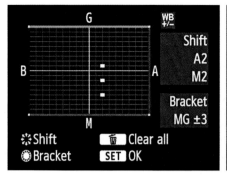
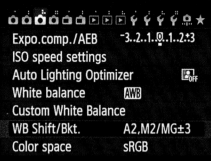

Figure 7-21: Bracketing white balance.

6. **Use the Multi-controller or Quick Control dial to highlight White Balance.**

   The White Balance Options are displayed (see the right image in Figure 7-21).

7. **Press Set and then use the Multi-controller or Quick Control dial to highlight Custom (see Figure 7-22).**

8. **If you've enabled White Balance Bracketing in Step 5, press the Drive button and select Continuous Drive.**

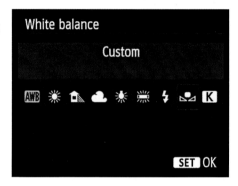

Figure 7-22: Applying the custom white balance.

9. **Press the Shutter button fully to take a picture.**

   The color shift is applied to your custom white balance. The colorcast is no more, quoth the raven. If you've enable White Balance Bracketing, your camera takes three pictures with the bracketing you specify in Step 5.

To remove White Balance Compensation, repeat the preceding Steps 1–3 and then press the Info button.

Flash Photography and Your EOS 6D

Your EOS 6D does not have a built-in flash. If you have the yen to flash your subjects, you'll have to insert a supported flash unit in the camera hot shoe. When you use a supported flash unit, the camera automatically calculates the amount of flash power needed to illuminate the scene and properly expose the image. The supported flash units are more powerful than the pop-up flash you may have used on other cameras, but they do have their limitations. Don't expect to turn night into day when photographing the Grand Canyon with a wide-angle lens and a flash unit. However, the flash will come in quite handy when photographing people in dim light. The following Canon flash units will work with your camera: 270EXII, 320EX, 430EXII, 600 EX or 600EX-RT. Some photographers use a 600EX or 600 EX-RT (wireless radio transmission) as master units to control multiple flash units. The other units listed function as slave units, enabling the photographer to set up sophisticated lighting scenarios similar to studio settings. Unfortunately, a tutorial on every lighting scenario you could conceive with your camera is beyond the scope of this book.

In the upcoming sections, I show you how to use auxiliary flash units, and how to modify the amount of light your flash unit delivers.

Using an Auxiliary Flash Unit

When you need to add some light to a scene or totally illuminate a subject with a supported flash unit, you must insert it into the camera hot shoe and power on the unit. After you do this, your camera senses the flash unit and automatically calculates the amount of light needed to illuminate the scene, or to fill in the shadows. You can perform flash photography using any shooting mode, however, you'll have the most options when you use the flash with Aperture priority or Shutter Priority mode. To use an auxiliary flash with your camera:

1. **Slide a supported flash unit into the hot shoe.**

   There is only one way to insert the unit into the hot shoe. If in doubt, look at the contacts at the bottom of the flash unit and then look at the contacts on the hot shoe, and you'll immediately see the correct orientation.

2. **Lock the flash unit into the hot shoe.**

   The flash unit will either have a thumbscrew that you turn, or a lever that you flip to lock the unit securely in the camera. If you cannot lock the flash unit, check to make sure the unit is fully inserted into the hot shoe.

3. **Power on the flash unit.**

   When you power on a supported flash unit, the camera and flash communicate.

4. **Take some pictures.**

   Figure 7-23 shows a Canon 430 EXII mounted on the hot shoe of a Canon EOS 6D ready for action.

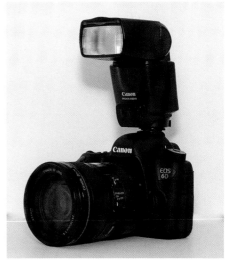

Figure 7-23: Flash photography is fun.

When you use an external Speedlite, the light source is relatively small in comparison to your subject. If your subject is near a wall, or not facing the camera directly, the flash will cast harsh shadows. When you use an external flash unit, it's always best to use a diffuser, which softens the light and makes it appear as though it is emanating from a much larger source. If you compare the light you get when photographing in direct sunlight, the light is fairly harsh and casts hard-edged shadows. That is because the sun is a relatively small light source. This is similar to your flash unit with no diffuser. Compare direct sunlight with the light you get on an overcast day. The clouds diffuse the sunlight and make it a much larger light source. You get the same thing when you add a diffuser to your camera flash. You can purchase a flash diffuser from your favorite camera retailer, or purchase one online. I highly recommend the LumiQuest (www.

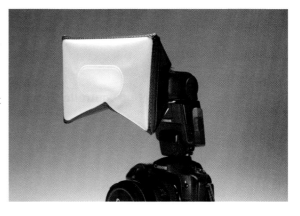

Figure 7-24: Using a flash diffuser.

lumiquest.com) line of flash diffusers. They're affordable and are easy to attach to your flash (see Figure 7-24).

Chapter 7: Using Advanced Camera Features

Using Fill Flash

Many photographers think that you use either ambient light or flash to illuminate a scene or subject. However, you can use camera flash to fill in the shadows when you're photographing a subject that is in shade, or a subject that is backlit. This is known as Fill Flash. When you use Fill Flash, the camera automatically determines how much power is needed from the flash to augment the ambient light. To use Fill Flash, simply attach a flash unit to the camera as outlined in the previous section, and use one of the Creative Modes to shoot your pictures. I usually choose Aperture Priority mode (Av on the camera mode dial), which enables me to control the depth of field when using Fill Flash. For example, when photographing flowers in shaded conditions, create your images in Aperture Priority mode using an f-stop of f/6.3 or 7.1. This gives you a limited depth of field and the Fill Flash illuminates your subject perfectly. The light from the flash is also warmer than the shaded light. As mentioned in the previous section, it's a good idea to use a diffuser when using any flash.

Controlling the External Speedlite

When you mount a Canon EX Speedlite in the camera hot shoe, you can control the output with the camera menu and much more. If you have an EX II Speedlite, you have gobs of control. The following steps show the options you have available with an EX II Speedlite. The options may be different for your Canon Speedlite. Refer to your Speedlite manual for additional instructions. To control flash with camera menu commands:

1. **Insert a supported Canon Speedlite in the camera hot shoe as outlined in the previous section, and press the Menu button.**

   The previously used menu displays.

2. **Use the Multi-controller to navigate to the Shooting Settings 2 tab.**

3. **Use the Multi-controller or the Quick Control dial to highlight External Speedlite Control (see the left image in Figure 7-25) and then press the Set button.**

   The External Speedlite Control menu displays (see the right image in Figure 7-25).

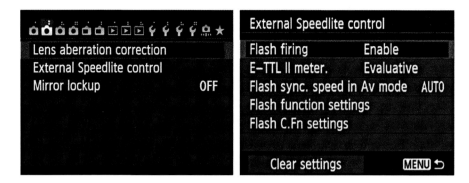

Figure 7-25: I'm in control, Mr. Speedlite.

4. Use the Multi-controller or Quick Control dial to highlight the desired command and then press Set to see the options.

The following is a brief rundown of each option:

- *Flash Firing:* Your options are to Enable or Disable flash firing. The only possible use I can see for this menu command is if you have a flash unit on your camera at all times and want to disable it when you're shooting outdoors and using the flash to fill in the shadows. When I'm using a flash unit to fill in the shadows and no longer need it, I either remove it and put it back in my camera bag or power off the flash unit. But I guess the lads in Canon engineering saw fit to cover every possible scenario.

- *E-TTL Meter:* This option determines how the camera meters the scene, which determines the amount of illumination the flash uses to properly expose the picture. Your options are Evaluative or Average. These options are identical to the metering options that I discuss in the "Choosing a Metering Mode" section earlier in this chapter.

- *Flash Sync in Av Mode:* Choose from Auto, 1/180 to 1/60 auto, or 1/180. This option determines the shutter speeds that will be chosen when you use an external Speedlite with your camera. For more information see the upcoming Changing the Flash Sync in Av Mode section of this chapter.

- *Flash Function Settings:* The options displayed vary depending on the flash unit you have attached to the camera. From this menu option you can enable second-curtain shutter sync, flash exposure compensation, flash bracketing, flash zoom, and so on.

- *Flash C.Fn Settings:* This option enables you to control the external Speedlite's custom functions from the camera menu. The options vary depending on the model flash you have attached to the camera. Refer to your flash manual for information about the flash custom functions you can control.

5. **After changing the desired flash settings, press the Shutter button halfway.**

   You're back in shooting mode and ready to put your new flash settings to work.

Changing the flash-sync speed in Av mode

When you're shooting in Aperture Priority (Av) mode, by default the camera shutter speed is set between 30 seconds and 1/180 of a second when the flash is enabled. The flash duration is very short and fires when the shutter opens, which gives you a sharp image of your subject. However, if the shutter speed is slow, you see motion trails if your subject moves during the long exposure. This can be very artistic. However, if you want to eliminate the possibility of motion trails, you can use a custom function to change the shutter speed used when a flash unit fires. Choosing one of the options that uses a higher shutter speed prevents motion trails, but the background will be dark. To change the flash-sync speed when shooting in Av mode:

1. **Navigate to the External Speedlite control menu (see the left image in Figure 7-26) as discussed in the previous section.**

2. **Use the Multi-controller or Quick Control dial to highlight Flash Sync in Av Mode, and then press Set.**

   The Flash Sync in Av mode options are displayed (see the right image in Figure 7-26).

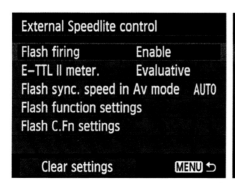
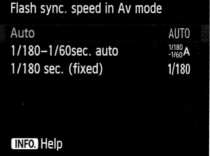

Figure 7-26: Choosing a flash-sync speed.

3. **Use the Multi-controller or the Quick Control dial to highlight one of the following:**

   • *Auto:* The camera chooses a shutter speed between 30 seconds and 1/180 of a second when a flash unit is used in Av mode.

   • *1/180–1/60Sec. Auto:* The camera automatically chooses a shutter speed between 1/60 of a second and 1/180 of a second when a flash unit is used in Av mode.

   • *1/180Sec. (Fixed):* The camera sets the shutter speed to 1/180 of a second when a flash is used in Av mode.

4. **After choosing an option, press Set.**

   Your flash unit is set to the desired flash-sync speed.

Using Flash Exposure Compensation

When you add a Speedlite to your camera, you're in complete control. If you review an image photographed with flash on your camera LCD monitor and notice that there's too much or too little flash, you can rectify the problem with flash exposure compensation, which enables you to increase or decrease the amount of power from your flash by up to 3 stops in 1/3 stop increments. To use flash exposure compensation:

1. **Navigate to the External Speedlite control menu as discussed in the "Controlling the External Speedlite" section earlier in this chapter.**

2. **Use the Multi-controller or Quick Control dial to highlight Flash Function Settings and press Set.**

   The Flash Function settings are displayed.

3. **Use the Multi-controller or Quick Control dial to highlight Flash Exposure Compensation (see the left image in Figure 7-27) and then press Set.**

   The Flash Exposure Compensation menu is displayed (see the right image in Figure 7-27).

4. **Use the Quick Control dial to increase or decrease the power from the flash unit in 1/3 stop increments and then press Set.**

   The change is applied.

5. **Press the Shutter button halfway to return to picture shooting mode.**

   Remember to set Flash Exposure compensation back to 0 after you've shot the pictures that need flash exposure compensation.

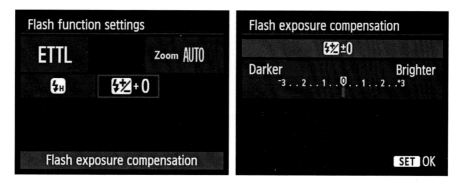

Figure 7-27: Using Flash Exposure Compensation.

Your flash unit may also have the option to bracket flash exposure. If this option is available, you'll see an FEB icon on the Flash Function Settings menu. When you choose this option, you capture three images: one with the flash exposure the camera deems optimum for the current lighting conditions; one image with negative flash exposure compensation, and one image with positive flash compensation. If your flash unit has this option, refer to the flash manual for additional information.

When you're photographing a person and there's a colorful background behind her, set camera Exposure Compensation to -1 stop, and set Flash Exposure Compensation to +1 stop. Your subject will be perfectly exposed, but the background will be slightly underexposed, which results in wonderfully saturated colors. This technique also works well when you photograph subjects such as flowers.

Using second-curtain sync

When you use an external Speedlite it fires when the shutter opens. This is all well and good when you're photographing people or objects that are standing still. However, when you use flash to photograph a moving object, the duration of the flash is much shorter than the shutter speed of the camera, especially when you're photographing in dim conditions or at night. The movement of the object after the flash fires shows up as a blur of motion, but the blur is going away from the object. When you enable second-curtain sync, the flash fires just before the shutter closes, creating a natural-looking motion trail that goes to the object instead of away from it. To enable second-curtain sync:

1. **Navigate to the External Speedlite control menu as discussed in the "Controlling the External Speedlite" section earlier in this chapter.**

2. **Use the Multi-controller or Quick Control dial to highlight Flash Function Settings and press Set.**

   The Flash Function settings are displayed.

3. **Use the Multi-controller or Quick Control dial to highlight First Shutter Synchronization, which is the default flash synchronization mode (see the left image in Figure 7-28) and then press Set.**

   The flash synchronization options are displayed.

4. **Use the Multi-controller or Quick Control dial to highlight Second Shutter Synchronization (see the right image in Figure 7-28) and then press Set.**

   You're now ready to photograph images using second-curtain synchronization.

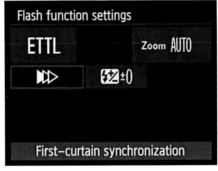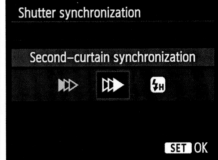

Figure 7-28: Enabling second curtain synch.

There is also an option for High Speed Synchronization on this menu. When you choose High Speed Synchronization the flash will fire at all shutter speeds. This option is useful when you're shooting in Aperture Priority mode using Fill Flash.

Modifying Flash Zoom

When you use a Speedlite, the camera detects the focal length of the lens you have on the camera and sends this information to the flash unit, which sends a beam of light at your subject that has the same angle of coverage as the lens. However, you have the option to modify the flash zoom. For example, if you're photographing flowers with an 80mm focal length, you can set the flash zoom to 105mm, which means the flash beam of light has a narrower range of coverage than your zoom lens, which effectively acts as a spotlight. To modify flash zoom:

1. **Navigate to the External Speedlite control menu as discussed in the "Controlling the External Speedlite" section earlier in this chapter.**

2. **Use the Multi-controller or Quick Control dial to highlight Flash Function Settings and press Set.**

   The Flash Function settings are displayed.

3. **Use the Multi-controller or Quick Control dial to highlight Zoom Auto, which is the default (see the left image in Figure 7-29) and then press Set.**

   The flash zoom options are displayed (see the right image in Figure 7-29).

4. **Use the Multi-controller or Quick Control dial to highlight the desired focal length, and then press Set.**

   The flash zoom is modified.

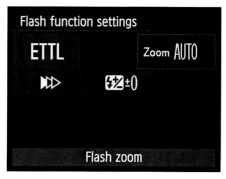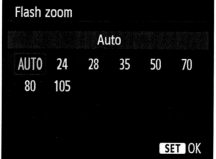

Figure 7-29: Modifying flash zoom.

Locking the flash exposure

Another handy lighting option at your disposal is locking the flash exposure to a certain part of the frame. This option is handy when your main subject isn't in the center of the frame or you want to throw some extra light on a specific part of the scene you're photographing. To lock flash exposure:

1. **Insert a supported flash unit into your camera's hot shoe.**

   If you fast forwarded to this section and don't know how to attach a flash to the camera, rewind to the "Using an Auxiliary Flash Unit" section of this chapter.

2. **Move your camera until the center autofocus point is centered over the part of the scene where you want to lock flash exposure.**

3. **Press the AE/FE Lock button.**

The camera fires a pre-flash to calculate exposure for the area over which you pointed the autofocus point. The flash icon in the viewfinder flashes on and off, and the FE lock icon appears (see Figure 7-30).

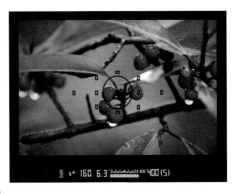

Figure 7-30: Locking flash exposure.

4. **Recompose the scene through the viewfinder and then press the Shutter button halfway to achieve focus.**

A green dot appears in the right side of the viewfinder when the camera achieves focus.

5. **Press the Shutter button fully to take the picture.**

The flash unit fires, properly exposing the area over which you locked flash exposure.

If you're really into controlling your Canon Speedlite through the camera, check out the External Flash C.Fn (Custom Function) Setting menu. This menu has options for custom functions that you can use to gain further control over your Speedlite. The available functions vary depending on the Speedlite you own. Refer to your Speedlite manual for more information.

Clearing Flash Settings

If you find that you've enabled lots of different flash options and don't want to go through the hassle of going through each and every menu option, or you forget which settings you've enabled, you'll be glad to know there is a menu command to clear settings. To clear all flash settings in one fell swoop:

1. **Navigate to the External Speedlite control menu as discussed in the "Controlling the External Speedlite" section earlier in this chapter.**

2. **Use the Multi-controller or the Quick Control dial to highlight Clear Settings and then press Set.**

The Clear Settings menu appears.

3. **Use the Multi-controller or the Quick Control dial to highlight the settings you want to clear.**

   Unless your flash unit has custom functions, select Clear Flash Settings (see Figure 7-31).

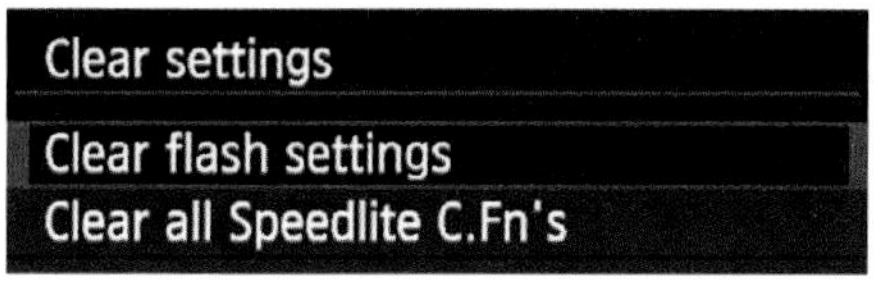

4. **Press Set.**

   All flash settings are cleared. Now wasn't that easier than going through each menu?

Clear settings

Clear flash settings

Clear all Speedlite C.Fn's

Figure 7-31: Clearing all flash settings.

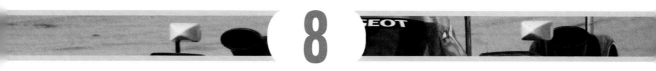

Mastering Your EOS 6D

*I*n earlier chapters, I show you all the bells and whistles on your camera that you can use in your photography. Bells and whistles are cool, but if you don't know when to ring or blow them, they don't do you much good. In this chapter, I cut to the chase and show you how to use these features for specific types of photography. Of course, you may not be interested in all the types of photography I discuss in this chapter. But I like to practice several different photography disciplines.

I find that different disciplines keep me on my toes and keep my work fresh. Not to mention that they help me get to know my camera better. Try diversifying and shooting different subjects — you might like it. At any rate, in this chapter, I show you what settings to use for specific types of photography. I also sprinkle in some tips that will take your photography to the next level.

Choosing the Optimal Settings for Specific Situations

Your camera has settings for every conceivable type of photography. In the early chapters of this book, I show you the SCN modes, where the camera takes the bull by the horns and uses automatic settings. But the camera doesn't really know if you're photographing a pet rock or the Grand Canyon. When you take off the training wheels and start using the really cool settings your camera has, you're in control, and with practice (plus the sage advice of your friendly author), you'll create some great images. All you need to do is attach the right lens to the camera and you're ready for action. You can take pictures of just about any object, from a small insect to a racing car traveling at a high rate of fuel consumption. But the trick is knowing what settings to use for a specific picture-taking situation. For example, say you're photographing your significant other and want her to be the center of attention with a soft blurry background. That's easy to achieve with the right camera setting and the right lens.

In addition to the right settings, you have to be creative so your photograph of a known person, place, or thing doesn't look like someone else's photograph of the same person, place, or thing. To take great pictures, you have to examine everything in the viewfinder and determine whether it's something you should include in the photograph. With a bit of thought and keen observation, you'll notice that light pole sticking out of your significant other's head and ask her to move to a different position, or you'll move to a different position.

Photographing Action

Your camera is well-equipped to photograph action, whether your subject is a flock of flying birds or the Blue Angels in formation. When you photograph an object in motion, your goal is to portray motion artistically. The camera settings and lens you use depend on the type of subject you're photographing. If you're photographing a marathon runner, you want to depict the beauty and grace of his fluid stride and athletic body. If you're photographing a racecar, your goal is the same. You want to depict the beauty of a beautifully sculpted racecar at speed. So the type of settings you use depends on whether your subject is moving toward you or parallel to you, and whether your subject is moving very fast or very slow.

Photographing fast-moving subjects

When people see my photographs of racecars, they always assume I'm using a fast shutter speed because the car looks so clear and they can see every detail, including the driver's name on the side of the car. But I do just the opposite. I shoot with a relatively slow shutter speed when the car is traveling parallel to me. To photograph a fast-moving subject:

1. **Attach a telephoto lens to your camera.**

   The focal length of the lens depends on how far away your subject is. When I photograph racecars, I use a Canon 70–200 mm f/4 lens. If the cars are relatively close to me, I can zoom out and still get the whole car. If they're far away, I zoom to 200mm, which brings the action to me.

2. **Point the camera where your subject will be when you take the picture and then zoom in.**

   If you're photographing an automobile race, you can compose your picture a lap before you take it. I generally zoom to almost fill the frame with the car and then zoom out a little, leaving a little distance in front of the car to give the impression that the car is going somewhere.

3. **Press the Drive button and then rotate the Main dial to switch to AI Servo focus mode so that your camera focuses continually on your subject as it moves toward or away from you.**

   If your camera has a hard time keeping fast-moving subjects in focus, you can focus manually on the spot where the object will be when you take the picture.

4. **Switch to a single autofocus point in the center of the frame.**

   When you use multiple autofocus points, the camera may focus on an object other than the one you want to photograph. For more information on choosing an autofocus point, see Chapter 7.

5. **Press the Mode Lock and then rotate the camera shooting Mode dial to Tv (Shutter Priority mode), and then press the Shutter button and rotate the Main dial to select a shutter speed of 1/160 second.**

   You may have to use a slightly higher shutter speed if you're using a lens with a focal length of 200mm or longer. The aperture really doesn't matter with this technique. The background is stationary, but the car and camera are moving at the same relative speed. Therefore the background will be a blur caused by the motion of the camera relative to the background. However, if you are photographing a race on an overcast day, and the f-stop value is lower than f/6.3, increase the ISO setting until you have an f-stop of f/6.3 or smaller. If you shoot with too large an aperture, the side of the car will be in focus, but the driver's helmet will be out of focus.

6. **Spread your legs slightly and move your elbows to the side of your body. Cradle the barrel of the lens with your left hand and position your right forefinger over the Shutter button.**

   This helps stabilize the camera as you pan with your subject. In this position, you're the human equivalent of a tripod.

7. **Pivot from the waist toward the direction from which your subject will be coming.**

8. **When your subject comes into view, press the Shutter button halfway to achieve focus.**

   Sometimes the camera has a hard time focusing on a fast-moving object, such as a fighter jet traveling at several hundred miles per hour. If this is the case, switch to One-Shot AF mode, switch your lens to manual focus, and focus on the place where your subject will be when you press the Shutter button. Press the Shutter button just before your subject reaches the spot on which you've focused.

9. **Pan the camera with your subject to keep it in frame.**

   When you're photographing an object in motion, a good idea is to keep more space in front of the object than behind it. This shows your viewer the direction in which your subject is traveling.

10. **Press the Shutter button when your subject is in the desired position and follow through.**

    If you stop panning when you press the Shutter button, your subject won't be sharp. Figure 8-1 is a photograph of a racecar racing through a corner. I used the panning technique to catch the essence of speed. At this point, the car was traveling well over 100 mph.

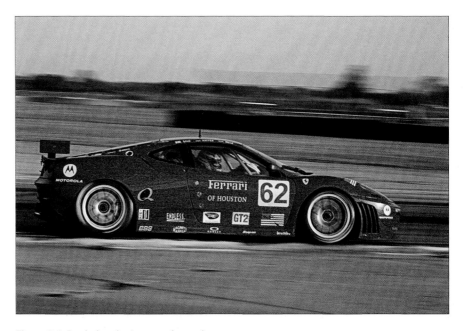

Figure 8-1: Depicting the beauty of speed.

Freezing action

When your subject is traveling toward or away from you at a fast rate, your goal is to freeze the action. Another time you want to freeze action is when you want the photo to depict the beauty and grace of your subject. An example of this is a closeup of a tennis player with the ball just leaving her racket or a waterskier slicing through the water. To freeze action:

1. **Attach a telephoto lens to your camera.**

   The focal length of the lens depends on how far away your subject is. I generally use a focal length that is 300mm or longer when photographing racecars coming toward me. This puts some distance between me and the subject. A telephoto lens also does a great job of compressing the background. For example, if you're photographing a gaggle of racecars, a long focal length makes them look like they're closer to each other than they actually are.

2. **Point the camera where your subject will be when you take the picture and then zoom in.**

   When you compose the picture, leave some room in front of your subject to give the appearance that it's going somewhere. I generally try to include some of the background to give viewers an idea of the locale in which the photograph was taken.

3. **Press the Drive button and then rotate the Main dial to switch to AI Servo focus mode so that your camera focuses continually on your subject as it moves toward or away from you.**

   Your camera may have a hard time focusing on a fast-moving vehicle. I had this problem when photographing the start of an automobile race. The cars were traveling well over 100 mph at the place I wanted to photograph them, so I switched to manual focus and focused on an expansion joint. I snapped the shutter just before the car crossed the expansion joint. (For more information on switching focus modes, see Chapter 7.)

4. **Press the AF Point Selection button and then use the Multi-controller to a single autofocus point in the center of the frame.**

   With multiple autofocus points, the camera may focus on something other than your subject. (For more information on switching to a single autofocus point, see Chapter 7.)

5. **Press the Mode Lock and then rotate the shooting Mode dial to Tv (Shutter Priority mode) and then press the Shutter button and rotate the Main dial to choose a shutter speed of 1/1000 of a second.**

   Choose a higher shutter speed when trying to freeze the motion of something like a pitcher throwing a fastball. When you set the shutter speed, make note of the f-stop. If you can get a 5.6 or 7.1 f-stop, the background will be recognizable but not in sharp focus. You may have to experiment with different ISO speed settings to achieve the optimal shutter speed and aperture combination. Note that if you're shooting in low ambient light, you may see the maximum aperture (smallest f/stop number) blinking in the viewfinder, which means the image will be underexposed at the current shutter speed. Either choose a slower shutter speed, or increase the ISO until the aperture stops blinking.

6. Press the Drive button and then rotate the Main dial to switch to Continuous mode.

With this mode, you can capture a sequence of images as long as your finger is on the Shutter button at approximately 4.5 fps (frames per second). This is a great way to capture a sequence of your dog catching a Frisbee. For more information on choosing a Drive mode, see Chapter 6.

7. Press the Shutter button halfway to achieve focus.

A green dot appears on the right side of the viewfinder when you achieve focus. When shooting in AI Servo autofocus mode, the camera updates focus as your subject moves toward or away from you.

If the dot is flashing, the camera can't achieve focus. You may experience this when you try to focus on a subject that's traveling very fast. If this happens, switch to One-Shot AF mode, switch the lens to manual focus, and then pre-focus on the place your subject will be when you take the picture.

8. Press the Shutter button fully to take the picture.

If you switched to manual focus, press the shutter button just before the subject moves to where you focused. Figure 8-2 was photographed at the start of an automobile race. In this case, I switched to manual focus and focused on an expansion strip in the race track (which began life as a WWII airport).

To get the knack of this technique, photograph one of your family members bouncing a ball or photograph your son or daughter throwing a knuckleball at baseball practice.

Photographing slow-moving subjects

I cover freezing motion and capturing the essence of speed in previous sections in this chapter. Here I show you techniques to photograph subjects that move slower, such as horses, runners, and bicyclists. When you freeze the motion of subjects like these, the end result is kind of boring. When you photograph slow-moving subjects like runners or cyclists, you can use blur creatively to capture a compelling photograph of your subject. This technique also works great for photographing birds in flight. To photograph slow-moving objects:

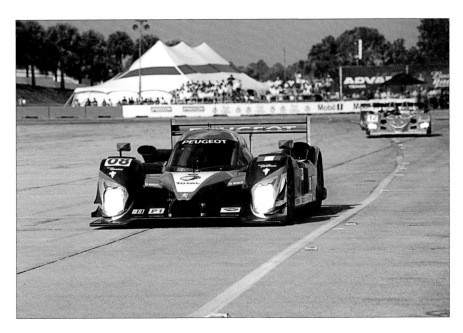

Figure 8-2: Freezing motion.

1. **Attach a telephoto zoom lens to your camera.**

   You can do this technique with a lens with a shorter focal length of 50mm. However a longer focal length compresses the background. I like to use my 70–200mm lens when photographing slow-moving subjects.

2. **Point the camera where your subject will be when you take the picture and zoom in.**

3. **Press the AF button and then rotate the Main dial to switch to AI Servo autofocus mode.**

   After the camera locks focus, your camera updates focus continually as your subject moves toward you. (For more information on switching autofocus modes, see Chapter 7.)

4. **Press the AF Point Selection button and then use the Multi-controller to switch to a single autofocus point in the center of the frame.**

   When you use multiple autofocus points, the camera may inadvertently focus on an object other than the one you want to photograph. (For more information on switching to a single autofocus point, see Chapter 7.)

5. **Press the Mode Lock, rotate the shooting Mode dial to Tv (switch to Shutter Priority mode), press the Shutter button, and then rotate the Main dial to select a shutter speed of 1/30 second or slower.**

   This shutter speed is a good starting point, but don't be afraid to choose a slower shutter speed. I often photograph runners and bicyclists at a shutter speed of 1/6 second.

6. **Spread your legs slightly and move your elbows to the side of your body.**

   This stabilizes the camera, which is important when you're shooting at a slow shutter speed.

7. **Pivot from the waist toward the area from which your subject will be coming.**

8. **When your subject comes into view, press the shutter button halfway to achieve focus.**

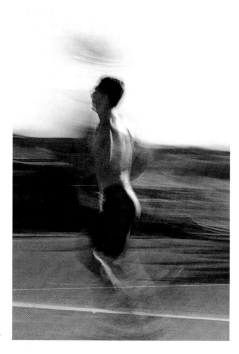

Figure 8-3: Using motion blur creatively.

   A green dot appears in the right side of your viewfinder when you achieve focus. When you shoot in AI Servo autofocus mode, the camera updates focus as your subject moves.

9. **Pan the camera with your subject and then press the shutter button when your subject is at the desired spot.**

   Remember to follow through.

When you use this technique, certain parts of your subject are in relatively sharp focus, but body parts, such as a runner's arms and legs, are a blur of motion (see Figure 8-3).

Photographing Landscapes

If you live in an area like mine, where you can discover lots of lovely land-scapes — thank you, Joni — capturing compelling pictures of the landscapes is an excellent way to use your camera. Landscape photography is a time-honored tradition. The fact that you own a camera capable of capturing images with a 20.2 megapixel resolution means that you can create some very big prints of your favorite landscapes. My home is decorated with photographs I've shot since moving to the Gulf Coast of Florida in December 2008. To photograph landscapes:

1. **Attach a wide-angle zoom lens to your camera.**

   When you're photographing landscapes, you want to capture the wide expanse. Use a lens that can zoom out to a focal length that is 28mm or less. My favorite lens for shooting landscapes has a focal length that is 24mm.

2. **Press the Mode Lock, rotate the shooting Mode dial to Av (Aperture Priority mode), press the Shutter button and then rotate the Main dial to choose the smallest aperture (highest f-stop value) possible for the lighting conditions.**

   A small aperture gives you a large depth of field. When you're photographing something like the Grand Canyon, you want to see everything from foreground to background. When I photograph landscapes, I use an aperture of f/11.0 or smaller. Keep in mind, you may have to increase the ISO speed setting when photographing in cloudy or overcast weather. For more information on Aperture Priority mode, see Chapter 6.

3. **Press the Shutter button halfway to achieve focus.**

   A green light appears in the viewfinder when the camera achieves focus. Take note of which autofocus points glow red. In spite of the large depth of field you get with a small aperture, you don't want the camera focus-ing on items in the foreground.

4. **Press the Shutter button fully to take the picture.**

Landscape photography is rewarding. The preceding steps get you started in the right direction, but the time of day is also very important. If you think morning is for eating breakfast and the time before sunset is for eating dinner, you have it all wrong. These are the times you need to be chasing the clouds with your camera in hand. And yes, I do mean "chasing the clouds" because clouds add interest to any landscape. If you have a still body of water into which the clouds can reflect, you have an even more compelling picture. The light in the morning just after sunrise and the light just before sunset is warm, almost golden in color. That's why the hour after sunrise and the hour before sunset is the *Golden Hour*. This is when you need to photo-graph your landscapes (see Figure 8-4).

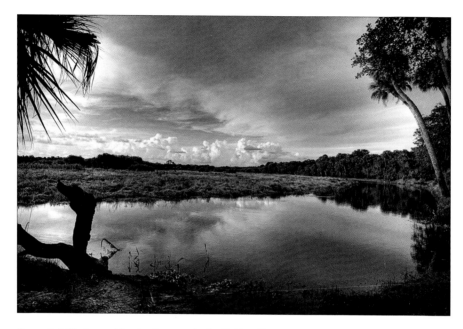

Figure 8-4: Photographing landscapes in the Golden Hour.

Composition is a very important part of photography, especially when you photograph a landscape. Your goal is to draw your viewer into the image. For more information on composing your photographs, check out the "Composing Your Images" section later in this chapter.

Photographing the Sunset

Sunset is an awesome time of day for photographers. The sun is low on the horizon, casting warm orange light. Add clouds to the equation and you have the recipe for great sunset pictures. When you photograph a sunset, the sun is obviously a key player, but you need other ingredients, such as clouds and an interesting landscape, for a great shot. Without clouds, you have a boring picture of an orange ball sinking in a cerulean sky. You can take pictures of sunsets with the skyline of your town in silhouette. You can get an even better sunset shot when you have a body of water such as a lake, a river, or an ocean. The water will reflect the colorful clouds. If the water is still, you have a wonderful mirror reflection of the clouds and the setting sun.

You can get some great sunset pictures in the final few minutes before the sun sets. After the sun sets, many photographers pack up their gear and head home. This is a mistake. As long as the clouds don't go all the way to the horizon, the sun will reflect warm colors on the underside of the clouds for about 10 to 15 minutes after setting. If you want really great sunset pictures, wait a few minutes after the sunset and get ready to take some pictures when the clouds are bathed in giddy shades of pink, orange, and purple (see Figure 8-5).

The camera settings for a sunset are almost identical to those you use for landscapes, with the exception of lens choice. If you're going for the grand view, use a wide-angle lens with a minimum of 28 mm or less, and choose the smallest possible aperture for a large depth of field. Sometimes you may need to go the other route and choose a telephoto focal length and a fairly large aperture for a limited depth of field.

Recently I photographed a sunset at a picturesque beach a few minutes from my home. I used my Canon 24–105mm F 4.0 L lens and zoomed to 105mm, with an aperture of f/7.1. I focused on some nearby sea oats. The sea oats were in silhouette and in sharp focus, the clouds were a little soft, and the sun was a soft out-of-focus orange orb, as shown in Figure 8-6. But due to the telephoto lens, the sun is relatively large in the resulting photo, which makes it clear I took the photo as the sun was setting.

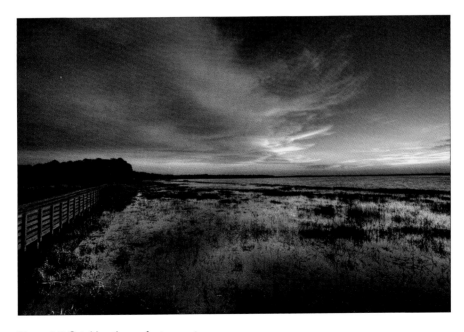

Figure 8-5: Catching the perfect sunset.

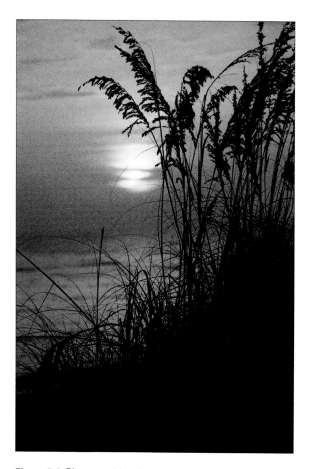

Figure 8-6: Photographing the sun.

When you photograph a sunset, the camera metering system may make the scene much brighter than it actually is. If you notice this when reviewing the image on the camera LCD monitor, lock exposure on the sky and then take the picture. Alternatively, you can use exposure compensation to reduce exposure by one stop or more. (For more information on exposure compensation and locking focus, see Chapter 6.)

When you photograph the sun, don't look directly at the sun through your viewfinder or you may damage your vision. If you photograph sunsets with Live View mode or with the mirror locked, don't point the camera at the sun for a long period of time because you may damage some of the sensitive components in your camera.

Developing a style

Photographers are attracted to different subjects and do things in different ways. Casual photographers tend to produce similar images, but die-hard photographers like to do things differently. Die-hards have a different way of seeing things, and therefore, produce different-looking images, even when they photograph the same subjects. They experiment with different lenses, different vantage points, different lighting, and so on.

Each year thousands of photographs are taken of Yosemite National Park, yet most of them pale in comparison with the memorable images photographed by Ansel Adams. The key to developing your own style is to study the work of the masters. If you're a landscape photographer, check out Ansel Adams's work. If you like the gritty, down-to-earth, street-journalism style of photography, look at Henri Cartier-Bresson's work. The next step is to shoot what you love as often as you can.

Photographing People and Things

You have a great camera that can do many things. Photographing people and the world around you is another great way to use your camera. When you photograph people and things, your goal is to create a compelling photo of the object or person, a portrait if you will. In the upcoming sections, I offer some advice for photographing people and things.

Photographing people and pets

With the right lens, your camera can capture stunning photos of people or pets. You can photograph formal or candid portraits, or use Live View mode to shoot from the hip. When you photograph people and pets, here are some things to keep in mind:

- Use a telephoto lens with a focal length that is 85mm or longer.

- Switch to Aperture Priority (Av) mode. (For more information on Aperture Priority mode, see Chapter 6.)

- Switch to a single autofocus point or the middle autofocus zone. (For more information on modifying autofocus, see Chapter 7.)

- Choose your largest aperture (smallest f-stop value). Choosing a large aperture gives you a small depth of field. Your subject is in focus, but the background is a soft, out-of-focus blur.

- If you're taking the picture indoors, photograph your subject against a solid color wall. You can also tack a solid color bed sheet to a wall and use that as a backdrop.

✔ If you're photographing your subject outdoors, photograph her against a nondescript background, such as distant foliage. If you photograph your subject with a telephoto lens with a large aperture and shoot *wide open* (photographer-speak for using your largest aperture), the background will be a pleasant out-of-focus blur that won't distract your viewer's attention from your subject (see Figure 8-7).

✔ If possible, don't use a flash when photographing people because this produces a harsh light that isn't flattering for portraits. Available light from a window is your best bet if you photograph indoors and diffuse shade is best if you photograph the portrait outdoors. Photographing portraits on a cloudy overcast day is also ideal. If you do use a flash, use it with a diffuser, which spreads the light out and makes it appear as though your subject is illuminated with a larger light source. You can find flash diffusers at your favorite camera retailer, or purchase them online. A company called LumiQuest (www.lumiquest.com) manufactures a line of very portable and very affordable flash diffusers.

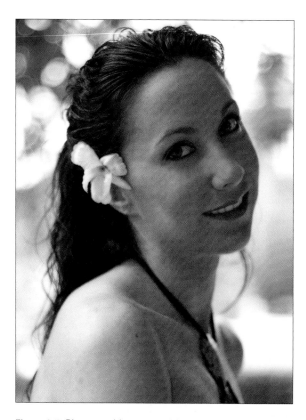

Figure 8-7: Photographing your subject against a plain background.

✔ When you're shooting portraits of a friend, relative, or your pet, take lots of pictures. Your subject will give you more natural expressions as he relaxes.

✔ If you have a Canon Speedlite, mount it in the hot shoe and then bounce it off a white surface, such as a wall or the ceiling. When you bounce the flash off a large surface, you end up with a soft diffuse light similar to that of a cloudy day.

✔ When using flash to illuminate your subject, make sure she's not too close to the wall; otherwise you'll get a nasty shadow.

✔ Use Live View mode when you want candid shots of friends or your pet. After enabling Live View, place the camera on a table with the end of the lens just off the table. When you see something interesting happen, take a picture. Your friends won't be as intimidated by the camera on the table as they would if you held the camera to your face.

✔ Never photograph pets with flash. The bright light scares them and the light reflecting from the back of their eyes makes them look like they're possessed.

✔ When you photograph a person or a pet, make sure the eyes are in focus. To do so:

  1. *Switch to a single autofocus point when photographing a head-and-shoulders portrait.*

  2. *In the viewfinder, align the autofocus point with the person's (or pet's) eye that is closest to the camera, and press the Shutter button halfway to achieve focus.*

  3. *Recompose the shot and take the picture.*

  Remember that the eyes are the windows to the soul.

You need to consider lots of things when you photograph people and pets, much more than I can include in this book. If you want more information on portrait photography, check out *Digital Portrait Photography For Dummies* by yours truly.

Exploring selective focus

When you own a camera like the EOS 6D and a lens with a large aperture with an f/stop value of 2.8 or smaller, you can create some wonderfully artistic photos by using the *selective focus* technique. When you take pictures with the largest aperture on a lens with a focal length 85mm or longer, you have a wonderfully shallow depth of field. You can use this to your advantage by focusing on one spot that will be your center of interest. The rest of the image will be out of focus, and your viewer's attention will be drawn to the point in sharpest focus. To create images with this technique:

1. **Switch to a single autofocus point and Aperture Priority mode.**

    See Chapter 7 for more on autofocus points and see Chapter 6 for more on the Aperture Priority mode.

2. **Look through the viewfinder and position the autofocus point over your center of attention.**

3. **Press the shutter button halfway to achieve focus and then recompose the image.**

    I photographed Figure 8-8 with a Canon 85mm f/1.8 lens. I switched to a single autofocus point and focused on the Harley Davidson badge.

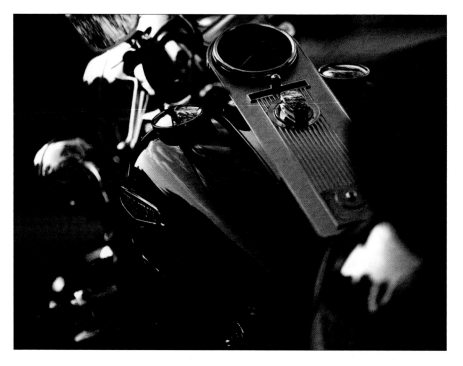

Figure 8-8: The selective focus technique with a telephoto lens and a large aperture.

Exploring macro photography

Extreme close-up photography, also known as *macro photography,* can be a tremendous source of enjoyment. With a macro lens, you can get close to small insects, flowers, and other objects that look interesting when magnified to life-size proportions. Keep the following in mind when working with macro photography:

✏ Canon makes a wonderful lens for macro photography — the 100mm EF f/2.8 lens — which works on your EOS 6D. You can also choose from lots of third-party macro lenses available for your camera. Tamron makes a great 90mm macro lens and 180mm macro lens.

✏ Focus is extremely important because when you use a macro lens and get very close to your subject, you're dealing with a very limited depth of field.

✏ Macro photography is almost impossible to do when the weather is windy because your subject keeps moving in and out of focus. If it's not too windy, switch the autofocus mode to AI Focus. If the camera achieves focus and the item you're photographing moves, the camera switches to AI Servo and updates focus.

✏ When you decide to get small and go macro, shoot in Aperture Priority (Av) mode (see Chapter 6) and choose the smallest aperture possible for the lighting conditions. This gives you a slightly larger depth of field.

✏ A good tripod is a handy accessory when shooting macro photography because it keeps the camera steady. If you're not using a tripod, shoot at a higher shutter speed than you normally would. Keep as steady as possible, focus, and gently squeeze the Shutter button when you exhale.

Photographing Wildlife

With a camera like the EOS 6D, you can capture stunning photos of wildlife, whether the animals are moving or standing still. Photographing wildlife can be challenging, but the results are extremely rewarding. When you shoot wildlife with a camera and get a great shot, the animal lives to see another day and you have a wonderful trophy to matte and frame. The following sections offer some tips for photographing wildlife in different locations.

Photographing animals at state parks

The easiest way to find spots to photograph wildlife near your home is to Google *state park* followed by the name of the town or county in which you live. Another good source for information are the people in your local camera store or camera club. Be nosy and ask them where their favorite wildlife photography spots are. Make friends with them and ask whether you can tag along on one of their photo shoots. I live in an area that has many state parks. When I moved to my current stomping grounds I had the good fortune to find a photography buddy who has shown me many of the wonderful wildlife hot spots near my home. Here are some things I've figured out about photographing wildlife in a state park:

✔ **Photograph animals with a long lens.** Unless you're photographing large animals, you'll need a long lens with a focal length that is 300mm or greater. State parks are animal sanctuaries. Even though the animals are protected, they're wary of humans. A long lens is the only way you can get close-ups of the animals.

✔ **Switch to Shutter Priority (Tv) mode (see Chapter 6) and choose the proper shutter speed.** When you're photographing wildlife with a long lens, camera shake due to operator movement is magnified. Choose a shutter speed that's equal to the reciprocal of focal length of the lens you're using. If you're using a lens with a focal length that is 300mm lens, you have to choose a shutter speed that is at least 1/300 of a second. If your lens has image stabilization, enable it when photographing wildlife. You may have to increase the ISO speed (see Chapter 7) to get the proper shutter speed, especially if you're photographing wildlife in a forest or in dense foliage. A tripod is also useful to stabilize the camera.

✔ **Use a large aperture (small f-stop number) when you create wildlife portraits.** The shallow depth of field you get with a large aperture ensures that your viewer's attention is drawn toward the animal, and not the background (see Figure 8-9). To get the desired f-stop when you want to use a specific shutter speed, change the ISO setting.

✔ **Switch to a single autofocus point (see Chapter 7) and focus on the animal's eyes.** If the eyes aren't in focus, you've missed the shot. When you're shooting wildlife with a long lens and using a large aperture, you have a very shallow depth of field, which makes accurate focus a necessity. If the animal's eyes are in focus, your viewer assumes the entire animal is in focus.

✔ **Always travel with a photo buddy.** Many of the animals in state parks are fairly benign. However, some of the inhabitants can be dangerous if you're not careful. Many state parks have bears, alligators, and other animals that can be hazardous to your health when provoked. While you're in the moment photographing a bird, your buddy can watch your back and make sure a dangerous animal like an alligator isn't sneaking up on you. An alligator can pop out of the water like a rocket.

Stabilizing the camera when using long telephoto lenses

When you photograph wildlife with a long telephoto lens, any operator movement is magnified. The simple act of pressing the shutter button, no matter how gently you do it, vibrates the camera. The vibration degrades the resulting images slightly; it doesn't appear to be tack-sharp. A tripod is a huge help when using a long lens, but it doesn't stop the vibration. Here are two techniques you can use to minimize the vibration transmitted after you press the Shutter button.

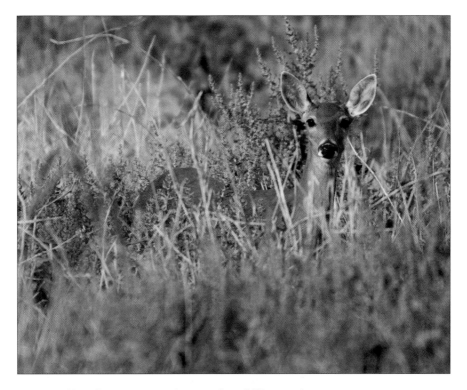

Figure 8-9: Use a large aperture when creating wildlife portraits.

Stabilizing the camera with the Self-Timer

An easy way to stop vibration from reaching the camera is to delay the shutter opening after you press the shutter button. You do this with the Self-Timer as follows:

1. **Press the AF button.**

2. **While looking at the LCD panel, rotate the Quick Control dial until the 2-Second Timer icon appears (see Figure 8-10).**

3. **Mount the camera on a tripod.**

4. **Compose your scene and press the Shutter button halfway to achieve focus.**

2-second timer icon

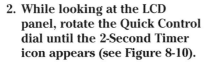
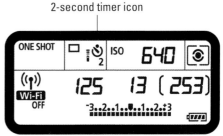

Figure 8-10: Stabilizing the camera with the 2-Second Timer.

When the camera focuses on your subject, a green dot appears in the viewfinder.

5. Press the Shutter button fully.

Press the Shutter button gently, don't stab it with your finger. After you press the Shutter button, the timer counts down. When you press the Shutter button gently, two seconds is enough time to stabilize any vibration transmitted to the camera.

Using Mirror Lockup to stabilize the camera

Your camera can also lock the mirror in the up position before the picture is taken. This helps minimize the transmission of any vibration that occurs when the mirror moves up prior to opening the shutter. This vibration can cause your image to be less than tack sharp. You can enable Mirror Lockup using a custom function as follows:

1. Press the Menu button.

The previously used menu displays.

2. Use the Multi-controller button to navigate to the Shooting Settings 2 tab.

3. Use the Multi-controller or the Quick Control dial to highlight Mirror Lockup (see the left image in Figure 8-11).

4. Press the Set button.

The options for Mirror Lockup appear on your camera LCD monitor (see the right image in Figure 8-11).

5. Use the multi-controller or Quick Control dial to highlight Enable and then press Set.

Mirror Lockup is enabled.

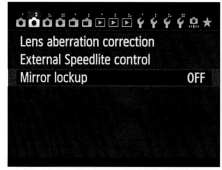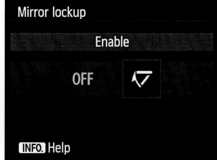

Figure 8-11: Enabling Mirror Lockup.

6. **Press the Shutter button halfway to return to shooting mode.**

7. **Compose the scene and then press the Shutter button halfway to achieve focus.**

   A green dot appears in the right side of the viewfinder.

8. **Press the Shutter button fully.**

   The mirror locks up.

9. **Press the Shutter button again.**

   The picture is taken and the mirror drops down.

When you're using Mirror Lockup in bright conditions, press the shutter button as soon as possible after the mirror locks up. Excessive exposure to bright light or the sun can damage the sensor. Make sure you disable Mirror Lockup as soon as you no longer need it.

Photographing animals at the zoo

If you live in a big city or don't have any nearby nature reserves, you can still get some great shots of wildlife at your local zoo. Visit the zoo on an off day when there will be fewer crowds to contend with and get there just before feeding time. The animals are likely to be more active prior to feeding time. When you find an animal you want to photograph, make sure no humans (or other signs that you're at a zoo) are in the frame. Switch to Aperture Priority (Av) mode (see Chapter 6) and choose your largest aperture. Move around to compose the best possible picture and then zoom in on the animal. Patiently wait until the animal does something interesting and then take the picture. Stick around for a few minutes, and the animal may do something else that's interesting or amusing. If possible, compose your image so that no telltale signs, such as fence posts or signs, give away that the image was shot at a zoo. If you're forced to take pictures with these objects, crop them out in your image-editing program.

Photographing birds

Birds run the gamut from downright ugly — the turkey vulture comes to mind — to beautiful and graceful. If you've ever witnessed a snowy egret preening, you've seen a truly elegant bird. When you photograph birds, it's almost like shooting a portrait of a person. Here are some tips for photographing birds with your EOS 6D:

✓ **If you're photographing flying birds, switch to the middle autofocus zone and switch to AI Servo autofocus mode (see Chapter 7).** When the camera achieves focus, it updates the focus as the bird flies.

✒ **If you're photographing flying birds, switch to Shutter Priority (Tv) mode (see Chapter 6), and choose a shutter speed of 1/250 of a second or faster.** This freezes the bird's motion. You can also go the other way and choose a slow shutter speed of 1/30 of a second. If you choose the slower shutter speed route, pan the camera with the bird and then the bird's wings will be blurred, giving you an artistic photograph of a bird in flight.

✒ **Photograph birds in the morning or late in the afternoon.** The light is warmer and more pleasing at these times of day. The harsh midday sunlight isn't a good light for any subject, even your fine feathered friends.

✒ **Use a long telephoto lens with a focal length that's the 35mm equivalent of 200mm or greater.** If the lens has a large aperture (small f-stop value), you're in business. The telephoto lens gets you close to your subject without spooking the bird. Even protected birds in a city park are unnerved by the sight of a human at close range. Shooting in Aperture Priority (Av) mode (see Chapter 6) and choosing a large aperture helps to blur the background. After all, you want photographs of birds, not the buildings in the background.

If you don't have a long telephoto lens, purchase a 2X tele-converter for your camera. This effectively doubles the focal length of any lens you attach to it. Unfortunately, it also doubles the f/stop, which lets less light into the camera. In spite of this, a good tele-converter is an excellent option, especially when you consider the price of a long telephoto lens.

✒ **Crouch down to the bird's level for a more natural-looking photograph.** This often means kneeling in wet grass. Wear a pair of old jeans when you photograph wildlife and watch where you kneel; you may kneel in a great blue heron's bathroom.

✒ **Photograph birds on a cloudy day or a foggy morning.** You'll have beautiful diffuse light that won't cast harsh shadows. If the sky is completely overcast, you have no shadows. Photograph birds in heavy fog and you have no signs of civilization (see Figure 8-12). When you photograph birds in low light, you may have to increase the ISO speed setting to get a shutter speed fast enough to take pictures while hand-holding the camera. Alternatively, you can use a tripod.

✒ **Take one shot and then move closer.** Get as close as you think you can without spooking the bird and then take a picture. With one picture in the bank, move closer and take another picture. If you approach the bird cautiously, you won't spook him and may end up getting an extreme close-up.

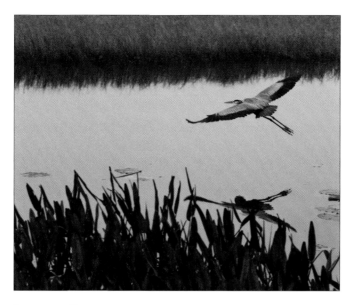

Figure 8-12: Photograph birds when it's cloudy or foggy.

Enhancing Your Creativity

Great photographs are made by creative photographers who stretch the envelope. You can enhance your creativity by trying new things. Schedule a time each week when you experiment with new techniques or new equipment. Julia Cameron, author of *The Artist's Way,* calls this an "Artist's Date." When I do this, I limit myself to one or two lenses and I often visit familiar territory. When you photograph a familiar place and the goal is to enhance your creativity, do things differently. Shoot from a different vantage point and use a different lens than you'd normally use for the subject.

When I was out on a recent "Artist's Date," I spotted brilliant flowers on the trail that I was hiking. Normally I'd photograph something like this from above and zoom in. Instead I put my Lensbaby Composer on the camera with the +4 and +10 macro attachments, placed the camera on the grass, and composed the scene through the camera LCD monitor while shooting in Live View mode (see Figure 8-13).

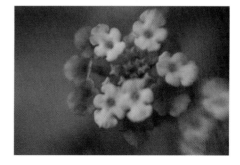

Figure 8-13: Look at things in a new way to enhance creativity.

Great photos always inspire me to get out the camera and take some pictures. Great photos can also help you become more creative. When you see a really great photo, dissect the image and try to figure out what the photographer did to make it so compelling. Was it a camera technique, or did the photographer do some editing after the fact to make the image pop? You can find great photos on the Internet in lots of places. One of my favorite places is `http://photo.net`. At this website, you'll find many types of inspirational photographs from portraits to drop-dead gorgeous landscapes. You can even join Photo.net and upload your own images. Next time you need something to spark your creativity, look at some great photographs.

You can enhance your creativity while you're taking pictures. Stretching the envelope is a wonderful way to create interesting photographs. The following points can help you stretch your creativity:

- ✔ **Simplify the scene to its lowest common denominator.** A great way to do this is to use a large aperture (small f-stop value) and focus your camera on the most important part of the scene. Or you can compose your picture so the viewer's eye is drawn to a single element in the image.

- ✔ **Look for patterns.** Patterns are everywhere. For instance, migrating birds in flight create a unique pattern; scattered leaves in the gutter create interesting random patterns; and flower petals create compelling symmetrical patterns. Of course nothing says you have to compose an image symmetrically.

- ✔ **Don't fall in love with your first shot.** Before moving on, think of other ways you can capture the scene. Perhaps you can move to a different vantage point, switch lenses, or select a different aperture. Milk a scene for all it's worth and remember to look down. An interesting photograph may be beneath your feet.

- ✔ **Explore your favorite subject and create a theme of photographs.** For example, if you're a cat lover, photograph your cat and then photograph the neighborhood cats. When you photograph the same subjects or places frequently, you think of new ways to create interesting pictures. Your creative juices start flowing and before you know it, you see your favorite subject in a different way. Photographing your favorite subjects and photographing them often helps you master your camera.

My favorite subject happens to be landscapes. I live near the ocean and not very far from a picturesque river, so lately this has been my theme.

Composing Your Images

A photographer's job is to create a compelling image, an image that makes the viewer take more than a casual glance. When you compose an image properly, you draw your viewer into the image. Lots of rules exist for composing a photo. I mention many of them in this section. Your job as a photographer is to figure out which one best suits your subject. This section is designed to make you think about composition when you look through the viewfinder of your EOS 6D. You can use the camera viewfinder grid or one of the Live View grids as a visual reference. For more information on the Live View grid, see Chapter 5.

When you compose an image, look for naturally occurring curves that you can use to draw your viewer into the photograph. Curves are everywhere in nature: Birds have curved necks, and roads and paths have curves. The trunk of a tree curves to cope with Mother Nature like the trees in the tundra regions of the Rocky Mountain National Park. Look for naturally occurring curves and compose your image so that the curve draws the viewer's eye into the picture.

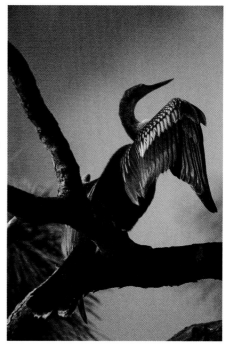

Figure 8-14: Using curves as part of your composition.

Many photographers take pictures in *Landscape* format — the image is wider than it is tall. When you're photographing a scene like a waterfall, a person, or anything that's taller than it is wide, rotate the camera 90 degrees. This is known as *Portrait* format. The photograph of the Anhinga bird in a pine tree (see Figure 8-14) is an example of shooting in Portrait format. A couple other compositional elements are in this picture: The branch leads your eye into the photo, the bird's beak is diagonal to the other elements in the picture, and then there's the lovely curve of the bird's neck . . . .

Many photographers place the horizon line smack-dab in the middle of the picture. Boring! When you're photographing a landscape, take a deep breath and look at the scene. Where is the most important part of the scene? That part of the scene should occupy roughly two-thirds of the image. For example, if you're photographing a mountain, the mountain base should be in the lower third of the image. When you're photographing a sunset, place the horizon line in the lower third of the image to draw your viewer's attention to the sky. In Figure 8-15, I wanted to draw the viewer's eye to the massive thunderhead in the distance, so I placed the horizon line in the lower third of the image.

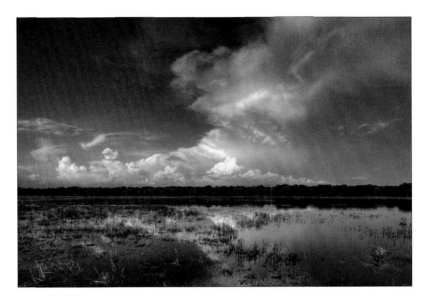

Figure 8-15: Placing the horizon line.

When you're composing an image, you want to draw the viewer's eye to a center of interest in your photo. In a composition rule known as the *Rule of Thirds,* imagine your scene is divided into thirds vertically and horizontally, creating a grid, as shown in Figure 8-16. Compose your picture so a center of interest intersects two gridlines. The grid you can enable in the viewfinder doesn't quite get the job done, but it does give you a point of reference. Figure 8-16 shows a grid overlay inside a facsimile of your EOS 6D viewfinder. Notice where the boy is placed in the sunset image. The

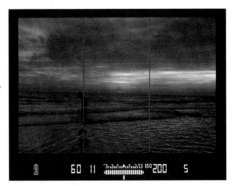

Figure 8-16: Aligning an image according to the Rule of Thirds.

middle of his body intersects two gridlines. This image, therefore, is composed according to the Rule of Thirds.

Visualizing Your Images

Anybody can point a camera at something or somebody, press the shutter button, and create a photograph. The resulting photograph may or may not be good, but that's not really photography. True photography is studying your subject and then visualizing the resulting photograph in your mind's eye. When you visualize the photograph, you know the focal length needed to capture your vision, the camera settings to use, and the vantage point from which to shoot your image.

Seeing, Thinking, and Acting

To take a good picture, you need a great camera like the EOS 6D. But even the EOS 6D doesn't guarantee you'll get a good, or even a mediocre, picture. Getting a good picture is all about you: Your unique personality, vision, and creativity is what separates your photographs from those taken by the guy down the street who also owns an EOS 6D. Have you ever looked at two photographs of the same subject, yet they look completely different? That's where the skill and unique vision of each photographer comes into play as well as the photographer's comfort level with his equipment. Compare Ansel Adams's fine-art photographs of Yosemite to tourist snapshots from there, and you'll see what I mean.

Being in the moment

Some people think of photography as a religion. They approach their equipment and their subject with reverence, awe, and wonder. I'm sure you've seen photographs that have brought out those feelings in you. There's no reason you can't create your own jaw-dropping images. One of the best skills you can develop is being *in the moment* — experiencing the present moment and not thinking about anything else but the subject you're about to photograph. If you're distracted by things you have to do later, you can't devote your total focus to the subject you're photographing. When you aren't thinking about anything in particular but are instead observing what's around you, you notice things that'd normally pass you by. When you're in the moment, you notice small details, such as the photogenic pile of leaves in the gutter or the way the sun dapples through the leaves to create an interesting pattern on the wall. You get better pictures when you're focused on what you're doing and not fretting about what you're going to cook for dinner or wear to work the next day.

Practicing 'til your images are pixel-perfect

If you use your camera only once in a blue moon, your pictures will show it. Letting your gear gather dust in the closet won't help you become a better photographer. Instead, use your camera every chance you get. Consider joining a local camera club because networking with other photographers is a wonderful way to get new information. You may also find a mentor there. Simply strike up a friendship with an experienced photographer and tell her you want to tag along the next time she does a photo shoot.

The best way to practice photography is to take pictures of people, places, and things that interest you every chance you get. Practice your photography when you see something that inspires you, such as a compelling image in a magazine or a picture on the web. With that inspiration fresh in your mind, grab your camera and take lots of pictures of similar subjects.

I often do a photo walkabout. I grab one or two lenses, my trusty camera, and my imagination and then drive to a part of town I haven't photographed. I then park the car and start exploring. This photo walkabout gives me a chance to learn how to use a new piece of gear or experiment with a new technique, which enhances my creativity. Figure 8-17 shows an image I created with a 90mm macro lens shortly after I received it.

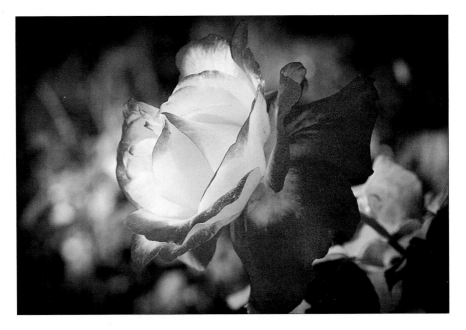

Figure 8-17: Practice makes perfect.

Becoming a student of photography

When you decide to seriously pursue photography, you can find a lot of resources. Great portrait photography is all around you. For instance, you'll find portraits of the rich and famous in magazines like *People* and *US Weekly,* or you can find great pictures of places in magazines like *Outdoor Photographer* or *National Geographic.* You can find great pictures of things in magazine advertisements. Your local newspapers and magazines are also great resources for great images.

When you see an interesting image in a magazine, study it carefully. Try to determine the type of lens the photographer used and then try to determine whether the photographer shot the picture in Aperture Priority or Shutter Priority mode. After you ascertain which shooting mode the photographer used:

- **In Shutter Priority mode,** try to determine whether the photographer used a fast or slow shutter speed.

- **In Aperture Priority mode,** try to determine whether the photographer used a large or small aperture.

Also try to determine how the photographer illuminated the subject. Did he use available light, camera flash, or fill flash. If you study great images carefully, you can get a rough idea of the settings the photographer used to take the picture.

Another great way to understand portrait photography is to study the masters:

- **Annie Leibovitz or Greg Gorman:** If you're into portrait photography, study their work.

- **Arnold Newman:** Google him if you like to study the work of the old portrait-photography masters. He created some wonderful environmental portraits.

- **Henri Cartier-Bresson:** If you like the gritty style of street photography, Google him.

- **Ansel Adams or Clyde Butcher:** If you enjoy landscape photography, study their work. Clyde Butcher is affectionately known as the "Ansel Adams of The Everglades."

You can also find lots of examples of great photography at www.photo. net. Other photography sites such as Flickr (www.flickr.com) or 500PX (www.500px.com) can be sources for inspirational photography.

Never leave home without a camera

You can't ask a photo opportunity to wait while you go home to get your camera. Photo opportunities happen when you least expect them. Therefore never leave home without a camera.

If you're nervous about taking your expensive EOS 6D with you wherever you go, I don't blame you and I actually feel the same way. That's why I bought a relatively inexpensive point-and-shoot camera that I carry with me everywhere I go. When I see something I want to photograph, I reach in the glove box of my car, grab my trusty point-and-shoot camera, and snap the picture.

Canon makes the PowerShot G15, a wonderful point-and-shoot camera with professional features; it's a great camera to augment your EOS 6D. The G15 won't fit in your shirt pocket, but it will fit in your pants pocket, coat pocket, or your glove box. The Canon PowerShot S100 is another great option for a second camera.

Some photographers think the cameras in cell phones are a joke. However, if you have one of the new smartphones, you may have a competent camera. The newer iPods and iPads also have good cameras. If your portable device doesn't have a great camera, you can still use it to create a digital sketch of a scene you want to photograph at a later date with your EOS 6D. As one photographer is fond of saying, "the best camera is the one that's with you."

Waiting for the light

Landscape photographers arrive at a scene they want to photograph and often patiently wait for the right light or until a cloud moves into the frame to get the perfect picture. Sometimes they'll backtrack to a spot at a time when they know conditions will be better. Good landscape photographers are very patient, which is a virtue that all photographers need to cultivate. When you arrive at a beautiful scene but the light is harsh, stick around a while or come back later when you know the lighting will be better.

Also wait when you're shooting candid pictures. Minutes may pass with nothing exciting happening, but don't put away the camera yet. If you wait patiently, something will happen that piques your interest and compels you to press the Shutter button.

Defining Your Goals

Before you snap the Shutter button, get a clear idea of what the final image will look like. If you don't have a goal for the picture or the photo shoot, you're wasting your time, and if you're photographing a person, you're wasting your time and your subject's time. Of course, the goal doesn't have to be a great image. You can go on a photo shoot to experiment with new ideas, master a new technique, or experiment with a new lens. After all, practice makes perfect.

When you know why you're taking the picture, you'll know what settings to use, how to light the photo, which lens to use, and so on. If you're creating an image for a friend or a client, adhere to the standard rules of composition, but also take a couple of pictures using a unique vantage point or a slightly different composition than you'd normally use; you may end up with some interesting pictures your client will like. However, if you're creating photographs for yourself, the sky's the limit and you can get as creative as you want. You can shoot from different and unique vantage points, tilt the camera, break the composition rules, use an unorthodox lens, and so on.

What's your center of interest?

When you create a picture of a person or place, decide what the main point of interest is and how you'll draw the viewer's eye there. For some photos, the point of interest may be a person's face or a landmark, such as the Lincoln Memorial. If you're creating a portrait of a pianist, a picture of him playing the piano would be appropriate and your center of interest could be his hands on the keys.

Sometimes, you have more than one center of interest. When this occurs, you can compose the photo in such a manner that one center of interest leads the viewer's eye to the other center of interest. For example, if you're photographing a cellist on a beach near San Francisco's Golden Gate Bridge, you have two centers of interest — the musician and the bridge. Your job is to marry these two centers of interest to create a compelling image and guide your viewer's eye through the photo. You also need to compose the photo so that one center of interest doesn't dominate the other.

What's your best vantage point?

The decision you make on your best vantage point depends on what you're photographing. In most instances, you want to be eye to eye when photographing a person. If you're photographing a landscape and the sky or a mountain is the dominant feature, choose a vantage point that causes the sky or mountain to dominate the upper two-thirds of the image. If you're photographing a scene in which a lake or the ocean is the dominant feature, lie on your belly and compose the photo so that the water feature occupies the bottom two-thirds of the image. Yup. The old Rule of Thirds is at work. Figure 8-18 shows a unique vantage point for an image of a historic district in Sarasota, Florida.

What else is in the picture?

The only time you aren't bothered by other objects is when you shoot a portrait against a solid color background, such as a wall or a cloth backdrop. But even then, you have to notice everything in the viewfinder or LCD monitor. If your subject's too close to the background, you may notice wrinkles from a cloth backdrop or texture from a wall. If this happens, ask your subject to move forward and then shoot the picture in Aperture Priority mode with your largest available aperture. Focus on your subject, and the bothersome details in the background will be out of focus.

When you're taking pictures on location, you often have unwanted objects, such as telephone poles in the background. Sometimes you have to decide whether to include the distracting elements in the image and then delete them in an image-editing application, but that takes time. If you can move your subject slightly and make the distracting elements disappear, that's always your best option. You can also move to a different place in the same general area with a pleasing background and no distracting elements.

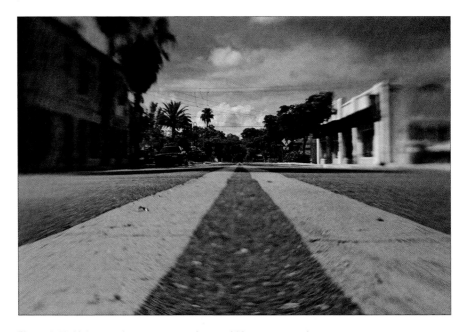

Figure 8-18: Using a unique vantage point to add interest to an image.

When you're photographing a landscape, take a careful look in the frame. Are power lines visible? Are ugly buildings or trash in the frame? If so, move slightly until the distracting elements are no longer in it.

The genius of digital photography

Immediacy is the genius of digital photography. The old days of waiting for your film to be developed and returned from the lab are gone. You know if you got the shot as soon as it appears on your camera's LCD monitor. You also never have to pay for film again. Ever.

With these advantages comes a curse: If you're not careful, the very genius of digital photography can turn you into a bad photographer. You don't pay for film, so you tend to shoot more images, which is a good thing if you take good photographs. But if you just shoot everything that pops up in front of your camera, you're going to get a lot of bad photos that end up in the trash. To take advantage of the genius of digital photography, be in the moment and do your best to make every image a keeper. Get it right in the camera and don't rely on image-editing applications to fix a bad image. Image-editing applications like Photoshop are designed to enhance a correctly exposed, well-composed image and make it better. I cringe when I hear a photographer say, "I'll Photoshop it." Photoshop is not a verb; it's a tool.

Practice also enters into the equation. When you know your camera like the back of your hand and you apply all your attention to your photography, you're well on the way to utilizing the genius of digital photography to its fullest and capturing compelling photographs.

Part III

Editing and Sharing Your Images

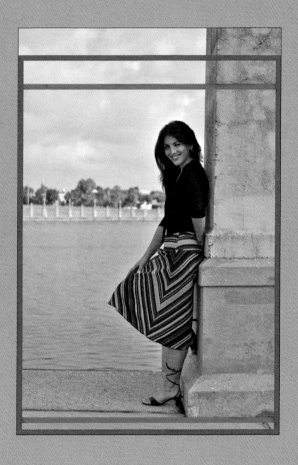

Check out the article "Creating a Book with Your Images" online at www.dummies.com/extras/canoneos6d.

In this part . . .

✔ Learn how to use Canon software to edit your images.

✔ Discover how to edit JPEG files with ImageBrowser EX.

✔ Get familiar with editing RAW files in Canon Digital Photo Professional.

✔ Find out how to print files from the ImageBrowser EX and the Canon Digital Photo Professional applications.

✔ Check out the article "Creating a Book with Your Images" online at www.dummies.com/extras/canoneos6d.

9

Editing Your Images

*T*aking pictures is lots of fun. But eventually you fill up all your cards. Then it's time to download them to your computer and view your images on a large monitor to see what you have. You can do this with third-party software, such as Adobe Photoshop Lightroom, Apple's Aperture, Adobe Photoshop Elements, or Adobe Photoshop. If you don't have an image-editing application on your computer, you can install *ImageBrowser EX,* the software Canon provides with the camera. ImageBrowser EX isn't as powerful as Lightroom or Photoshop, but you can get a lot done with the application.

You have a two-pronged attack for organizing and editing your work. Canon ImageBrowser EX is a utility you use to download and organize your work. You can also edit JPEG files in ImageBrowser EX. But if you use the RAW format to capture your images, you need to bring in the heavy artillery. Canon Digital Photo Professional 3.7 gives you the tools to edit your RAW images and export them. In this chapter, I show you how to use both applications.

Introducing the Canon ImageBrowser EX

The Canon ImageBrowser EX application is your first weapon for organizing images. You use the utility to download your images, rate your images, rename your images, and more. If you can't get 'er done in ImageBrowser EX, you have options to launch Canon Digital Photo Professional. Both applications are present on the Canon EOS Digital Solution Disk that was included with your camera. If you've installed the software, you're ready to play. If not, give your eyes a break and install the software. Figure 9-1 shows the Canon ImageBrowser EX in all its glory.

ImageBrowser EX shows thumbnails of your images in a main window. The top of the application contains task buttons that you use to organize and edit your images. The main window is divided into three sections: the section on the left is used to navigate to images and folders, the middle section displays image thumbnails, and the section on the right displays image information. You can change the view of the middle window to suit your workflow as I show you in upcoming sections.

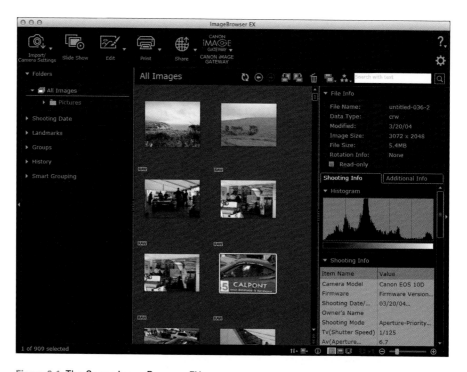

Figure 9-1: The Canon ImageBrowser EX.

Downloading Your Images

The first step in your image-editing journey is downloading images. You can download images directly from the camera or from a memory card reader. I suggest the latter. A memory card reader gets the job done faster. To download images to your computer from the camera:

1. **Connect the USB (Universal Serial Bus) cable supplied with your camera to your computer and to the camera (see Figure 9-2).**

2. **Click the Import/Camera Settings button, which is on the left side of the workspace.**

   The button expands to show the available tasks (see Figure 9-3).

3. **Click the Connect to EOS Camera.**

   The EOS Utility 6D application appears in the ImageBrowser EX window (see Figure 9-4).

   The dialog box in Figure 9-4 automatically appears when you insert a memory card in a card reader, even if the ImageBrowser EX application is not open. After the images are downloaded, ImageBrowser EX opens by default.

Attach small end of USB cable here

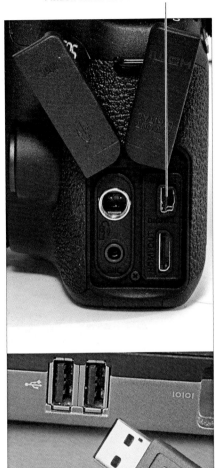

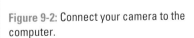

Figure 9-2: Connect your camera to the computer.

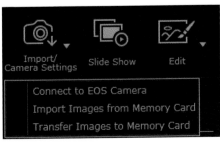

Figure 9-3: The Import/Camera Settings commands.

4. **Click the desired option.**

If you click Download Images, the images will be downloaded into your computer's default location for downloading images — which is not necessarily a good thing, because they're just dumped in with everything else in the folder. I recommend you click Select and Download Images, which gives you the option of creating the folder into which the images are downloaded. If you follow my advice, the dialog box shown in Figure 9-5 appears.

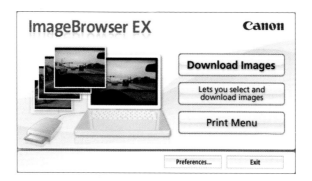

Figure 9-4: Downloading with the EOS Utility 6D application.

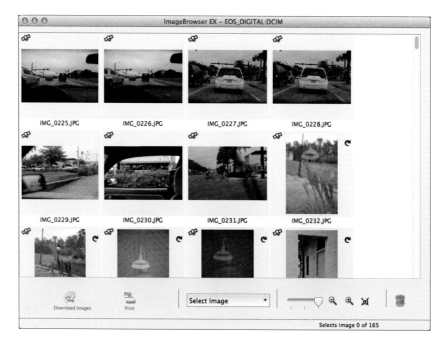

Figure 9-5: Selecting images to download.

5. Select the images you want to download.

At this stage, you can just click the images you want to download, and the images you don't download will get lost in pixel heaven when you reformat the card. However, I suggest you choose Select All from the drop-down menu. It's much easier to decide whether to delete an image when you can see it full-size on your computer screen.

6. Click Download Images.

The Download Images Dialog box appears (see Figure 9-6). This dialog box shows the default settings for downloading images. Notice the option to open ImageBrowser EX after the download is completed. This is for photographers who just insert a card into a card reader, or connect a camera with a card to the computer, which opens the download utility. Also notice that the images are downloaded into the default folder for images on your computer. This is all well and good if you only shoot a couple of hundred pictures a year, but I have the feeling that you bought this camera because you want to shoot lots of pictures. Therefore, it makes sense to sort the images into specific folders, either by month, by week, or by individual photo shoot.

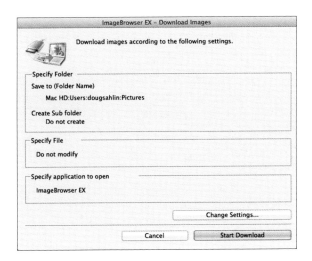

Figure 9-6: Downloading images.

7. Click Change Settings.

The Change Settings dialog box appears (see Figure 9-7), which gives you the option to specify a different folder. The option to download the images into a subfolder is the option I suggest you take. This organizes the images in a folder based on the month, day, and year the images were photographed.

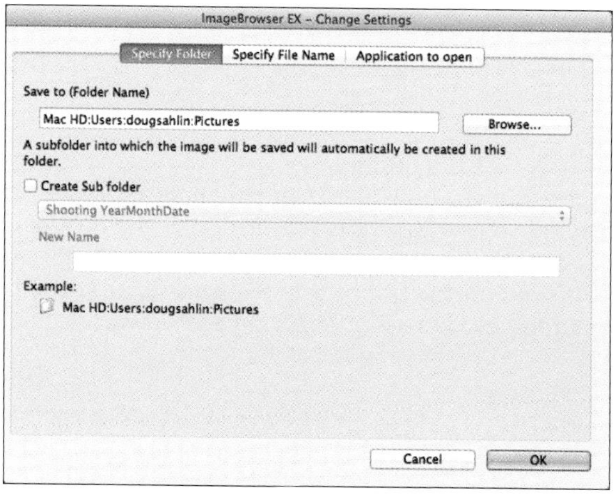

Figure 9-7: Changing download settings.

8. **Specify the desired folder or choose the option to create a subfolder.**

Note that there is an option that enables you to create a subfolder. After you enable the option, click the drop-down menu and choose the desired option. I suggest you choose Shooting YearMonthDate (see Figure 9-8). This option lets you store the images in a subfolder that you can easily identify. There is also an option to give the image a new name. You might think this is wise, but if you choose this option, you'd only download one image, because then all images will have the same name. I show you how to give the image a meaningful name in the next step.

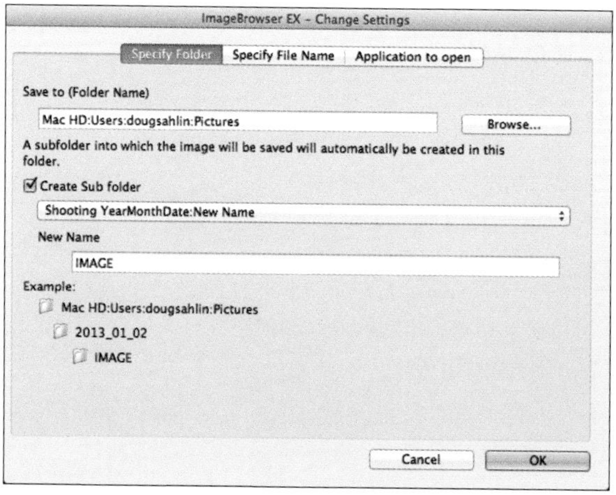

Figure 9-8: Specifying a folder into which to store the images.

9. Click Specify File Name.

The Specify File Name tab opens.

10. Choose Shooting YearMonthDate + Prefix + Sequence Number from the drop-down menu.

This option allows you to fine-tune the filename. The default prefix is IMG, which of course stands for image. Select IMG and then enter a prefix name that makes sense to you and will help you identify the person or place in the photographs. Figure 9-9 shows the new name for a card full of images I created at Myakka State Park.

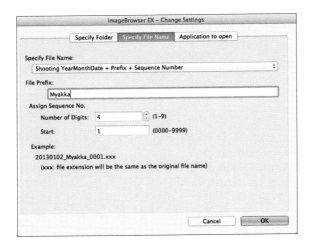

Figure 9-9: Renaming the images.

11. Click Start Download.

A dialog box appears, showing you the progress of the download. The access lamp on your camera flashes while the images download.

After the download is complete, the images appear in the ImageBrowser EX's main window (see Figure 9-10).

The Thumbnail mode is the default viewing mode. You can switch to a different viewing mode by clicking the desired icon at the bottom of the window. Any images or movies you protected in the camera have a lock icon above them, indicating they're protected in ImageBrowser EX as well.

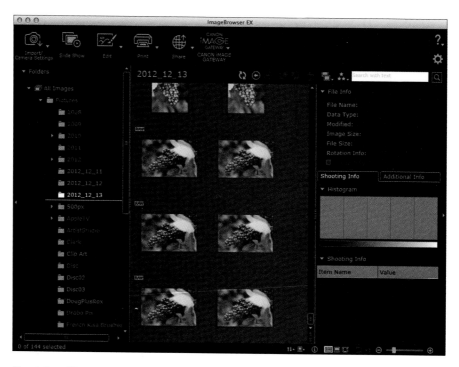

Figure 9-10: The downloaded images appear in the main window.

Using external card readers

The USB cable that shipped with your camera makes it possible to download images to your computer; however, downloading images uses your camera's battery power. If you attempt a download with a low battery, you run the risk of corrupting the images or the memory card if the battery exhausts its power during a lengthy download. You can also download your images with an external card reader. Connect an external card reader to a computer USB port and you're ready to download images with ImageBrowser EX or a different application. Many card readers accept multiple image-card formats. Choose a card reader that has a port for the SD cards your camera uses.

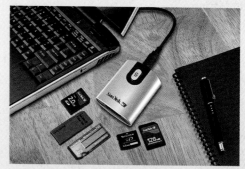

Courtesy of SanDisk

You will have to change the settings as outlined in this section to specify the desired prefix each time you download images. This may seem like a lot of work, but it beats hunting for a needle in a haystack.

If you plan to do all of your image management with ImageBrowser EX, do not move images to different folders by using your computer operating system. If you do, ImageBrowser EX won't know where they are.

The only time you can rename more than one image with ImageBrowser EX is upon import. I strongly advise you to give each of your images a meaningful name when you download them, as outlined in the previous section.

Rating and Keywording Images

If you download images as suggested in the previous section, ImageBrowser EX downloads your images into folders arranged by the date they were photographed and adds the prefix you specify upon download. This will prevent you from having to find the proverbial needle in the haystack. You can also rate images and add keywords to images, which makes them easier to find as well.

The first thing I do after downloading images from a photo shoot is to rank them and add keywords. In the days of film, photographers would put their slides on a light box and give them a rating from one to five stars, with five-star images being the best of the lot. You can assign each image a rating of up to five stars with ImageBrowser EX.

Using keywords (tags in ImageBrowser EX) is another method of identifying images. You can add a keyword to an image that reflects the type of photography, the place in which the image was photographed, the name of the person in the photograph, and so on.

If you're like me, you shoot a lot of images at the same place, and they have the same basic keywords. You can add keywords to multiple images as follows:

1. **Click the folder into which the images were downloaded.**

   You find the folders listed by date in the All Folders tab.

2. **Select the images that you want to add keywords to.**

   You can select contiguous images in the ImageBrowser EX window by pressing the Shift key, clicking the first image you want to select, and then clicking the last image you want to select.

3. **After selecting the desired images, right-click.**

   The context menu appears (see Figure 9-11).

4. **Choose Add tag.**

   The ImageBrowser EX dialog box appears (see Figure 9-12). You can assign multiple keywords to the selected images. Place a comma between each keyword and the next.

5. **In the text box, type a keyword that helps you identify the image.**

   I generally start with adding the town where I shot the image to the Places category.

6. **Click OK.**

   The keyword is added to the properties of each image.

7. **Repeat Steps 4 and 5 to add any additional keywords that help describe the photographs.**

   You could add the person's name, the word *sunset* if it was a sunset shot, and so on.

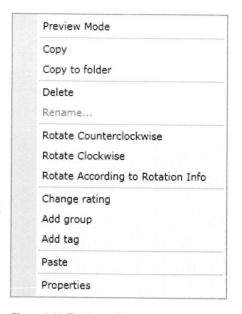

Figure 9-11: The ImageBrowser EX context menu.

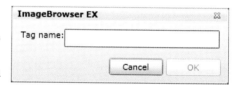

Figure 9-12: Adding keywords to multiple images.

Another manner in which you can sort images is by ranking them. You can rank an image from 1 to 5 Stars. To rank images:

1. **Click the folder into which the images were downloaded.**

   You find the folders listed by date in the All Folders tab.

2. **Select the images that you want to rank.**

   You can select contiguous images in the ImageBrowser EX window by pressing the Shift key, clicking the first image you want to select, and then clicking the last image you want to select.

3. **Right-click.**

   The context menu appears (refer to Figure 9-11).

4. Pause your cursor over Change Rating.

The rating submenu appears (see Figure 9-13). You can assign a rank of 1–5 to the selected images or reject them.

5. Click the desired rating.

ImageBrowser EX assigns the keywords and ranks the images in one operation. How cool is that?

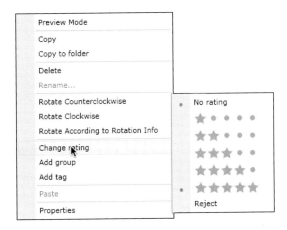

Figure 9-13: Rating images, how rank.

Adding Comments to Images

You can also add comments, which appear as *metadata* with the Additional Info of your images. Metadata is data, such as shooting information, that's recorded with the image when you shoot it and data you add, such as keywords and comments. You can add whatever comment you want that will help you remember the image. To add a comment to an image:

1. Select the image in ImageBrowser EX and then click Additional Info.

2. Scroll down until you see the Comments text box (see Figure 9-14).

3. Type the comment.

The comment is applied to the image.

You can only apply a comment to one image at a time.

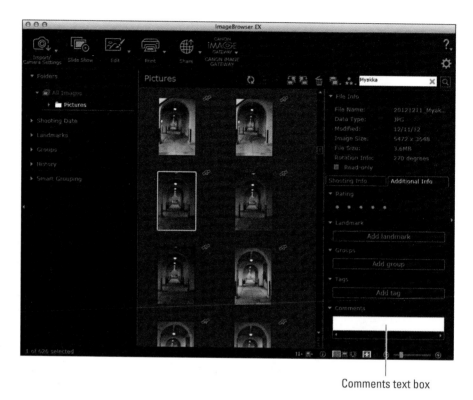

Comments text box

Figure 9-14: Applying a comment to an image.

Adding Information to a Single Image

Metadata is very powerful. When you add metadata to an image, it's easier to find. The information can also be used if you decide to branch out and try to sell some of your images in the stock-photo agencies. The more metadata you have, the easier it is to find a specific image. To add information to a single image:

1. **Launch ImageBrowser EX and then navigate to the image to which you want to add additional information.**

   As a rule, I find it's easier to do this right after a photo shoot when all the information is fresh in your mind. After you select the image, the shooting information is shown in the Shooting Info tab (see Figure 9-15).

2. **Click the Additional Info tab (see Figure 9-16).**

   In the Additional Info tab, you can add the following information to the image metadata:

Shooting Info tab

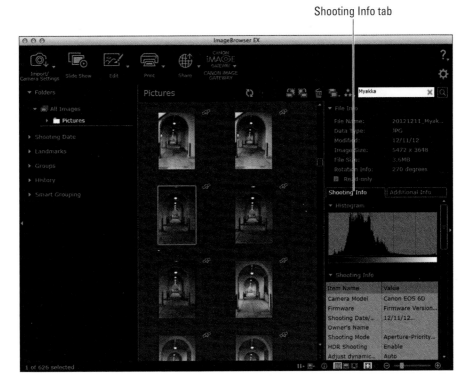

Figure 9-15: All the shooting info that's fit to print.

- **Landmark:** When you photograph images of places that are land-marks, you enter the name of the landmark here to create a new folder in the Landmarks section of the Folders tab. After creating the folder, you then drag the applicable images into the folder. This applies the landmark information to each of the images and creates a bookmark in the landmark folder, which you can use to quickly locate images you've taken of the landmark. To me this seems redundant. If you do a good job of adding keywords (tags in ImageBrowser EX–speak), you can easily find any image you want no matter how many images you download to your computer.

- **Groups:** Here's another way for you to further segment your images. When you create a group, you create a folder into which you can drag images. The images still stay in their original folders, but the group folder is a bookmark to all images you add to a spe-cific group. For example, if you do pet photography, you can create a group for Dogs and a group for Cats and whatever other type of image you photograph. A word of caution though: If you plan to photograph venomous snakes, do so with a 500mm lens. It takes the fear out of getting close. But seriously, the group option seems redundant to me as well. It's another step you don't have to take if you do a good job of keywording your images.

- **Tags:** This is very important metadata you should add to each image. I include the town in which the image was photographed, the state in which the image was photographed, and any other pertinent information I think should be added. For example, if the image is a photograph of wildlife, I add wildlife as a tag. Separate each tag with a comma. At the risk of being redundant, if you do a good job of keywording (tagging) your images, you'll be able to find them easily.

- **Comments:** Here's another useful metadata tag you can add to images. You can add a comment that will help you remember the weather conditions that were prevalent when you created the image, other photographers you were with, and so on.

3. **Select another image to which you want to add information.**

    Applying tags to multiple images is definitely the efficient way to work. However, sometimes you need to add information to special images.

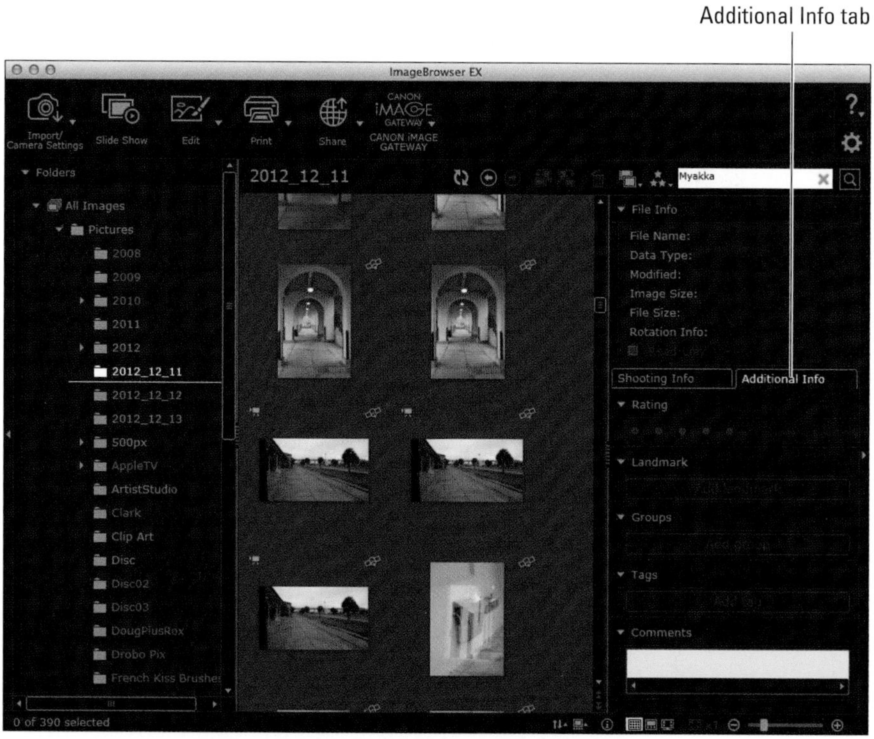

Figure 9-16: Adding information to images with the Additional Info tab.

Changing Your View

ImageBrowser EX is quite versatile. You have three different ways to view your images. You can view images in Thumbnail mode, Preview mode, and Full Screen mode. The mode you choose depends on the task you're performing. You can perform all tasks in Thumbnail and Preview modes. In Thumbnail mode, you can perform changes to multiple images. In Preview mode, you work on one image at a time.

To view images in Thumbnail mode:

1. **Click the Thumbnail Mode icon.**

   The view shows very small thumbnails (see Figure 9-17). Click the thumbnail to reveal information about the image.

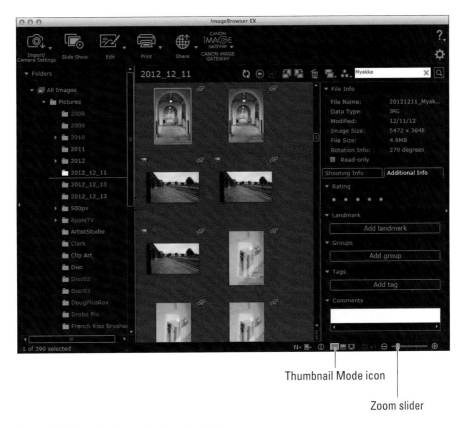

Thumbnail Mode icon

Zoom slider

Figure 9-17: Viewing images in Thumbnail Mode.

2. Drag the Zoom slider to increase magnification.

The thumbnails become bigger.

3. Click the Information icon to hide the image information and view thumbnails only (see Figure 9-18).

The larger images make it easier for you to decide which images you're going to edit and which images need additional information.

4. Double-click the thumbnail to view it the Preview Mode (see Figure 9-19).

Preview mode shows one large image and a filmstrip of thumbnails below it. Some photographers find it useful to winnow (photographer-speak for choosing which images to keep and which ones to toss in the trash can) images in Preview mode. When you view images in Preview mode, you can use the left and right arrow keys above the filmstrip to preview different images in the folder. You can also click the Preview Mode icon to view images in Preview Mode.

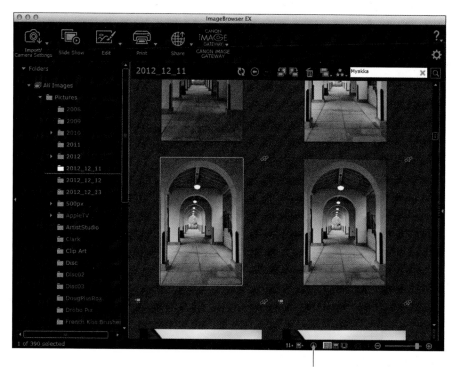

Information icon

Figure 9-18: The better to see you, my lovely thumbnail.

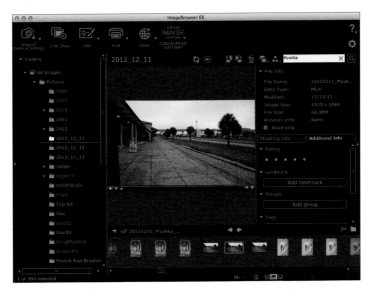

Figure 9-19: And now for your viewing edification: Preview Mode.

Backing Up Your Work

You work hard to capture great photographs with your EOS 6D. Your work in ImageBrowser EX and Canon Digital Photo Professional fine-tunes your images, but a computer crash or hard drive failure will wipe out all your images in a heartbeat. You can save images to a CD, but that's 700MB, less than a memory card. I suggest you invest in a good external hard drive and use an application to back up your work. After you back up images to the external hard drive, take it offline, which minimizes wear and tear on the hard drive.

I know some photographers who leave their external hard drives online all the time. And some of them have paid the price when the drive crashed and burned. Do a Google search for a backup program for your operating system. Most companies that sell backup programs will let you download a fully functional trial version of the software. Try a couple, and when you find one you like, buy it. Unfortunately, I'm not in a position to make a recommendation because I use proprietary software to back my images up to an 8TB external hard drive array.

Organizing Your Images

By default, your images are downloaded into the Pictures folder. You can, however, organize your work by creating new folders, moving images into different folders, and deleting images.

To create a new image folder:

1. In the ImageBrowser EX All Folders tab on the left side of the workspace, select the root folder in which you want to create a subfolder.

2. Right-click and then choose New Folder from the context menu.

A new folder is born.

3. Enter a name for the folder and then click OK.

Your new folder is empty (see Figure 9-20), but I show you how to fill it if you read further.

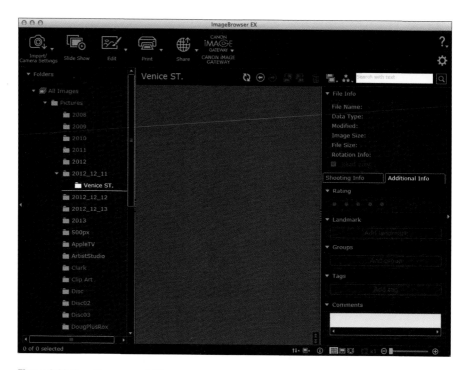

Figure 9-20: Creating a new folder.

To move images to another folder:

1. Click the Thumbnail icon to switch to Thumbnail mode.

Your new folder and the images in the root folder display.

2. Drag images from the root folder into the new folder.

Alternatively, you can select the image and drag it into the desired folder, as displayed in the All Folders tab.

To delete one or more images:

1. **Select the images and press the Delete key, which looks like a trashcan.**

   A dialog box appears asking you to confirm deletion.

2. **Click OK.**

   The images are deleted.

Editing JPEG Images in ImageBrowser EX

You can view all images you download in ImageBrowser EX, but you can edit only JPEG images. You can select RAW images in ImageBrowser EX and then edit them in Canon Digital Photo Professional. When you opt to edit a JPEG image in ZoomBrowser, you can correct red-eye, adjust sharpness, crop the image, apply an auto-adjustment, and insert text. I can't cover all the image-editing tools in ImageBrowser EX — doing so is beyond the scope of this book. However, in the following sections, I cover the most important ones.

You can adjust the color of a JPEG image in ImageBrowser EX. You can also change the brightness and saturation. You can even adjust the RGB (Red, Green, Blue) channels and levels as well as use the Tone Curves Adjustment menu option to adjust brightness for different tone values. To adjust image color:

1. **Select the image you want to edit and then click the Edit button.**

   The menu drops down to reveal the editing options.

2. **Click Edit Image.**

   The Edit drop-down menu appears (see Figure 9-21).

3. **Select Adjust Color and Brightness.**

   The Color/Brightness Adjustment dialog box appears (see Figure 9-22).

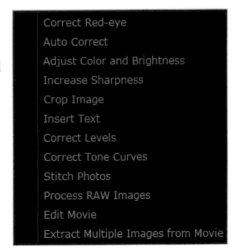

Figure 9-21: Editing an image in ImageBrowser EX.

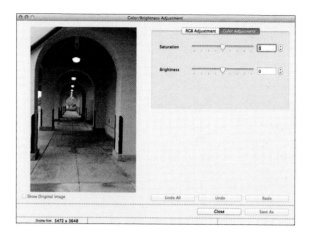

Figure 9-22: Adjusting image brightness and saturation.

4. Drag the sliders to adjust brightness and saturation.

The settings you choose are a matter of personal taste. Don't go too far over the top with saturation though because you might create some colors that can't be printed. It's also a good idea not to increase saturation when editing images of people. When you increase saturation, you amp up all colors including the red tones, which affects the skin color of people in the photograph.

5. After you make your adjustments, click the Save As button.

A dialog box appears, telling you that some shooting information might be lost. Click OK and the Save As dialog box appears (see Figure 9-23). You can only save the image as a JPEG file. However you can rename it and specify the folder in which the edited image is saved.

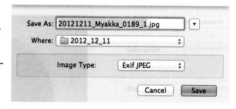

Figure 9-23: Saving your edited image.

6. Enter a filename and specify the folder that the image will be saved to.

Image editing is destructive. I urge you to give the image a different filename and store it in a different folder. That ensures you'll have the original image to edit at a later date.

In addition to adjusting the brightness and saturation, you can adjust the color for the red, green, and blue channels by choosing an option from the Color Adjustment tab (refer to Figure 9-22). This is fairly advanced image editing, as is one of the other options on the list, Correct Levels. The Tone Curve Adjustment option lets you adjust tonality in specific brightness ranges. This option is useful and fairly easy to master. To adjust the tone curve of a JPEG image:

1. **Select the image you want to edit and then click Edit.**

   The menu drops down to reveal the editing options.

2. **Select Correct Tone Curves.**

   The dialog box refreshes to show the Tone Curve Adjustment dialog box (see Figure 9-24). The diagonal line is the tone curve. The line isn't a curve now because it's applying brightness information in a linear fashion: from shadows (the left side of the curve), to midtones (the middle section of the curve), and then to highlights (the right end of the curve). When you add points for different tonal values along the curve and drag them to adjust brightness, you see a curve.

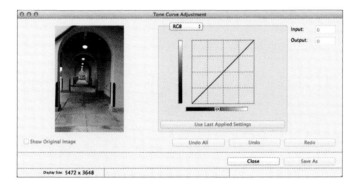

Figure 9-24: The Tone Curve dialog box.

3. **Click a point on the curve to make an adjustment for that tonal value.**

   Click a point near the bottom of the curve to modify the brightness of shadow areas, a point in the middle of the curve to change the brightness of the midtones, and a point near the top of the curve to change the brightness level for highlights. After you click a point, you see values in the Input and Output text boxes (see Figure 9-25).

4. **To adjust a point, drag it up to make the tonal range brighter or down to make the tonal range darker.**

   You can also change the value in the Output text box. A typical use for a tone curve is to apply more contrast to the image, with one point near the bottom of the curve, one point in the middle of the curve, and one point near the top of the curve. Study Figure 9-25 and note the input and output values for the shadow, midtone, and highlight points. I haven't changed the value for the middle point, which is smack-dab in the middle of the tonal value range. Doing so would increase the overall brightness of the image. Brightening the highlights and darkening the shadows increases image contrast.

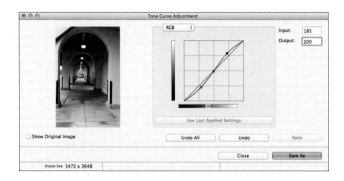

Figure 9-25: Adjusting the tone curve.

5. **After you make your adjustments, click Save As and then in the Save As dialog box, follow the prompts to save the image.**

When editing an image, you can compare the edited image with the original by clicking Show Original Image in the lower-left corner of each editing task's dialog box.

Sharpening an Image

You can sharpen an image in ImageBrowser EX. When you sharpen an image the application locates image edges and applies additional contrast to make the image appear sharper. To sharpen a JPEG image:

1. **Select the image you want to edit and then click the Edit button.**

   The menu drops down to reveal the editing options.

2. **Select Increase Sharpness.**

   The Sharpness dialog box appears (see Figure 9-26).

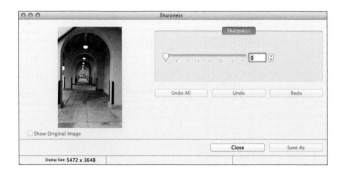

Figure 9-26: Sharpening an image.

3. Drag the slider to sharpen the image.

You can oversharpen an image. As you drag the slider, pay attention to the edges. If you see something that looks like a halo or a white spot on an edge, you've gone too far.

Working with RAW Files in Digital Photo Professional

When you capture an image with the RAW file format, you have more data to work with. The images have a greater bit depth than JPEG images, which means you have more colors to work with. I use Adobe Photoshop Lightroom to edit and sort my RAW images. I find it's very intuitive, and I can edit a massive amount of images in a short amount of time.

Adobe Photoshop and Adobe Photoshop Elements have a Camera RAW editor that enables you to edit RAW images. If you're just experimenting with the RAW format or don't have one of the aforementioned applications, you can edit your work in Canon Digital Photo Professional. You can jump from ImageBrowser EX directly to Canon Digital Photo Professional, or launch the application and begin editing.

The following steps show you how to edit RAW files in Canon's Digital Photo Professional:

1. Launch Digital Photo Professional.

When you install Canon software, several shortcuts are sprinkled on your desktop. You can either click the Digital Photo Professional shortcut on the Windows desktop or the Macintosh Dock or launch the application from your computer menu. In Windows, you'll find Digital Photo Professional in the Canon Utilities Folder on your Start menu. If you use a Macintosh computer to edit your images, you'll find the application icon in the Canon Utilities folder in the Applications folder. Alternatively, you can select a RAW image in ImageBrowser EX and then choose Edit⇨ Process Raw Images.

Any of those methods launches Digital Photo Professional (see Figure 9-27). The application displays thumbnails for all images that reside in the same folder as the image you select in ImageBrowser EX. A soup-to-nuts tutorial of Digital Photo Professional is beyond the scope of this book; however, the following steps show you how to process a RAW image in the application.

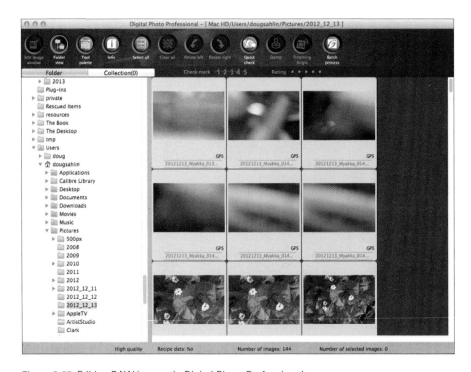

Figure 9-27: Editing RAW images in Digital Photo Professional.

2. **Select the image you want to edit.**

   The images you download with ImageBrowser EX are stored in subfolders of the Pictures folder. The default name of the folder is the date that the image was photographed. You'll find the folders on the left side of the interface.

3. **Click Edit Image Window.**

   The image opens in another window. Notice the icons on top of the Edit window (see Figure 9-28). These are your tools for editing an image in Canon Digital Photo Professional. Here you find a Stamp tool that enables you to clone pixels from one part of the image to another. There's also an icon to launch the Tools Palette, which appears in the right side of the window.

   Unfortunately, a detailed tutorial of every tool is beyond the scope of this book. The application does offer help that you can use if you decide to explore some of the more esoteric commands. The following steps show you how to tweak an image with the application.

4. **Drag the Brightness Adjustment slider to brighten or darken the image.**

   As you drag the slider, you see the image change in real time.

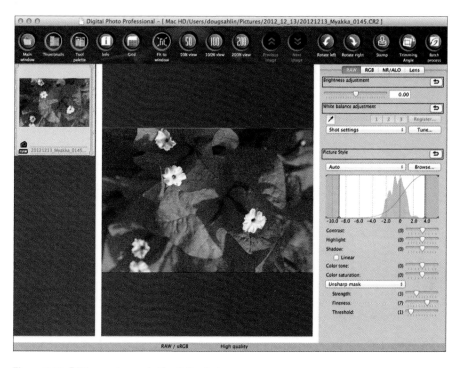

Figure 9-28: Editing an image in the Edit window.

5. **To quickly adjust the white balance, click the eyedropper in the White Balance Adjustment section, and then click an area inside the image that should be pure white, black, or gray.**

After you click inside the image, the white balance changes. If you don't like the results, click again. Alternatively, you can click the drop-down arrow and choose an option from the White Balance Adjustment drop-down list. You can choose Shot Settings to return the image to the white balance as determined by the camera or choose Auto to let Digital Photo Professional adjust the white balance. On the drop-down menu, you find the same white balance options found on your camera — Daylight, Cloudy, Shade, and so on — are also found in this drop-down list.

If you're really adventurous, click the Tune button to open a color wheel that you use to fine-tune the white balance and remove any colorcast. You may not get great results, so use this at your own risk.

6. **Choose an option from the Picture Style drop-down list.**

The picture style the image was photographed with displays on the Picture Style button. But these are RAW files, which can be folded, spindled, and mutilated. You can choose a different picture style from the drop-down list to change the look of the image. Alternatively, you can click Browse, which opens a folder of Picture Styles created by those wild and crazy engineers at Canon. As always, if you don't like the preset you choose, you can always revert to Auto, or whichever style you used to capture the image by clicking the curved arrow to the right of the style currently listed in the Picture Style window.

7. **Drag the Contrast, Highlight, and Shadow sliders to fine-tune these tonal areas.**

   You can increase or decrease contrast for all tonal ranges. As you make your changes, the image updates in real time and the curve in the window above the sliders updates as well.

8. **Adjust the Color Tone and Color Saturation sliders.**

   Drag the sliders while reviewing the thumbnail. When what you see is what you like, stop dragging the sliders. NOW!

9. **Adjust image sharpness with the Unsharp Mask option.**

   This option will seem right at home if you've used an Unsharp Mask command in another image-editing application. The amount of each option you use varies depending on the image you're editing. If you're not happy with the results, click the drop-down menu, choose Sharpness, and then drag the slider to increase image sharpness.

10. **After you make your adjustments, click Tool Palette to hide the Tool Palette and display the edited image in the main window.**

Digital Photo Professional doesn't store the changes after you close the application. Therefore, you need to save the changes by saving the image in another file format. When you launch Digital Photo Professional again, you can apply different edits to the RAW file and save the image with the new changes using a different filename. To save your edited work:

1. **With the image you just edited still selected, choose File⇨ Convert and Save.**

   The Convert and Save dialog box appears (see Figure 9-29).

2. **Enter a filename and location for the edited image.**

   If desired, you can use the same filename. The file format in which you can save the image won't overwrite the RAW file. You can save the new file in the same folder or create a new folder in which to store your edited images.

3. **Choose a file type.**

   You can save the file in any of the following formats:

   - *Exif-JPEG:* Saves the edited image as a JPEG file.
   - *Exif-TIFF (8Bit):* Saves the edited image as an 8-bit TIFF file.

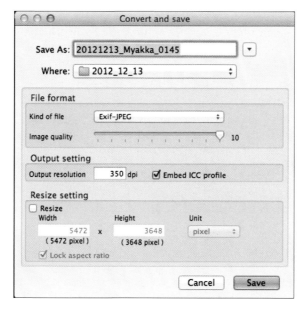

Figure 9-29: Converting a file to a different format and saving it.

- *TIFF (16Bit):* Saves the edited image as a 16-bit TIFF file. The file size of this format is considerably larger than the 8-bit TIFF format, but you have more information to work with if you edit the image in an application like Photoshop.

- *Exif-TIFF (8Bit) + Exif-JPEG:* Saves an 8-bit TIFF file and a JPEG file.

- *TIFF (16Bit) + Exif-JPEG:* Saves a 16-bit TIFF file and an 8-bit JPEG file.

If you choose a JPEG option, you can specify the quality.

4. **Accept the default JPEG quality of 10 or drag the slider to specify a different quality.**

The default setting of 10 produces a high-quality image at the expense of a large file size. If you specify a lower quality, the image quality is poorer and the file size is smaller. When you specify a lower quality, Digital Photo Professional compresses the file and data is lost.

5. **Accept the default resolution of 350 dpi (dots per inch) or enter a different resolution.**

With most printers, you can get by with a resolution of 300 dpi.

6. **Accept the default option to embed the ICC (International Color Consortium) profile or click the check box to reject the option.**

Your best option is to embed the profile with the image.

7. **(Optional) Select the Resize check box.**

   If you use this option, the Width and Height text boxes appear with the current dimensions of the image. The Lock Aspect Ratio check box is selected by default. If you deselect this option and change one value, the other value won't change and the image won't look right.

8. **(Optional) Enter a new value for width or height.**

   When you enter one value, Digital Photo Professional does the math and supplies the other value as long as you enable the Lock Aspect Ratio option. (You did enable it, didn't you?)

9. **Click Save.**

   Your changes to the image(s) are saved.

10

Creating Prints from Your Images

*P*rinters have come a long way. Back when I started printing my own images, printer ink cartridges had three inks. Then printers graduated to cartridges with six inks. Now the really good printers have up to twelve cartridges, which enables you to print stunning color as well as black-and-white prints. You can also get prints made at a wide variety of sources, from your local drugstore or supermarket to an online printer that specializes in creating beautiful prints in sizes from 4 x 6 inches to as large as 36 x 24 inches.

Your camera has an 20.2-megapixel capture, which means you can create very large prints. In this chapter, I explore the wonderful world of printing the images you capture in your EOS 6D.

To Print or Not to Print?

Modern photo-quality printers are a wonderful thing. They print rich, wonderful colors with crisp delineation among them. But good photo-quality printers don't come cheap, and neither do the ink cartridges. Modern printers have multiple cartridges. If you've been printing a lot of images that use, say, red or cyan ink, you'll exhaust that cartridge much sooner than the other cartridges in your printer. And you never seem to have a spare cartridge of the color that runs out.

In addition to the problem of running out of ink at an inopportune moment, don't forget the expense involved. If you use a third-party fine-art paper, it soaks up ink like a sponge. Then, when you run out of one color in one cartridge in the middle of a print job, you have a double whammy: You've wasted lots of ink and a sheet of very expensive paper. Fortunately, you can get good color prints in lots of other ways. The following list shows a few options:

- **Superstore printing services:** Many superstores, such as Costco and Sam's Club, have do-it-yourself printing. Simply bring a memory card to the store, put it in the machine, and review the images on the card. Many of the in-store kiosks have options such as cropping images to a specific size. After you select images from your card, you can place your order. In many instances, you can do your shopping in-store and come back an hour later for your prints.

- **Drugstores:** Many drugstores offer the printing of digital images. Simply bring your memory card to the store, insert it in their machine, choose the images you want to print, and place your order.

- **Online printing services:** Lots of online printing services offer many options in addition to standard prints. If you want standard prints, no problem. A full online printing service can print anything from wallet-size images to huge wall posters. You say you want to put a picture of your cat on a coffee mug? No problem. Upload the image and you'll get your cat's mug on a mug within a matter of days. Other services include photo books, images on mouse pads, and so on. One of my favorite online printing sources is Mpix (www.mpix.com). They offer all the aforementioned services and much more.

When you edit images for print, you rely on your monitor to preview the image. If the colors in your monitor are slightly off, what you see on your monitor is not what you will get when you print the image or send the image to a third-party printer. The best way to ensure consistent and accurate color is to calibrate your monitor. A monitor calibrator (*colorimeter* in techno-speak) is attached to your computer screen and a software program generates colors and shades of gray. The colorimeter measures the colors displayed on your computer screen and compares them to the values in the software program. When the calibration process is completed, the software generates a profile that adjusts the colors on your screen to match the known values generated by the software. If you decide to calibrate your monitor, do so every couple of months as the colors in your monitor change as it ages. As of this writing, X-Rite's Color Munki Smile is a good device with a reasonable price tag.

Finding Images

After you download lots of images and edit them, you end up with lots of images in lots of folders. Even though the folders are organized by date and each one has the date as the actual folder name, and even though you've renamed the images, looking for a single image (or group of images) is like looking for the proverbial needle in the haystack. You can search for images by image type, star rating, and keywords. You can choose any or all those criteria. When you need to find images of Aunt Millicent, you can easily find them with ImageBrowser EX (see Chapter 9) by following these steps:

1. **Launch ImageBrowser EX and select the root folder for your images.**

   There's no place to start like the start.

2. **Click the Filter by File Category, and choose an option from the drop-down menu (see Figure 10-1).**

   Choose the desired option.

3. **Click the Filter by Rating icon to search for images by star rating.**

   After you choose this option, a drop-down list becomes available. You can choose to search for one-, two-, or three-star images, one- and two-star images, two- and three-star images, or one- and three-star images.

4. **Enter the desired keyword in the Search with Text text box.**

   You can only enter one keyword at a time.

5. **Click the Search icon that looks like a magnifying glass.**

   The images that match your criteria are displayed in the window as thumbnails.

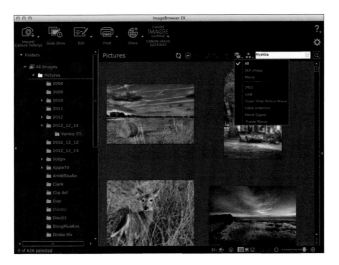

Figure 10-1: It's all in your file.

Leaving Some Breathing Room

Your EOS 6D produces images with an aspect ratio of 3:2, which is perfect if you print your images on 4-x-6-inch photo paper. However, if you print your images on different-size papers, the aspect ratio of those papers doesn't match the aspect ratio of your camera. For example, if you print images on 8-x-10-inch paper, the aspect ratio is 4:5. If you take a picture and don't leave any breathing room at the edges, you can't crop to 8 x 10 without cutting out part of your subject. When you take pictures, keep this in mind: Leave a little breathing room and you can crop to different aspect ratios without losing important parts of your image. Figure 10-2 shows an image that has plenty of breathing room. The complete image is perfect for a 4 x 6 print. The red rectangle shows the image cropped for a 5-x-7-inch print, and the blue lines show the image cropped for an 8-x-10 inch print. Breathing room is a wonderful thing.

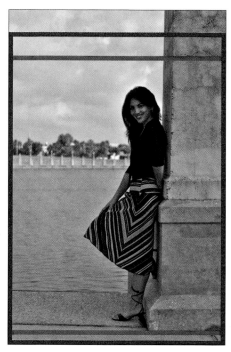

Figure 10-2: Leave a little wiggle room for different aspect ratios.

Image size and resolution considerations

Whether you print an image on your home computer printer or use an online printing company, it's important that you send an image that's large enough to print on the media size you choose. Also important: Match the resolution of the printer as closely as possible. To find the ideal resolution, check with the company that's doing your printing or check your computer printer manual. If you're printing the image, a resolution of 200 dots per inch (dpi) gives you acceptable results. If you choose a resolution of 300 dpi,

you'll get a better-looking image because the pixels are smaller and you'll get a better color variation. So how does this equate to image size? If you want to print an 8-x-10-inch image at 200 dpi, the image dimensions must be 1600 x 2000 pixels, and of course, the image must have a resolution of 200 dpi. If you want to print an 8-x-10-inch image at 300 dpi, your image must be 2400 x 3000 pixels. To do the math for a different image resolution, multiply the size in inches by the resolution to get the document size in pixels. Your image should be larger than this. Unfortunately, neither ImageBrowser EX nor Digital Professional Pro has a menu command to change the image size. If you have Photoshop Elements, you can easily perform this task. If you decide to invest the paltry sum Adobe charges for Photoshop Elements, *Photoshop Elements 11 For Dummies,* by Barbara Obermeier and Ted Padova, is a good book to reference. If you own an earlier version of Photoshop Elements, Wiley has *Photoshop Elements For Dummies* books dating all the way back to version 2.

Cropping an Image in ImageBrowser EX

You can crop an image to get rid of unwanted pixels. When you crop an image, you end up with a smaller image size as well. To crop an image in ImageBrowser EX:

1. **Select the image you want to edit and then click the Edit button.**

   The menu drops down to reveal the editing options.

2. **Select Crop Image.**

   The Cropping dialog box appears (see Figure 10-3). You have two methods of trimming an image. The first is to simply drag the handles until you've cropped away any unwanted pixels. This method is fine when you create an image for the Web or to send via e-mail. However, when you want to print an image on photo paper with set dimensions, you need to use the second method — crop to an aspect ratio from the Advanced Options choices. The following steps show you how to crop manually.

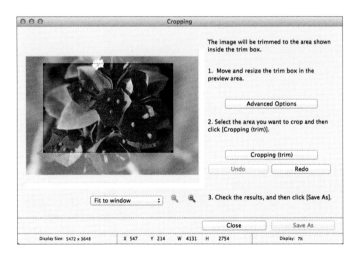

Figure 10-3: Cropping an image.

Creating photo books at Blurb

If you want to see your images in a custom photo book, you can make this a reality by visiting Blurb (www.blurb.com). Blurb is a popular online website for creating and selling photo books. You can create a great-looking photo book with Blurb's free BookSmart software, which you can download for free from http://www.blurb.com/booksmart. After you use the software to create your book, you can upload the photos to Blurb directly from the BookSmart software. You can also create a custom book in an application like Adobe InDesign and then upload it to Blurb as a PDF (Portable Document Format). After you upload the book, you have 14 days to order at least one copy of it. If you don't order a copy within 14 days, Blurb removes it from the website. Blurb offers hardcover and softcover books in the following sizes (in inches): 7 x 7, 8 x 10, 10 x 8,

12 x 12, and 13 x 10. You can also upgrade to premium paper, which looks absolutely stunning with high-resolution images. The minimum number of pages is 20, and the maximum number of pages you can put in a book is 440. You can put multiple photos on a page with BookSmart templates.

You can also choose to make your book public after you order one copy. When you make a book available to the public, you can specify the selling price. The following image is a copy of the book cover I created from images I shot at a local car show. Quite a few copies of this book have been ordered online. When your book sells, Blurb sends you the difference between your selling price and its established price minus a small handling fee.

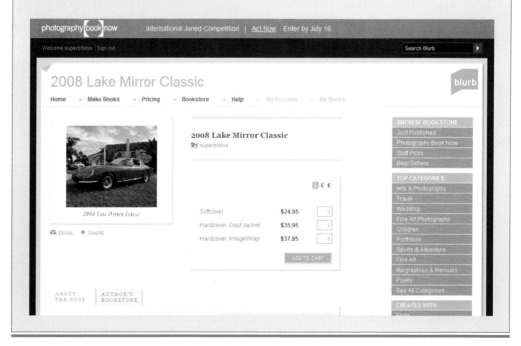

3. Drag the handles.

Drag any handle to trim the image to a different size. Click inside the trim box and then drag to move the box to trim to a different area of the image.

4. Click the Cropping button.

The image trims to size. If you don't like the results, click the Redo button.

5. Click the Save As button and then in the Save As dialog box, follow the prompts to save the image.

Cropping an image in ImageBrowser EX is an inexact science, but you can add precision to cropping if you use the Advanced Options and follow these steps:

1. Select the image you want to edit and then click the Edit button.

The menu drops down to reveal the editing options.

2. Select Crop Image.

The Cropping dialog box appears (refer to Figure 10-3). I showed you how to crop manually in the last set of steps. Now it's time to add precision to cropping.

3. Click Advanced Options.

The Advanced Options for cropping images appears (see Figure 10-4).

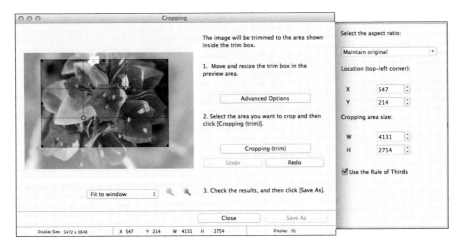

Figure 10-4: Advanced Cropping Options.

4. Choose an option from the Aspect Ratio drop-down menu.

You can maintain the original aspect ratio, or choose one that matches the media on which you're going to print the image. Your options are: Manual, Maintain Original, 1:1, 3:2, 2:3, 4:3, 3:4, 16:9, or 9:16. If you're not familiar with aspect ratio, it compares the proportion of the width compared to the height. When you choose 3:2, the image is cropped to a size that is 3 units high and 2 units wide. For example, if you wanted to print the image on 6-x-4-inch paper, you'd choose the 3:2 aspect ratio. Oddly there is no aspect ratio that matches the popular 10 x 8 print size.

5. If you want to crop the image according to the Rule of Thirds, click the Rule of Thirds check box.

This places an overlay of nine rectangles on top of the cropping rectangle. If you're not familiar with this rule of composition, a *Rule of Thirds power point* is where the edges of two rectangles intersect. Refer to Figure 10-4, and you see four small squares where the rectangles intersect. If you crop your image so that a center of interest in the form of an object or a person appears on one of the small squares, in theory your viewer will be drawn toward the center of interest.

6. Enter values for the X and Y coordinates for the upper-left corner of the cropping rectangle.

If you use ImageBrowser EX to do your cropping, you'll have no idea where these coordinates are. My recommendation is to use the cropping rectangle handles to crop the image by eye. The X and Y coordinates appear in these text boxes after you crop manually. You can tweak the position of the upper-left corner of the cropping rectangle by changing the values slightly until you can see the results you're after.

7. Enter the Cropping Area size.

This is the dimension in pixels of the cropped image. This requires a bit of math on your part. Your camera has a default resolution of 240 pixels per inch. Therefore, you'll have to multiply the desired width and height by 240 and enter these values in the W and H text boxes. For example, if you want to print a 6 x 4 image, you enter 1440 (6 inches x 240) in the W text box and 960 in the H text box. Unfortunately, even if you choose the desired aspect ratio, you cannot enter the width and have ImageBrowser EX automatically figure the height. For this type of sophistication, you'll need a full-fledged image-editing application like Adobe Photoshop or Adobe Photoshop Elements.

8. Click Cropping.

The image is cropped to your specifications.

9. Click Save As.

The Save As dialog box appears. The image is saved using the JPEG file format.

10. **Enter a name for the image, and specify the folder in which to save the image.**

    Use a different name for the image, especially if you're cropping a JPEG image. If you use the same name and save it in the same folder, you over-write the original, which is not a good thing.

Printing an Image

After you trim an image to size, it's time to print it. If you're printing the image on your local printer, you can do so from within ImageBrowser EX or Digital Photo Professional. You can print a single image or a contact sheet. I show you how to do both in the upcoming sections.

Printing an image from ImageBrowser EX

You can print an image you select in ImageBrowser EX on your local printer. You get the best results when printing a JPEG image. If you attempt to print a RAW image from within ImageBrowser EX, the application uses an embed-ded JPEG thumbnail that was designed to be used as an image preview. If you try to print large images from RAW files, you probably won't be happy with the results. You get the best results when you print RAW images from within Digital Photo Professional. To print an image from ImageBrowser EX:

1. **Launch ImageBrowser EX and then select the image you want to print.**

   You can select the image while viewing a folder in Thumbnail or Preview mode.

2. **Click the Print button and then select Print Images.**

   The Photo Print dialog box appears (see Figure 10-5).

3. **Click the Printer drop-down arrow and choose the desired printer.**

   Your default printer appears on the button. If you have more than one printer, you'll find them on this drop-down list.

4. **Click the Page Setup button.**

   A dialog box with properties for your printer appears. Use this to match the media size to what you have in your printer tray, specify page layout, and so on. The options vary depending on the printer you use. Choose the desired options and close the dialog box.

5. **(Optional) To display the shooting date and time on the image, click the Shooting Date/Time drop-down arrow.**

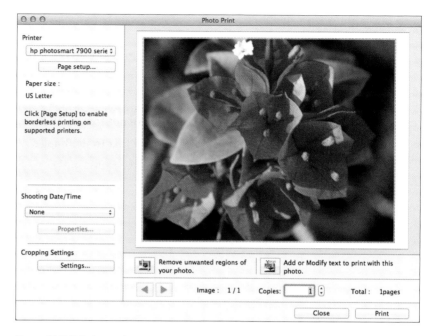

Figure 10-5: Printing an image.

When you choose this option, a drop-down menu becomes available with the following options: None (the default), which does not print the date and time; Date/Time, which prints the date and time; Date; or Time. Personally, I never print the date and time on a photo. The date and time are with the image metadata. If you choose this option, a preview of the date and time appear on the preview of what the final print looks like.

6. (Optional) If you choose to display the date on the image, click Properties.

This opens the Shooting Date/Time Settings dialog box (see Figure 10-6). The options, which enable you to change the text outline, text color, time and date separator, and the position where the date and time appear on the image are fairly

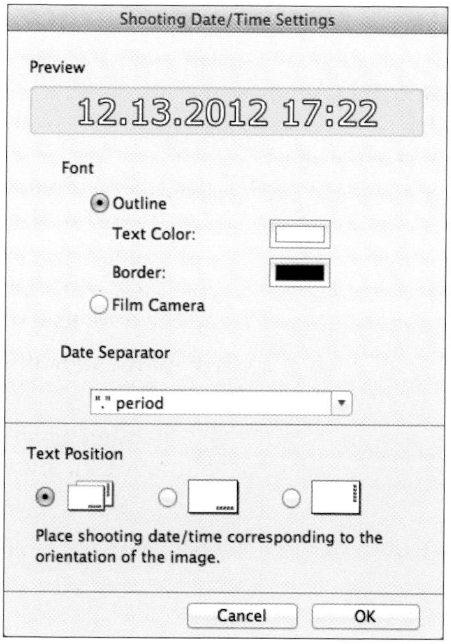

Figure 10-6: Modifying the way the date and time appear on the image.

self-explanatory. I'll do my bit to help save a rain forest by not wasting paper to record the obvious.

7. **(Optional) Click the Cropping Settings button if you want to trim the image.**

   The Cropping Settings dialog box opens. From this dialog box you can choose to automatically crop the image, which eliminates a white border around the image, or choose not to crop the image.

8. **Click the Insert Text button to add text to the image.**

   The Insert Text dialog box opens (see Figure 10-7).

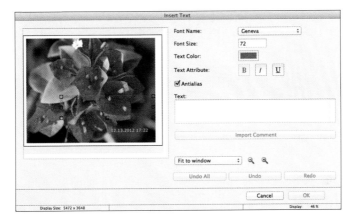

Figure 10-7: Adding text to the image.

9. **Click inside the image where you want the text to appear and then type the text in the text box.**

   Four handles appear around the text box. The text box resizes while you type. After you click inside the image you can enter text into the image and the options to change the font type, size, and color appear.

10. **Accept the default font type as well as size and color, or specify different options.**

11. **If you added comments to the image, the Comments button is available. Click the button to add the comments to the text box.**

12. **Click inside the text box and drag it to the desired position and then click OK.**

    You return to the Photo Print dialog box.

13. **Specify the number of copies to print.**

    The default is one copy; however, you can print additional copies by entering the desired amount in the text box or by clicking the spinner buttons.

14. **Click the Print button.**

    The selected printer prints the image.

Printing an image in Digital Photo Professional

If you want to print RAW images, you can do so from Digital Photo Professional. The process is pretty straightforward. You can specify the printer and then modify the printer properties to suit the media you're using. To print an image from Digital Photo Professional:

1. **Launch Digital Photo Professional, select the image you want to print, and then choose File⇨Print.**

   The Print dialog box appears (see Figure 10-8).

2. **Choose the desired printer from the Printer drop-down list.**

   This menu shows every available printer on your computer or in your network.

3. **Choose the desired Preset from the drop-down menu.**

   This menu shows the various paper options available for your printer. When you choose a preset, the printer sends the proper amount of ink to create the best possible print for the paper you've chosen.

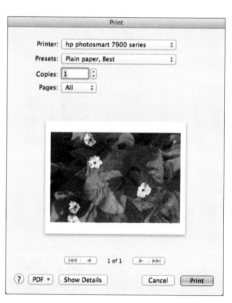

Figure 10-8: Printing an image from Digital Photo Professional.

4. **Specify the number of copies to print.**

   You can specify the number of copies by entering a value in the text box or by using the spinner buttons.

5. **If the image is larger than the media, select the Fit Image to Print Area check box, and then click the OK button.**

   The selected printer prints your image.

TIP

You can also save the image in PDF format by clicking the PDF button and choosing the desired options from the drop-down menu.

Printing a Contact Sheet in ImageBrowser EX

You can print a *contact sheet* of selected images. The contact sheet is a handy reference that shows information about each photo as well as a thumbnail image for each photo. Many photographers file these as reference material. They're also useful for showing images to prospective clients. After all, looking at an image tells you a lot more than looking at a filename. To print an index sheet in ImageBrowser EX:

1. **Launch ImageBrowser EX and then select the images you want to include on the index sheet.**

   If you choose RAW images, ImageBrowser EX uses the thumbnail image for the index sheet because ImageBrowser EX can't decode RAW files. This may result in poor image quality. If you primarily shoot RAW images, you can print a contact sheet as I show you in the next section.

2. **Click the Print button, and then choose Contact Sheet.**

   The Print Contact Sheet dialog box appears (see Figure 10-9).

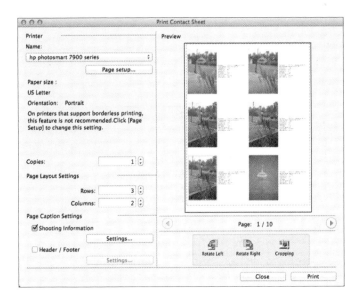

Figure 10-9: Printing a contact sheet.

3. **Choose a printer from the Name drop-down list.**

   Your default printer is listed on the button, and any additional printers connected to your computer appear on the drop-down list.

4. **Click the Page Setup button.**

   A dialog box with the printer properties appears. The properties differ depending on what type of printer you use.

5. **Specify the desired options from the Page Setup dialog box and then click OK.**

   The dialog box closes.

6. **Enter the number of copies in the Copies text box.**

   Alternatively, you can click the spinner buttons to specify the number of copies.

7. **In the Page Layout Settings section, enter the desired number in the Columns and Rows text boxes.**

   This setting determines how the images display on the sheet. The default setting gives you three rows and three columns. If you choose a larger number, the images will be smaller.

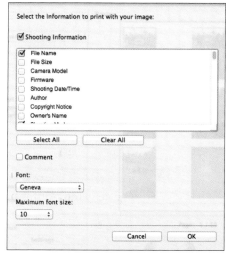

8. **(Optional) Deselect the Shooting Information check box (it's enabled by default) so that only images appear on the sheet.**

   If you deselect this check box, skip to Step 12.

9. **If you left the Shooting Information check box selected, click the Settings button.**

   The Shooting Information Settings dialog box appears (see Figure 10-10).

Figure 10-10: Modifying Shooting Information options.

10. **Select the Shooting settings you want displayed under each image and then select the Comment check box to print any image comments on the contact sheet.**

11. **Accept the default font (Geneva) or choose a different font from the drop-down list and then click OK.**

    The Shooting Information Settings dialog box closes.

12. **(Optional) Select the Header/ Footer check box to include a header and footer on each sheet.**

    If you don't select the Header/ Footer check box, skip to Step 15.

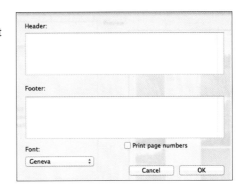

Figure 10-11: Entering information for the index sheet header and footer.

13. **If you selected the Header/ Footer check box, click the Settings button.**

    The Header/Footer Settings dialog box appears (see Figure 10-11).

14. **Type the desired text in the Header and Footer text boxes, change the font if desired, and then click OK.**

    The Header/Footer Settings dialog box closes.

15. **To change the orientation of an individual image, click it and then click one of the icons below the preview window.**

    You can rotate the image right, left, or crop the image. The third option seems rather foolish to me as the object of a contact sheet is to show a thumbnail version of the complete image, not a cropped copy. If you do choose to crop the thumbnail, a dialog box opens with a preview of the image and cropping handles you can drag to crop the thumbnail.

16. **Click the Print button.**

    The selected printer prints the contact sheet.

Printing a Contact Sheet in Digital Photo Professional

If you need to print a contact sheet of RAW images, you can easily do so in Digital Photo Professional. You can specify how many rows and columns are on the sheet and much more. To print a contact sheet in Digital Photo Professional:

1. **Launch Digital Photo Professional and then choose File⇨Print Contact Sheets.**

   The Contact Sheet dialog box appears (see Figure 10-12).

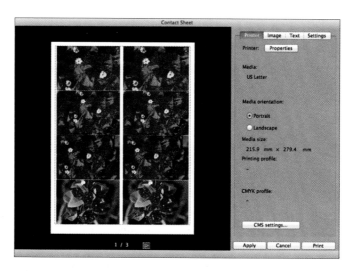

Figure 10-12: Printing a contact sheet.

2. **Click Properties.**

   The Page Setup dialog box appears (see Figure 10-13).

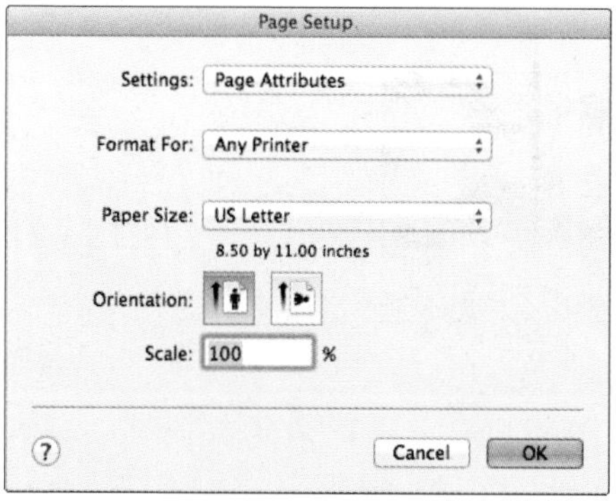

Figure 10-13: Setting page properties.

3. **Click the Format For button.**

   A list of printers connected to your computer appears.

4. **Select the desired printer from the drop-down list.**

   This closes the Properties dialog box.

5. **Accept the default paper size (8 1/2 x 11), or Click the Paper Size button.**

   This displays a list of paper sizes.

6. **Select the desired paper size.**

7. **Accept the default orientation (Portrait) or select Landscape.**

   This option determines whether the sheet is taller than it is wide *(portrait),* or wider than it is tall *(landscape).*

8. **Accept the default scale (100%) or enter a different value.**

   If you enter a larger value, part of the contact sheet will be cut off.

9. **Click OK to apply the settings and exit the Page Setup dialog box.**

10. **Click the CMS Settings tab.**

    The Color Match Settings dialog box opens. This lets you specify a printer profile or CMYK (Cyan, Magenta, Yellow, Black) simulation profile.

11. **Select the desired options from the drop-down list and then click OK to exit the Color Match Settings dialog box and return to the Contact Sheet dialog box.**

12. **Click the Image tab (see Figure 10-14).**

    The size and formatting options for the contact sheet are displayed.

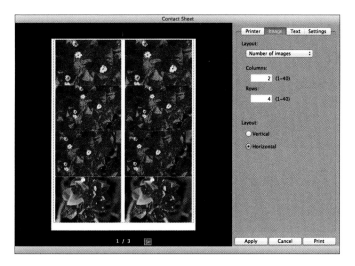

Figure 10-14: Specifying image options.

13. **Accept the default layout (Number of Images), or choose Size from the drop-down menu.**

    The default option sizes the contact sheet to the page. If you choose Size, you can specify the size of the contact sheet, which determines how much of the page is contact sheet and how much of the page is blank. The default unit of measure is millimeters. If you want to use the size option and prefer to set the size up in inches, go to Step 20 to open the Settings tab, and then choose inches as the unit of measure.

14. **If you accept the default option (Number of Images), enter the desired value in the Columns and Rows text boxes.**

    This determines how many columns and rows of images are displayed on each page of the contact sheet.

15. **Choose the desired layout.**

    Your options are Vertical or Horizontal.

16. **Click the Text tab (see Figure 10-15) and then enter the desired information in the Header and Footer boxes.**

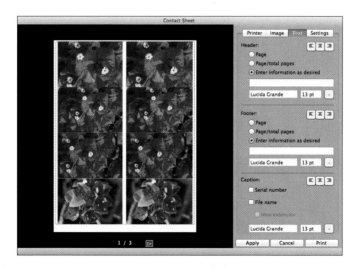

Figure 10-15: Specifying text options.

Alternatively, you can display the page number, or you can display the page number and the total number of pages.

17. **Accept the default font face and size for the header/footer, or click the ellipsis (. . .) button to the right to specify a different font face and size.**

18. **(Optional) Choose an option in the Caption section.**

    You can display the serial number or the filename.

    If you don't choose a Caption option, skip to Step 20.

19. **Accept the default font face and size for the caption, or click the ellipsis (. . .) button to specify a different font face and size.**

20. **Click the Settings tab (see Figure 10-16).**

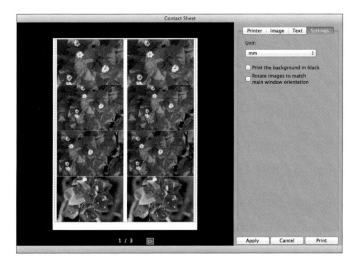

Figure 10-16: Specifying the final settings.

21. **(Optional) Click the Unit drop-down list and choose Inches as the unit of measurement.**

    Don't do this if your preferred unit of measure is millimeters.

22. **(Optional) Select the Print Background in Black check box.**

    Choose this option, and the background behind the images is black.

23. **(Optional) If desired, select the Rotate Images to Match Main Window Orientation check box.**

    If you don't use this option, images aren't rotated if they don't have the same orientation.

24. **Click the Print button.**

    The selected printer prints the contact sheet.

Using third-party papers

Lots of companies manufacture paper for printing digital images. Some of them are more economical than the paper available from your printer manufacturer, and others are more expensive and suitable for creating fine art prints. For example, papers with a high rag content make your images look like artwork instead of photos. When you print images from an application such as Photoshop Elements, the printer determines how much of each ink is laid on the paper to create the resulting image. However, when you use *third-party* paper (paper not manufactured by the company that made your printer), your printer has no way of knowing how much ink to lay on the paper to replicate what you see on your computer screen. When this is the case, you need to get an ICC (International Color Consortium) profile for the paper and your printer. Many manufacturers of fine-art photo paper, such as Ilford and Hahnemuhle, have profiles you can download for your printer and their paper. They also supply instructions on where the profile needs to be stored on your system and how to use the profile with many popular image-editing applications, such as Photoshop and Photoshop Elements.

Part IV

the part of tens

Enjoy an additional Canon EOS 6D Part of Tens chapter online at www.dummies.com/extras/canoneos6d.

In this part . . .

- Get familiar with creating custom menus that contain your favorite commands.

- Find out how to register user settings and make them available whenever you select a user setting on the camera Mode dial.

- Explore adding copyright information to images.

- Utilize Wi-Fi and GPS features of the Canon EOS 6D. Also, discover some cool projects you can do with your camera.

- Enjoy an additional Canon EOS 6D Part of Tens chapter online at www.dummies.com/extras/canoneos6d.

11

Ten Tips and Tricks

In This Chapter

▶ Creating custom menus

▶ Adding copyright info

▶ Adding your name as author to the camera

▶ Creating and registering picture styles

▶ Editing movies in-camera

▶ Updating your firmware

▶ Registering camera settings

▶ Restoring camera settings

▶ Leveling your camera

▶ Customizing your camera

When the weather is dismal and you're fresh out of ideas for shooting macro or still-life photography in your house, you can always photograph your pet rock. Or better yet, you can do some cool things with your camera, such as creating a custom menu or a custom picture style. In this chapter, I show you some cool tips and tricks that you can do on a rainy day.

Creating a Custom Menu

Do you have a set of menu commands you use frequently? How cool would it be not to have to sift through all 4,000 commands in your camera menu? That's right, you can cut to the chase and create your own custom menu with your very own favorite commands. If I've piqued your curiosity, read on. To create a custom camera menu:

1. Click the Menu button.

The last-used menu displays.

2. Use the Quick Control dial to navigate to the My Menu Settings tab (see the left image in Figure 11-1).

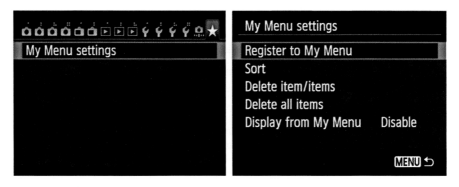

My Menu settings

My Menu settings
Register to My Menu
Sort
Delete item/items
Delete all items
Display from My Menu   Disable

MENU↩

Figure 11-1: Gonna make your very own menu.

3. Press the Set button.

The My Menu Settings dialog box displays. The Register option is highlighted when you first open the menu (refer to the right image in Figure 11-1).

4. Press Set.

A list of menu commands displays (see the left image in Figure 11-2).

Select item to register

Image quality
Beep
Release shutter without card
Image review
Lens aberration correction
External Speedlite control

MENU↩

Select item to register

Register in My Menu
External Speedlite control

Cancel   OK

Figure 11-2: Choosing commands to register.

5. **Use the Multi-controller or the Quick Control dial to highlight a command and then press Set to register it.**

   A dialog box appears asking whether you want to register the command in your custom menu (refer to the right image in Figure 11-2).

6. **Use the Multi-controller or the Quick Control dial to highlight OK and then press Set.**

   The command is grayed out on the list.

7. **Repeat Steps 5 and 6 to add other commands to your menu.**

8. **After registering commands to your menu, press the Menu button.**

   You're returned to the My Menu Settings dialog box (see the left image in Figure 11-3). You have the following commands at your disposal:

   - *Sort:* Press Set and then your menu commands display. Select a menu command and press Set to display an up-and-down arrow next to the command. Use the Multi-controller or Quick Control dial to move the command up or down in the list and then press Set when the command is in the desired position. Repeat for other commands you want to move. Press the Menu button when finished.

   - *Delete Item/Items:* Press Set to display all commands on your menu. Use the Multi-controller or the Quick Control dial to highlight a command and then press Set to delete it from the list. This opens a dialog box asking you to confirm deletion. Use the Multi-controller or the Quick Control dial to highlight OK and then press Set. Press the Menu button to return to the My Menu Settings dialog box.

   - *Delete All Items:* Press Set to reveal a dialog box that asks you to confirm deletion of all registered items. Rotate the Quick Control dial to highlight OK and then press Set to finish the task.

   - *Display from My Menu:* Press Set to reveal the options. Use the Multi-controller or the Quick Control dial to highlight Enable and then press Set. The My Menu tab is selected. The last menu used opens first by default. However, if you put all your frequently used commands on a custom menu, you won't have to use the other menu tabs very often. The right image in Figure 11-3 shows a custom menu.

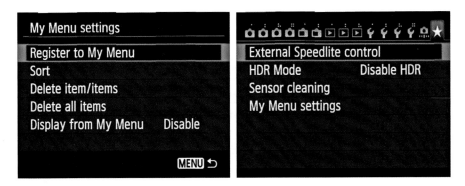

Figure 11-3: Setting My Menu Settings options.

Adding Copyright Information to the Camera

You can add your copyright information to the camera. The data you enter will be added to the EXIF metadata recorded with each image. To add copyright information to the camera:

1. **Press the Menu button.**

   The previously used menu displays.

2. **Use the Multi-controller to navigate to the Camera Settings 4 tab.**

3. **Use the Multi-controller or the Quick Control dial to highlight Copyright Information (see the left image in Figure 11-4) and then press the Set button.**

   The Copyright Information menu displays.

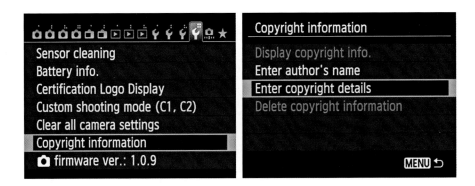

Figure 11-4: Adding your copyright to the camera.

4. **Use the Multi-controller or the Quick Control dial to highlight Enter Copyright Details (see the right image in Figure 11-4) and then press Set.**

   The Enter Copyright Details dialog box appears (see Figure 11-5).

5. **Enter the Copyright Details.**

   Press the Quick Control button to navigate to the character section of the dialog box. Use the Multi-controller to highlight a letter, and then press Set to add the letter to your copyright information. Continue in this manner until you've entered the desired text and year.

Figure 11-5: Entering copyright information.

6. **Press the Menu button to OK the changes (see Figure 11-5).**

   A dialog box appears, telling you that the Setting Screen will close after the text that was entered is saved to the camera.

7. **Use the Multi-controller or the Quick Control dial to highlight OK and then press Set.**

   You're returned to the copyright menu (see the left image in Figure 11-6).

8. **Use the Multi-controller or the Quick Control dial to highlight Display Copyright Info and then press Set.**

   Your copyright information is displayed (refer to the right image in Figure 11-6).

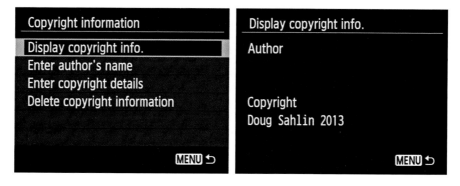

Figure 11-6: Viewing copyright information.

To edit your copyright information, follow the previous steps. When you get to Step 4, your current copyright information is displayed. Press the Erase button to delete letters, and then enter the revised information, using the Multi-controller to select letters; press Set to add each letter to your copyright information.

Adding Author Name to the Camera

You can add your name as the author of each image you capture with your camera. The information is added as EXIF data to each picture you take. To register your author information with the camera:

1. **Press the Menu button.**

   The previously used menu displays.

2. **Use the Multi-controller to navigate to the Camera Settings 4 tab.**

3. **Use the Multi-controller or the Quick Control dial to highlight Copyright Information (see the left image in Figure 11-7), and then press the Set button.**

   The Copyright Information menu displays.

4. **Use the Multi-controller or the Quick Control dial to highlight Enter Author's Name (see the right image in Figure 11-7), and then press Set.**

   The Enter Author's Name dialog box appears (see the left image in Figure 11-8).

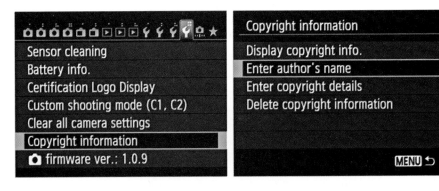

Figure 11-7: Adding your name to the camera information.

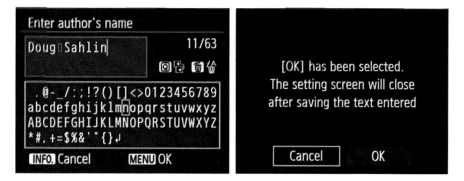

Enter author's name	
Doug⬚Sahlin|	11/63
	🔲 📸 🗑 🗑
. @ - _ / : ; ! ? ( ) [ ] < > 0123456789	
abcdefghijklmnopqrstuvwxyz	
ABCDEFGHIJKLMNOPQRSTUVWXYZ	
* # , + = $ % & ' " { } ↵	
INFO Cancel MENU OK	

[OK] has been selected.
The setting screen will close
after saving the text entered

Cancel   OK

Figure 11-8: Registering your name with the camera.

5. **Press the Quick Control button to enter the text selection box.**

   Use the Picture Style Selection button to navigate between the text box and the text selection box.

6. **Use the Multi-controller button to navigate to a letter or a number.**

   The character is highlighted with a gold rectangle.

7. **Press Set.**

   The character appears in the text box.

8. **Continue adding characters to complete your name.**

   Your completed author information appears in the text box (refer to the right image in Figure 11-8).

9. **Press the Menu button.**

   A dialog box appears, telling you that the Setting Screen will close after the text that was entered is saved to the camera.

10. **Use the Multi-controller or the Quick Control dial to highlight OK and then press Set.**

    You're returned to the copyright menu (refer to the left image in Figure 11-6).

    You can edit your name with the techniques from the preceding section.

Creating and Registering a Picture Style

If you like to use picture styles in your photography, you'll be glad to know that you can customize your favorite picture style. After customizing the picture style, you can register it as a User Defined picture style and it's available whenever you want to use it for pictures. To customize a picture style:

1. **Press the Menu button.**

   The last-used menu command is displayed.

2. **Use the Multi-controller to navigate to the Shooting Settings 4 Tab.**

   The Shooting Setting tab is displayed.

3. **Use the Multi-controller or Quick Control dial to highlight Picture Style (see the left image in Figure11-9), and press Set.**

   The pre-defined Picture Styles are displayed.

4. **Use the Multi-controller or the Quick Control dial to select one of the User Defined picture styles (see the right image in Figure 11-9).**

5. **Press Set.**

   The Picture Styles menu is displayed.

6. **Use the Multi-controller or Quick Control dial to highlight Usr Def 1 (see the left image in Figure 11-10) and then press Info.**

   The currently selected Picture style is displayed at the top of the dialog box with the settings you can modify.

7. **Press Set.**

   An arrow appears above and below the current Picture style.

⬛⬛⬛⬛⬛⬛⬛▶⬛▶⬛ 🎥 🎥 🎥 🎥 🔧 ★	Picture Style ◑.◑.⅙.◐
Picture Style Auto	⬛A Auto 3 , 0 , 0 , 0
Long exp. noise reduction OFF	⬛S Standard 3 , 0 , 0 , 0
High ISO speed NR ▪▫▫	⬛P Portrait 2 , 0 , 0 , 0
Highlight tone priority OFF	⬛L Landscape 4 , 0 , 0 , 0
Dust Delete Data	⬛N Neutral 0 , 0 , 0 , 0
Multiple exposure Disable	⬛F Faithful 0 , 0 , 0 , 0
HDR Mode Disable HDR	**INFO.** Detail set. **SET** OK

Figure 11-9: Customizing a picture style.

8. **Use the Multi-controller or Quick Control dial to select on of the preset picture styles that you will modify to create a custom style and then press Set.**

   If you're a portrait photographer, you could use the Portrait style as the basis for your custom style. The details for the picture set display on the camera LCD monitor (see the right image in Figure 11-10). You can customize the following:

   - *Sharpness:* You can increase or decrease image sharpness.

   - *Contrast:* You can increase or decrease the amount of contrast in the image.

   - *Saturation:* You can increase or decrease color saturation.

   - *Color Tone:* You can change the skin tone of people you photograph. You can make skin tones more yellow by moving the indicator to the left side of the scale, or more red by moving the indicator to the right side of the scale.

9. **Customize image sharpness (the first on the list), or use the Multi-controller or the Quick Control dial to highlight another detail, and then press Set.**

   The selected detail appears on the camera LCD monitor. You can now customize it (see the left image in Figure 11-11).

10. **Use the Multi-controller or the Quick Control dial to increase or decrease the amount of the detail.**

    Rotate the dial to the right to increase, or left to decrease.

11. **Press Set.**

    The change is applied, and you're returned to the Detail Set menu.

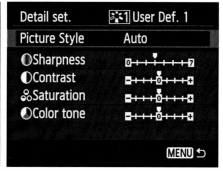

Figure 11-10: Customizing a picture style.

12. **Repeat Steps 6–11 to customize the other details in the picture style.**

    Customize the details that make sense to the style you're customizing. For example, you wouldn't change Color Tones when customizing the Landscape picture style. The right image in Figure 11-11 shows a customized set that's ready to be registered with the camera.

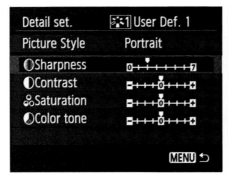 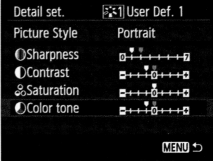

Figure 11-11: Customizing a picture style.

13. **Press the Menu button.**

    Your custom picture style is registered. The text above the style shows the style on which your style is based; it also shows the changes you've made to the base style, in blue.

14. **Press Set to choose the custom Picture style.**

    The custom picture style appears in the Picture Style menu box and will be applied to all images until you choose a different picture style. Note that you can have up to three custom picture styles.

You can also customize a Standard picture style. Follow the preceding steps but instead of selecting one of the User Defined styles, select one of the Standard styles and then press the Info button. Follow Steps 9–11 to customize the picture style to suit your taste.

Editing Movies in the Camera

When you review movies in your camera, they may need to be trimmed. You can cut footage from the beginning or end of a movie clip in the camera by following these steps:

1. **Press the Playback button repeatedly until you navigate to the movie you want to edit.**

   You can press the Index/Magnify/Reduce button to view four or nine thumbnails. Movies have a filmstrip icon around the border of the thumbnail.

2. **Select the movie you want to edit and then press the Set button.**

   The playback controls display.

3. **Use the Multi-controller or the Quick Control dial to highlight the Edit icon that looks like a pair of scissors (see the left image in Figure 11-12) and then press Set.**

   The editing controls display (see the right image in Figure 11-12). Cut Beginning is the first tool, which enables you to trim footage from the beginning of the movie clip.

4. **Press Set.**

   The Cut Beginning edit tool is available.

5. **Press the right side of the Multi-controller to fast-forward to the spot where you want the clip to begin and then press Set.**

   The icon that indicates where the movie begins displays above the clip.

6. **Use the Multi-controller or the Quick Control dial to highlight the Cut End tool and then press Set.**

   The tool for trimming from the end of the movie is highlighted.

7. **Press the left side of the Multi-controller left to rewind the movie to where you want the clip to end and then press Set.**

   The revised starting and ending points for the movie display above the clip (refer to the left image in Figure 11-13).

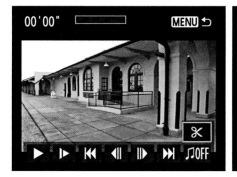
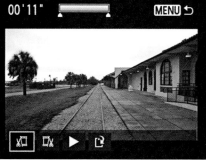

Figure 11-12: Editing a movie in camera.

8. **Use the Multi-controller or the Quick Control dial to highlight Save and then press Set.**

   The Save button is the icon to the right of the Play button in the image on the left image in Figure 11-13. After pressing the icon, a dialog box appears asking you whether you want to create a new file or overwrite the existing file (see the right image in Figure 11-13). If you still have footage on the original file you want to keep, make sure you create a new file.

9. **Use the Multi-controller or the Quick Control dial to highlight the desired option and then press Set.**

   Your movie clip is on the cutting-room floor.

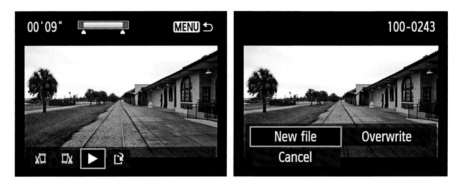

Figure 11-13: Trimming the beginning and ending of a movie clip.

Updating Your Camera's Firmware

Canon is constantly making changes to make its cameras better. Canon locates any potential problems based on user input and its own tests, and then takes this information and modifies the camera's firmware. *Firmware* is like the operating system for your computer. If you've registered your camera, Canon notifies you by e-mail when a firmware update is available. You can register your camera online or mail in the card provided with the camera documents. If you mail in the card, make sure you fill in the E-Mail section of the form to be notified of any changes. When you get the notification, follow the link to the firmware. You can also find out online whether your camera has a firmware update available. Open your favorite web browser and navigate to

```
http://www.usa.canon.com/cusa/consumer/products/cameras/slr_cameras/
                    eos_6d#DriversAndSoftware
```

Look at the Firmware section and you'll see whether any updates are available for your camera. If an update is available, follow the prompts to download the information to your computer. You then transfer the firmware program to an SD (Secure Digital) card to install it on your camera. Canon posts detailed instructions on how to install the firmware on one of the web pages associated with the download.

Make sure you have a fully charged battery in your camera when you update firmware. If the battery exhausts itself during the firmware upgrade, you may permanently damage your camera.

Registering Camera User Settings

Everybody has a preferred way of working. That's why you have preferences in computer programs and why you can register user settings to the Mode dial. The settings you register are available whenever you select a user setting on the camera Mode dial. For example, you may have custom settings that you use when you do flash photography, settings you use often but don't use every day. You can register these settings and they'll be there, even if you clear all camera settings. To register your favorite settings:

1. **Use the camera menu to choose the settings you use frequently.**

   For example, you can specify the image format and size, set up exposure compensation, or set any other settings you use frequently.

2. **Rotate the Mode dial to select your preferred shooting mode.**

   For example, you can rotate the dial to Av, if your favorite mode is Aperture Priority. After you select all your favorites, you're ready to register them.

3. **Modify any other settings you want to register.**

   For example, if you're setting up a custom menu for sports photography, you probably want to register a shutter speed that is fast enough to stop the action of the sport you photograph, and Continuous Drive mode. You might want to register an ISO setting as well.

4. **Press the Menu button.**

   The previously used menu displays.

5. **Use the Multi-controller button to navigate to the Camera Settings 4 tab.**

6. **Use the Multi-controller or the Quick Control dial to highlight Custom Shooting Mode (C1, C2), (see the left image in Figure 11-14), and then press the Set button.**

   The Custom Shooting Mode menu appears with the Register option highlighted (see the right image in Figure 11-14).

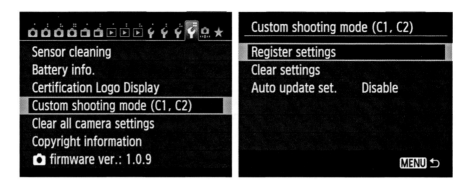

Figure 11-14: Preparing to register a setting.

7. **Press Set.**

   The Register settings menu appears (see the left image in Figure 11-15).

8. **Use the Multi-controller or the Quick Control dial to highlight the desired mode dial.**

   Your choices are C1 and C2. A dialog box appears, asking whether you want to register your settings to the selected mode dial (see the right image in Figure 11-15). If you have registered settings to a mode dial previously, make sure you don't select that same mode dial or you'll override the previous settings.

9. **Use the Multi-controller or the Quick Control dial to highlight OK and then press Set.**

   Your settings are registered to the selected mode dial.

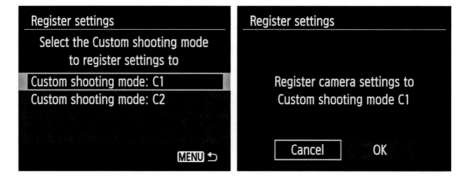

Figure 11-15: Registering user settings.

To erase user settings:

1. **Follow Steps 3–6, select Clear Settings, and then press the Set button.**
2. **Select the mode dial you want to clear from the next menu and then press Set.**

3. **Use the Multi-controller or Quick Control dial to highlight OK from the Clear Settings menu, and then press Set to complete the task.**

Restoring Your Camera Settings

Sometimes you need to do some spring cleaning and wipe the slate clean. If you have enabled more settings on your camera than you care to deal with, no longer use, or even know about, you can restore camera settings to factory defaults. This wipes out all your menu changes, your custom menu, and any picture styles you've registered or customized. So think twice before doing this. To restore your camera settings to the factory default:

1. **Press the Menu button.**

   The previously used menu displays.

2. **Use the Multi-controller to navigate to the Camera Settings 4 tab.**

3. **Use the Multi-controller or the Quick Control dial to highlight Clear All Camera Settings (see the left image in Figure 11-16) and then press Set.**

   A dialog box appears, asking you to confirm that you want to clear all settings (see the right image in Figure 11-16).

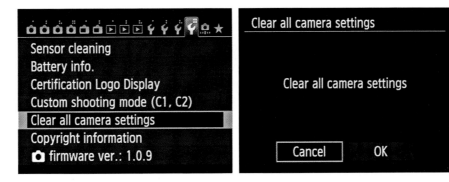

Figure 11-16: Clearing all your camera settings.

4. **Use the Multi-controller or the Quick Control dial to highlight OK and then press Set.**

   A dialog box appears, telling you the camera is busy. When it stops, the camera settings have been cleared.

Leveling Your Camera

The electronic level enables you to take pictures with your camera level and plumb. This ensures that the camera isn't tilted right or left, or up or down. The end result is you get images that look correct and not like they were photographed by a drunken sailor. When you're not shooting in Live View mode, the electronic level is most useful when you have the camera mounted on a tripod. To display the electronic level on your LCD monitor:

1. **Mount your camera on a tripod.**

   You can also use the electronic level when handholding the camera. However, it's more difficult to get accurate results, and you can't hold the camera as steady because it's away from your body.

2. **Press the Info button twice.**

   The electronic level displays on your LCD monitor. The left image in Figure 11-17 shows what the level looks like when the camera isn't level horizontally and not plumb.

3. **Adjust the legs of your tripod until a solid green line appears in the center of the level.**

   This tells you the camera is level and plumb (see the right image in Figure 11-17).

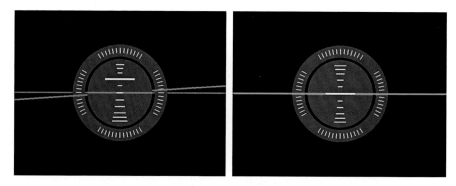

Figure 11-17: A level camera is a wonderful thing.

Customizing Your Camera

Many of the buttons on your camera can be customized to perform different takes. For example, you can change the task that the Shutter button performs when you press it halfway. Nine buttons on the camera are customizable. You may find it useful to customize some of these buttons. Instead of going through a long, boring Niagara-Falls-and-slowly-I-turn, step-by-step dissertation on how each button can be customized, I point you in the right direction with this short tutorial. Exploring each option for each button is another good rainy day project. If it's still rainy at night, shoot some reflections of city streets. Just make sure you're under cover when you do it so you don't damage your camera. To customize the buttons on your camera:

1. **Press the Menu button.**

   The previously used menu displays.

2. **Use the Multi-controller to navigate to the Custom Functions tab.**

   The last-used Custom Functions option is highlighted.

3. **Use the Multi-controller or the Quick Control dial to highlight the Custom Functions tab.**

   The last-used Custom Functions option is highlighted.

4. **Rotate the Quick Control dial to highlight C.Fn III: Operations/Others (see the left image in Figure 11-18).**

5. **Press Set.**

   The C.Fn III: Operations/Others custom functions display. Custom Controls is the fifth option (see the right image in Figure 11-18). As you can see, you can customize quite a few buttons. The default option is displayed to the right of the button. For example, the default task performed by the Shutter button when pressed halfway is achieving focus automatically. The following steps show you how to customize the button. The steps are similar for the other customizable buttons.

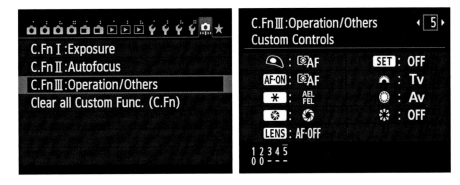

Figure 11-18: Customizing camera controls.

6. **Press Set.**

   The top of the camera is displayed next to the buttons that can be customized (see the left image in Figure 11-19).

7. **Use the Multi-controller or the Quick Control dial to highlight the button you want to customize. For this exercise, leave the Shutter button highlighted.**

   When you highlight a customizable button, a dark orange rectangle surrounds it. As you select different buttons, the button is highlighted on the camera image. The camera view also changes when you highlight a button that's on the front or back of the camera.

8. **After you highlight a button, press Set.**

   The options for the button display. The right image in Figure 11-19 shows the options for the Shutter button. The default task for the button is highlighted with an orange border.

9. **Use the Multi-controller or the Quick Control dial to highlight the desired option.**

   The task that the button performs is listed above the option.

10. **Press Set to finish customizing the button and then repeat Steps 7–10 to finish customizing camera buttons.**

11. **Press the Menu button when you've finished customizing buttons.**

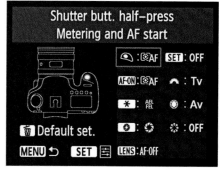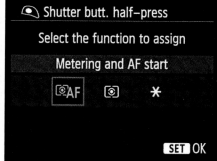

Figure 11-19: Customizing the Shutter button.

Ten (Plus One) Cool Projects

*A*h, another Part of Tens chapter. You guessed it — a list about stuff you can do with your camera, your images, and the software that came with it. In this chapter, I show you some interesting things, such as creating a makeshift tripod, creating abstract images, editing your images, going wireless, and more. So if you're up for extra bits of useful information, prop up your feet, get comfortable, and read on.

Strutting Your Stuff Online

Everybody likes to show off their work, and you can do this online in quite a few places. The granddaddy of photo-sharing sites is Flickr (`www.flickr.com`). This site enables you to post your images online, but it's more than just a photo-sharing site; it's a community as well. You can send your Flickr URL to other photographers to show off your work. Other members of the Flickr community can comment on your work. You can set up a free account and start uploading images to your personal gallery or set up a Pro account for $24.95 per year (see Figure 12-1).

Another great photo-sharing site is 500 PX (see Figure 12-2). 500PX is a lively community of photographers. To test the waters, you can sign up for a free account and (as of this writing) upload 10 images per week. If you like what you see, you can upgrade to a Plus membership for $19.95 per year, which gives you the option of selling your images online, with unlimited uploads per week. Such a deal!!

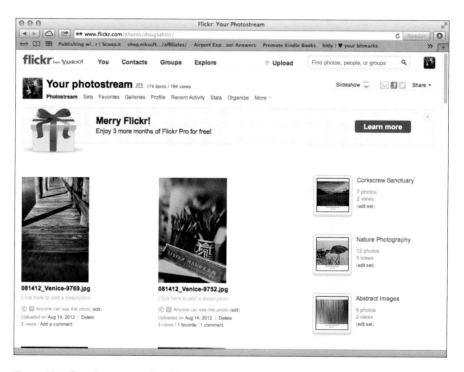

Figure 12-1: Showing your stuff on Flickr.

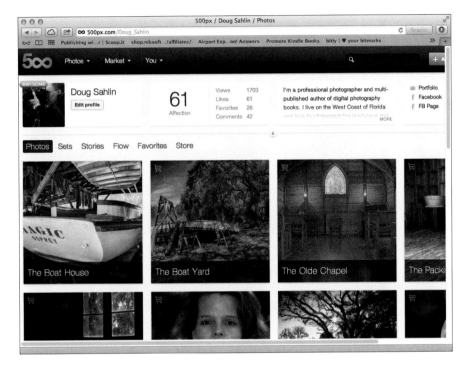

Figure 12-2: Strutting your stuff at 500PX.

Uploading Images to your Facebook Page

Another place you can show off your work online is at Facebook. If you
have a Facebook page (and who doesn't?), you can upload images from
ImageBrowser EX while creating an album for your Facebook Wall. Here's
how you do it:

1. **Launch ImageBrowser EX.**

2. **Select the images you want to upload to your Facebook wall.**

3. **Click the Share button and then choose Upload to Facebook Album.**

   The Canon Utilities Uploader for Facebook appears (see Figure 12-3).

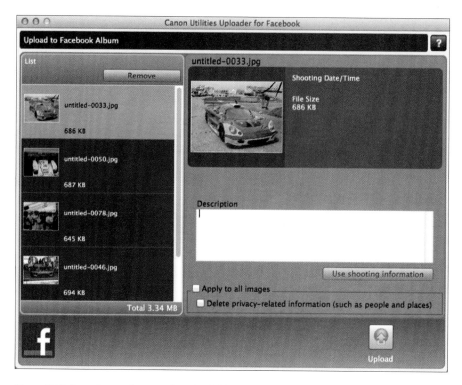

Figure 12-3: I'm going to show my Facebook friends some cool images.

4. Select an image and enter a description for the image.

This call's on you, Lou. Write whatever you normally write when you create a Facebook album of your images. You have the option to apply the same description to all images in the album.

5. If desired, click the Use Shooting Information button.

This adds shooting information to the description. Included are the camera model, shutter speed, aperture, and ISO. Upload this information at your own risk; other photographers may glean some wisdom from your post and steal your thunder.

6. If desired, click the Delete privacy related information (such as people and places) check box.

This disavows all records of the innocent or guilty parties in the image, which is useful if you shoot pictures of people who are part of a witness-protection program. Kidding!

7. **Review the information before uploading to Facebook.**

   Note that there is a Remove button in the left side of the dialog box. If you decide not to upload an image to Facebook, select it from the left column and click Remove.

8. **Click Upload.**

   When you upload for the first time, you'll be asked a series of questions regarding your Facebook page and Canon's Utilities application. It's all standard stuff. After you go through that rigmarole, you'll see the Upload Confirmation dialog box (see Figure 12-4).

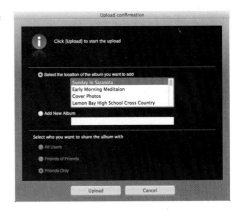

Figure 12-4: Set your controls for the heart of the sun.

9. **Select the album to which you want to add the images, or enter the name of a new album.**

   In most instances, you'll choose the latter. When you do, the utility creates the new album for your Facebook wall.

10. **After choosing an album, or entering the name of a new album, choose an option that determines who will see the album.**

    You can choose to make the album visible to all users, friends of friends, or friends only.

11. **Click Upload.**

    A dialog box appears, informing you about the status of the upload. After the upload is complete, another dialog box appears, telling you the upload is complete.

12. **When the Upload Is Complete dialog appears, click OK.**

    This closes the Canon Utilities Facebook Uploader and you can now edit more images, upload more images, or visit Facebook and review the album (see Figure 12-5).

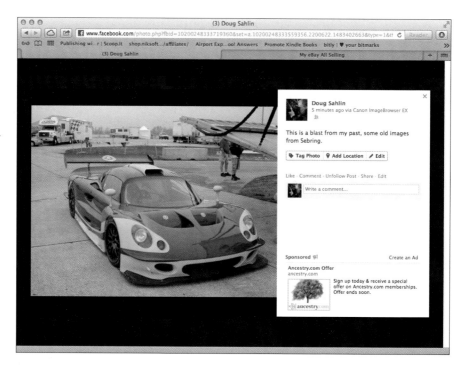

Figure 12-5: An album uploaded to Facebook is a thing of beauty.

Creating a Makeshift Tripod

Your EOS 6D can capture images in very low-light conditions. However, at times, you absolutely can't do without a tripod. But what do you do when you've left home without one? Here are some ways you can steady your camera without a tripod:

- **Switch to Live View mode and place the camera near the edge of a table.** If you can see the tabletop in the viewfinder or LCD monitor, move the camera closer to the edge.

- **Hold the camera against a wall.** Use this technique when you rotate the camera 90 degrees (also known as *Portrait mode*).

- **Lean against a wall and spread your legs slightly.** This is known as the *human tripod.* Press the Shutter button gently when you exhale.

- **Use a small beanbag to steady the camera.** You can just throw the beanbag in your camera bag; it doesn't take up much space. Place your camera on the beanbag and move it to achieve the desired composition. You can purchase beanbags at your local camera store.

As an alternative to the bean bag, you can carry a baggie filled with uncooked rice (cooked rice is messy and will spoil) in your camera bag. Place your camera on the bag and move it until you achieve the desired composition.

In addition to using one of these techniques, use the 2-Second Self-Timer. This gives the camera a chance to stabilize from any vibration that occurs when you press the Shutter button. These techniques are also great when you're on vacation and don't have the room to carry a tripod in your baggage.

Creating Abstract Images in the Camera

When you stretch the envelope, you can create some very cool images with your camera. A technique I like to use is controlled motion blur when photographing vertical objects such as tree trunks. If you're a nature photographer, this technique will spice up your portfolio. To create an abstract image:

1. **Attach the desired lens to the camera.**

   Choose a lens with a focal length of 80mm or greater.

2. **Rotate the Mode dial to Av (Aperture Priority).**

   You're using the aperture to control how long the shutter is open.

3. **Press the ISO button and then rotate the Main dial to set the ISO speed to 100.**

   You want the shutter to be open for a long time. The lowest ISO setting makes the camera less sensitive to light requiring a longer shutter speed.

4. **Rotate the Main dial to specify the smallest aperture (highest f-stop value) for the lens you're using.**

   This ensures that the shutter will be open for a long time.

5. **Find an interesting subject.**

   Closely spaced trees or tall grass are ideal subjects for this technique.

6. **Aim your camera at the base of the subject, and then press the Shutter button halfway.**

   The camera achieves focus.

7. **Press the Shutter button fully and slowly move the camera up.**

   The shutter opens, and the picture is taken. Depending on the ambient light, your lens may be open for several seconds. When you slowly move the camera up, you create abstract patterns of nature(see Figure 12-6).

8. Edit your pictures.

When you edit images in an application like Photoshop or Photoshop Elements, you can use filters to tweak the images. Figure 12-7 shows an abstract image created using this technique, as it appears after being edited in Photoshop.

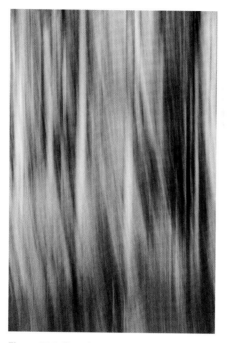

Figure 12-6: Creating an abstract image in camera.

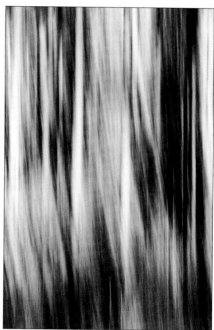

Figure 12-7: A tweaked abstract image.

Editing Your Images in Photoshop Elements

The software Canon provided with your EOS 6D will get the job done. But if you want a really powerful image-editing application on a beer budget, consider purchasing Adobe Photoshop Elements 11.0. This image-editing powerhouse gives you the power to manage your images, work with multiple keywords, find images, and much more. And that's just the Organizer. Elements is also a three-pronged image editor. You can edit images using the: Guided Edit Panel, Edit Quick mode, or Full Edit mode. If you're new to image editing, the Guided Edit panel guides you through the image-editing process. If you want the quick, down, and *Dirty Harry* version of the Editor, use the Edit Quick mode. As the title implies, this version enables you to quickly edit an image. If you want the full-course treatment from soup to nuts, edit your images in the Edit Full mode.

Photoshop Elements 11 gives you the power to crop, resize, color correct, adjust your image, and much more. If you're in an artsy-farsty state of mind, you'll find a plethora of filters you can use to edit your images. You can also use third-party filters, such as Nik Software, Alien Skin, and so on. Photoshop Elements 11 is too cool for school (see Figure 12-8). As of this writing, the application sells for a meager $99.99. So much power for such a small investment is a great deal, Lucille.

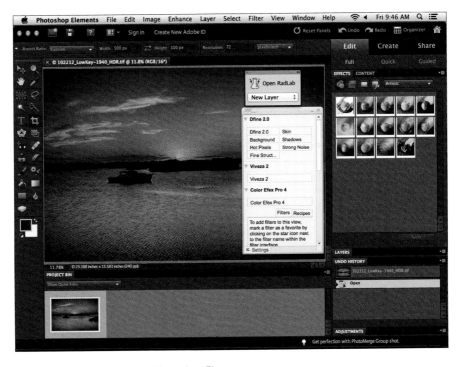

Figure 12-8: Editing images in Photoshop Elements

Creating Multiple Exposures In-Camera

Back in the days of film, photographers had to resort to trickery to expose two images on one piece of film. Your EOS 6D can create multiple exposures in camera and you don't have to resort to any kind of chicanery to get the job done. All you need to know is where to enable multiple-exposure photography in the camera menu, and then have a creative eye for subjects that would look good when combined on a single image. To create multiple exposures in camera:

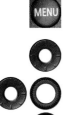

1. **Press the Menu button.**

   The last used menu displays.

2. **Use the Multi-controller to navigate to the Shooting Settings 4 tab.**

3. **Use the Multi-controller or the Quick Control dial to highlight Multiple Exposure (see the left image in Figure 12-9), and then press Set.**

   The Multiple Exposure menu options appear (see the right image in Figure 12-9) and the Multiple Exposure option is selected. (Multiple exposures are disabled by default.)

4. **With the Multiple Exposure option still selected press Set.**

   The option to enable Multiple Exposures appears (see the left image in Figure 12-10).

5. **Use the Multi-controller or the Quick Control dial to highlight Enable and press Set.**

   You're returned to the Multiple Exposure menu and are one step closer to shooting multiple exposures.

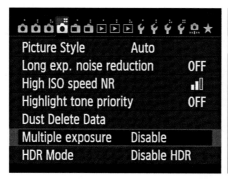

Figure 12-9: Multiple exposures in-camera. How cool!

6. **Use the Multi-controller or the Quick Control dial to highlight Multi-expos ctrl and press Set.**

   The Multiple Exposure options are displayed (see the right image in Figure 12-10).

7. **Use the Multi-controller or the Quick Control dial to highlight one of the following:**

   • *Additive:* Each exposure is added cumulatively to create the single image. You'll have to employ negative exposure compensation to decrease the exposure of each image so all of the images add up to a correctly exposed image. If you're combining two images, set exposure compensation to –1 stop; for three images, –1.5 stops; for four images, –2 stops.

- *Average:* Negative exposure compensation is applied to each image. The amount of negative exposure is determined by the number of images you're combining.

8. **Press Set.**

   You're returned to the Multiple Exposures menu and have one more decision to make.

9. **Use the Multi-controller or the Quick Control dial to highlight No of Exposures and then press Set.**

   The Number of Exposures option appears (see the left image in Figure 12-11). This determines how many images will be combined to create your multiple exposure.

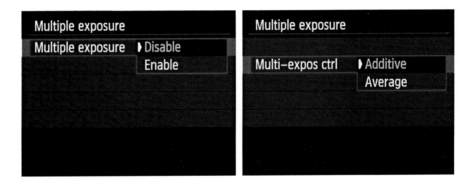

Figure 12-10: Decisions, decisions!

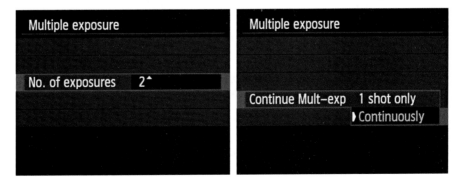

Figure 12-11: Determining how many images will be included in the final image.

10. **Use the Multi-controller or the Quick Control dial to select the number of images, and then press Set.**

    You can combine from 2 to 9 exposures to create your multiple exposure image. After you press Set, you're returned to the Multiple Exposure menu.

11. **Use the Multi-controller or the Quick Control dial to highlight Continue Multi-exp, and then press Set.**

    In this menu (see the right image in Figure 12-11) you choose whether to create one multiple exposure, or continuous multiple exposures. If you choose the latter option, you'll have to disable multiple exposures to return to single image exposures.

12. **Use the Multi-controller or the Quick Control dial to highlight the desired option, and then press Set.**

    The option is applied and you're returned to the Multiple Exposure menu.

13. **Begin multiple-exposure photography.**

If you shoot in LiveView mode, you'll see the exposures combined so far. You'll also be able to compose your multiple exposure after taking one or more shots. As you move the camera, the subjects in the frame are overlaid on the previous exposures. In the viewfinder, you'll see the Continuous Shooting icon with the number of frames remaining to be shot to complete your multiple exposure.

Choosing subjects for multiple-exposure images can be tricky. If you combine a busy subject, with another busy subject, your multiple exposure will look like a surreal Salvador Dali painting. That's fine if that's the look you're after, but if you want the subjects to be recognizable, I suggest you have one subject that is the main focal point of your multiple exposure, with the other images contributing to the overall look, but not distracting from the focal point. The easiest way to grasp multiple-exposure photography is to shoot lots of multiple exposures. Figure 12-12 is an example of a multiple-exposure image using two exposures.

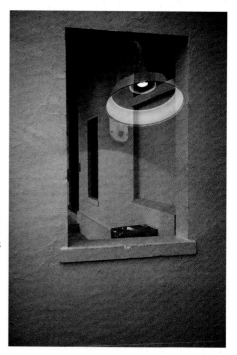

Figure 12-12: Creating multiple exposures for fun and profit.

Creating HDR Images

HDR images are all the rage. An HDR image combines multiple exposures of a scene with a wide dynamic range to create a single image that shows details in the shadow areas and bright areas of the image. Many photographers use camera-menu commands with expensive software to create HDR images, but you can create HDR images with your EOS 6D as follows:

1. **Press the Menu button.**

   The last-used menu displays.

2. **Use the Multi-controller to navigate to the Shooting Settings 4 tab.**

3. **Use the Multi-controller or the Quick Control dial to highlight HDR Mode (see the left image in Figure 12-13), and then press Set.**

   The HDR Mode menu is displayed (see the right image in Figure 12-13) and the HDR Mode option is selected.

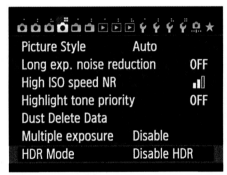
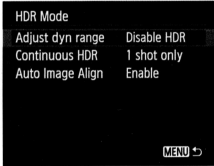

Figure 12-13: Creating HDR images starts in the camera menu.

4. **Press Set.**

   The HDR exposure options are displayed (see the left image in Figure 12-14).

5. **Use the Multi-controller or the Quick Control dial to highlight one of the following options:**

   • Auto: The camera sets the exposures based on the overall tonality in the scene. This is a good way to get started with HDR photography. If, after examining an HDR image, you notice that there's not enough detail in the overall image, you can choose one of the remaining options.

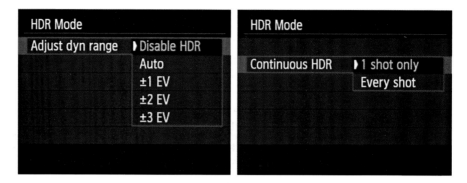

Figure 12-14: HDR, here we come.

- ±1 EV: The camera captures three images; one image is underexposed by 1 EV, one image is captured with the exposure deemed correct for the scene by the camera metering device, and one image that is overexposed by 1 EV.

- ±2 EV: The camera captures three images; one image is underexposed by 2 EV, one image is captured with the exposure deemed correct for the scene by the camera metering device, and one image that is overexposed by 2 EV. Use this option for scenes with a range of tones from shadows to bright lights.

- ±3 EV: The camera captures three images; one image is underexposed by 3 EV, one image is captured with the exposure deemed correct for the scene by the camera metering device, and one image that is overexposed by 3 EV. Use this option for scenes with an extreme dynamic range from very dark shadows to bright highlights.

6. **Press Set.**

   The exposure option you choose will be applied to the next HDR images you create and you're returned to the HDR mode menu.

7. **Use the Multi-controller or the Quick Control dial to highlight Continuous HDR and press Set.**

   The Continuous HDR options are displayed (refer to the right image in Figure 12-14).

8. **Use the Multi-controller or the Quick Control dial to highlight one of the following options:**

   - *One Shot:* Creates an HDR image the next time you press the Shutter button.

   - *Continuous:* Creates HDR images continuously until you disable HDR shooting.

9. **Press Set.**

   The option is applied and you're returned to the HDR mode menu.

10. **Use the Multi-controller or Quick Control dial to highlight Auto Image Align and then press Set.**

    The Auto Image Align options are displayed. Images are aligned by default. The only time I would suggest disabling this option is when you create HDR images with the camera mounted on a tripod.

11. **Press the Shutter button halfway to return to shooting mode and create some HDR images.**

    When you shoot HDR images, the camera captures three images as you specify through the camera menu. The camera does a good job of aligning the images, but you do need to hold the camera as steady as possible. If you're shooting in a low-light situation, and the shutter speed is too slow to create sharp images, increase the ISO until the shutter speed is fast enough to ensure a blur-free image, or mount the camera on a tripod. Figure 12-15 shows an HDR image. If this image had not been photographed with HDR, the details on the side of the boat would not be visible and the boat would be a black silhouette.

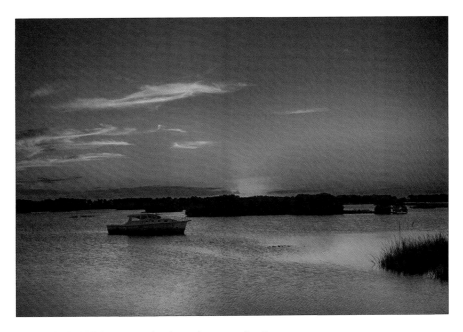

Figure 12-15: HDR increases the dynamic range of an image.

Going Wireless

Your EOS 6D has more cool features than there are Smiths in the New York phone book. Well almost. But I would be remiss if I didn't cover one very cool feature: Your EOS 6D is a Wi-Fi device. When you enable Wi-Fi with your EOS 6D, you can connect to an existing Wi-Fi network, transfer images to another EOS 6D, control your camera wirelessly with the EOS Utility that ships with your camera, upload images to Canon Gateway, and more. In this section, I show you how to enable wireless on your camera; then I show you how to control your camera remotely with your smartphone. To enable wireless on your EOS 6D:

1. **Press the Menu button.**

   The last-used menu displays.

2. **Use the Multi-controller to navigate to the Camera Settings 3 tab.**

3. **Use the Multi-controller or the Quick Control dial to highlight Wi-Fi (see the left image in Figure 12-16), and then press Set.**

   The Wi-Fi options are displayed (see the right image in Figure 12-16).

4. **Use the Multi-controller or Quick Control dial to highlight Enable, and then press Set.**

   You're ready to fly the friendly skies with Wi-Fi.

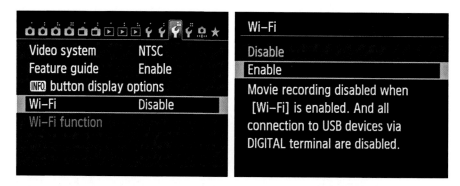

Figure 12-16: Enabling Wi-Fi.

You do use more of the camera battery when you enable Wi-Fi. Therefore I advise you to disable the Wi-Fi feature when you're not using it.

To use your camera Wi-Fi with other devices, you must give the camera a nickname. In essence, the nickname you give the camera is the name of the Wi-Fi hub emanating from the camera. To give your camera a nickname:

1. **Press the Menu button.**

   The last-used menu displays.

2. **Enable Wi-Fi as outlined in the previous steps.**

3. **Use the Multi-controller to navigate to the Camera Settings 3 tab.**

4. **Use the Multi-controller or the Quick Control dial to highlight Wi-Fi Functions (see the left image in Figure 12-17) and press Set.**

   When you choose this command for the first time, your only option is to register a nickname for the camera (see the right image in Figure 12-17).

5. **Use the Multi-controller or the Quick Control dial to highlight OK, and then press Set.**

   The Register Nickname menu appears . You can create a nickname with up to 16 characters.

6. **Press the Quick Control button to place the cursor in the bottom half of the dialog box — you know, the place with the letters and numbers.**

   Canon calls this a Virtual Keyboard.

7. **Use the Quick Control dial to navigate to the desired number or letter, and then press Set.**

   The number or letter appears in the upper part of the dialog box.

8. **Continue in this manner until you've spelled out the nickname.**

   Your author's nickname for his camera is shown in the left image in Figure 12-18.

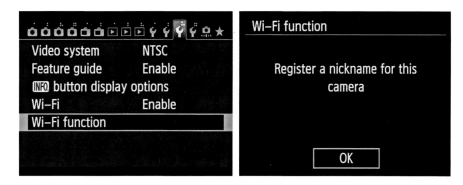

Figure 12-17: Hmm. The camera needs a nickname. Spike?

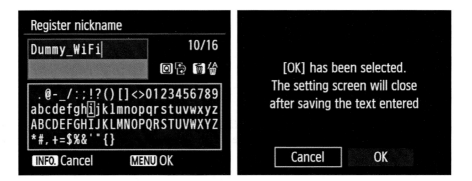

Figure 12-18: Registering a camera nickname.

9. **Press Menu when you've finished entering the nickname for your camera.**

   A dialog box appears, asking you to confirm the nickname (refer to the right image in Figure 12-18).

10. **Use the Multi-controller or the Quick Control dial to highlight OK, and then press Set.**

    Your camera nickname is now registered.

The next time you enable Wi-Fi functions, you see the menu shown in Figure 12-19. As you can see, there are quite a few functions you can enable. Unfortunately, many of them are particular to your home network, and you'll need to know the username and password to connect and use these functions. But not to worry, intrepid photographer/geek. After you select a Wi-Fi function, press Info to get some help setting up the camera with the function. In the next section, I show you what I think is the most important Wi-Fi function: the capability to connect the camera to your smartphone (or for that matter, to an iPod Touch).

Controlling Your Camera with Your Smartphone

If you've got a Smartphone you can control your camera with it. Or as your intrepid author found out, you can use an iPod Touch (Fourth Generation or newer) to control your camera. You can download an app that Canon has created to control your camera and view images stored on the memory card on the device screen. Now, how cool is that? The following steps show how to control your camera with an iPhone or an iPod Touch.

1. **Download and install the Canon remote app for your iPhone or iPod Touch.**

   The app is completely free. You can download it from this website, which will connect with iTunes on your computer:

   ```
   https://itunes.apple.com/us/app/eos-remote/
   id565839396?mt=8
   ```

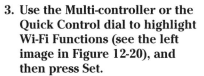

2. **Use the Multi-controller to navigate to the Camera Settings 3 tab.**

3. **Use the Multi-controller or the Quick Control dial to highlight Wi-Fi Functions (see the left image in Figure 12-20), and then press Set.**

   The Wi-Fi functions are displayed.

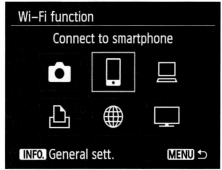

Figure 12-19: The Wi-Fi functions for your Canon EOS 6D.

4. **Use the Multi-controller or the Quick Control dial to highlight Smartphone (refer to the right image in Figure 12-20), and then press Set.**

   The Connect'n Method dialog box appears (see the left image in Figure 12-21).

5. **Use the Multi-controller to select Camera point mode, and then use the Multi-controller or Quick Control dial to select OK.**

   The Network settings dialog box appears (see the right image in Figure 12-21).

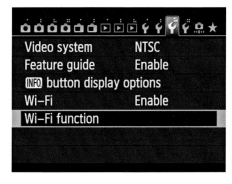
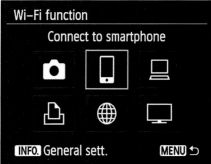

Figure 12-20: Connecting the camera to a smartphone.

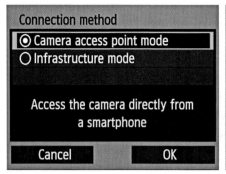 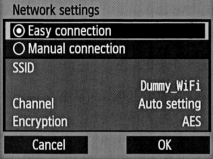

Figure 12-21: Connecting to the network.

6. **Use the Multi-controller to select Easy Connection and then use the Multi-controller or Quick Control dial to select OK.**

   A dialog box appears with the settings you need to connect your smartphone to the camera's Wi-Fi network (see Figure 12-22).

7. **Access your iPhone or iPod Touch network settings, and enter the camera network information to connect your device to the camera network.**

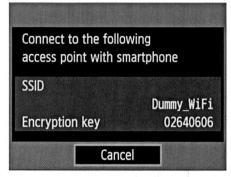

Figure 12-22: The settings to connect your smartphone to the camera network.

   After you enter the information, you see the nickname of the camera as the network to which your smartphone is currently connected.

8. **Start the EOS Remote app on your smartphone.**

9. **Click Camera Connection (see the left image in Figure 12-23).**

   The app detects your camera.

10. **Click the camera name.**

    Pairing begins (see the right image in Figure 12-23).

    After the camera and device are paired, you see a dialog box on your camera menu that asks you to confirm that you want to connect to the smartphone (see the left image in Figure 12-24).

11. **Use the Multi-controller or Quick Control dial to select OK and then press Set.**

    A dialog box appears, telling you that the settings have been configured, assigning them to Set_1 (refer to the right image in Figure 12-24). You can either accept or change the default settings name. If you're going to work with multiple devices, I suggest you change the settings name as shown in the following steps.

12. Use the Multi-controller or Quick Control dial to highlight Change Settings and then press Set.

The Virtual Keyboard appears.

13. Use the Virtual Keyboard to enter a new name for the settings.

This keyboard functions identically to the keyboard you used to set the camera nickname (see the left image in Figure 12-25).

14. Use the Virtual Keyboard to enter a new name for the settings.

If you are going to connect to lots of devices, it's a good idea to give each setting a unique name (see the right image in Figure 12-25).

15. Press Menu to apply the changes.

The dialog box changes to show that the settings have been configured with the new name (see the left image in Figure 12-26).

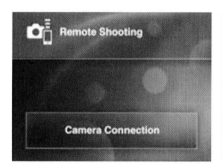
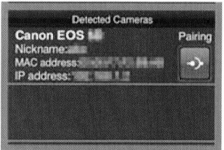

Figure 12-23: Pairing the camera with the smartphone.

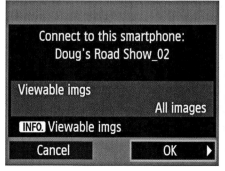
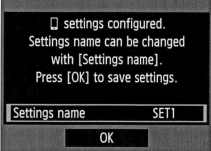

Figure 12-24: Another successful pairing.

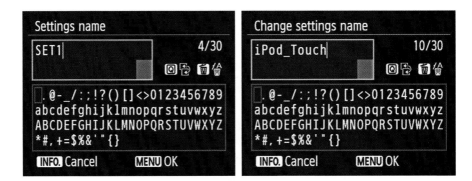

Figure 12-25: I now christen thee . . .

16. **Use the Multi-controller or the Quick Control Dial to highlight OK, and then press Set.**

The Connection screen appears (refer to the right image in Figure 12-26).

17. **Press Menu.**

You close the connection.

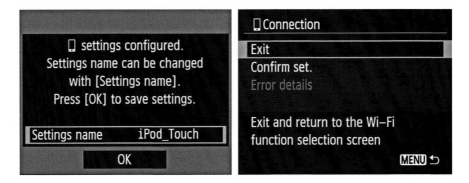

Figure 12-26: Saving the Settings with a new name.

That seemed like a lot of work to get connected, but the good thing is you only have to do it once. After you save the settings, you can easily connect your camera to your smartphone by following these steps:

1. **Launch the EOS app on your smartphone.**

2. **Use the Multi-controller to navigate to the Camera Settings 3 tab.**

3. **Use the Multi-controller or the Quick Control dial to highlight Wi-Fi Functions (see the left image in Figure 12-27), and then press Set.**

   The Wi-Fi functions are displayed.

4. **Use the Multi-controller or the Quick Control dial to highlight Smartphone (refer to the right image in Figure 12-27), and then press Set.**

   The Connect to Smartphone menu appears (see the left image in Figure 12-28).

5. **Use the Multi-controller or Quick Control Dial to highlight your Smartphone settings, and then press Set.**

   The Connect to Smartphone dialog refreshes (see the right image in Figure 12-28).

6. **Use the Multi-controller or Quick Control dial to highlight OK, and then press Set.**

   You camera is now available to your smartphone.

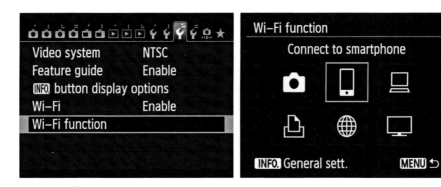

Figure 12-27: Connecting to your smartphone.

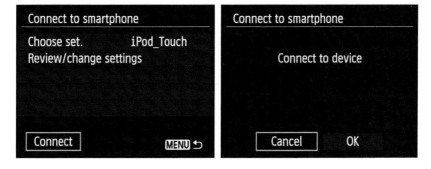

Figure 12-28: Using your connection settings.

7. On your Smartphone EOS Remote app, click Connect to Camera.

After you connect to the camera, you can use the EOS Remote app to trigger the Shutter button and view images stored on the memory card on your Smartphone.

This option is wonderful for the busy photographer working on location with the camera on a tripod. The photographer can work with subjects, showing them how to pose and so on. It's also great for a photographer photographing still-life images. The photographer can make changes to the still life and then use the Smart phone to take a picture. After the picture has been taken, the photographer can review it on the smartphone instead of walking back to the camera. This app saves time and shoe leather. How cool is that?

Enabling GPS

Your camera is equipped with a GPS receiver. When it's enabled, you can use this option to log the GPS coordinates of each place you photograph. The GPS coordinates are stored as metadata with each image. In addition, you can store a GPS log on the camera that you can use to create a map of the places you photographed. In order to log GPS coordinates, you must first enable GPS as follows:

1. Press the Menu button.

The last-used menu displays.

2. Use the Multi-controller to navigate to the Camera Settings 3 tab.

3. Use the Multi-controller or the Quick Control dial to highlight GPS (see the left image inFigure 12-29), and then press Set.

The GPS menu appears (see the right image in Figure 12-29). Select GPS is the only option available when GPD is disabled.

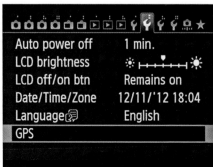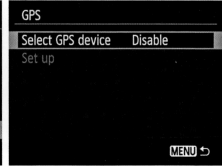

Figure 12-29: Enabling GPS.

4. **Press Set.**

The GPS menu expands; Internal GPS is the default option (see Figure 12-30).

5. **Press Set.**

You're ready to receive signals on the camera GPS from GPS satellites when you take a picture.

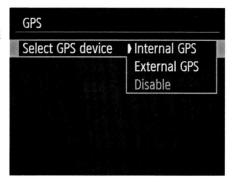

Figure 12-30: Select a GPS device.

When you enable GPS, you see the GPS icon in your viewfinder and on your LCD panel. If the GPS icon is flashing, the camera has not acquired a GPS signal. When the GPS signal is steady, your camera is receiving signals from a GPS satellite.

When you enable GPS, the camera uses default settings to refresh the GPS signal. You can change the refresh rate and view other information about the current GPS coordinates by following these steps:

1. **Enable Internal GPS as outlined in the previous steps.**

After you enable GPS the Set Up option becomes available (see the left image in Figure 12-31.

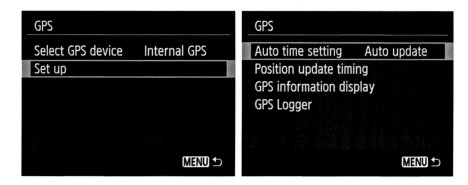

Figure 12-31: Setting up the Internal GPS.

2. **Use the Multi-controller or Quick Control dial to highlight Set Up, and then press Set.**

The Set Up options for the Internal GPS are displayed (see the right image in Figure 12-31. The first option is Auto Time Setting, which is set to Auto Update by default. If you disable this option, the GPS will acquire the signal and coordinates of the position where you enabled GPS, but will not update the signal as you move, which defeats the purpose of GPS. I suggest you leave this option at its default setting.

3. **Use the Multi-controller or Quick Control Dial to highlight Position Update Timing, and then press Set.**

   The Update Timing options are displayed (see the left image in Figure 12-32).

4. **Use the Multi-controller or Quick Control Dial to highlight the desired timing interval.**

   The default option is 15 seconds, which is fine for most photographers. However, if you have a tendency to spend a long time in one location, you can specify a longer interval for updates. If you specify a shorter interval for updates, GPS drains the battery quicker.

5. **Press Set.**

   The desired update timing interval is applied and you're returned to the GPS Set up menu.

6. **Use the Multi-controller or the Quick Control dial to highlight the GPS information display, and and press Set.**

   The GPS information display appears (see the right image in Figure 12-32). This information is useful when you first enable GPS at a specific location. The information provided is the longitude and latitude of your current position, the date and time (UTC, which is essentially Greenwich Mean Time). In addition the display shows you the relative strength of the satellite signal. If you see 3D listed next to the satellite strength, you can receive elevation information as well.

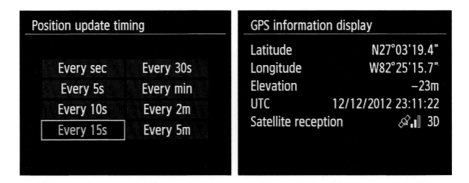

Figure 12-32: Setting the Update Timing interval and reviewing information.

Take the elevation information with lots of grains of salt; it's not that accurate, as you can see by the elevation listed in the display on the right side of Figure 12-32. According to this display, I'm 23 meters below sea level, and I can assure you I was high and dry. If you see 2D listed next to the satellite strength, you can only receive longitude and latitude information.

7. **After reviewing the information, press Set.**

   You're returned to the GPS Set up menu. The only other option is the GPS Logger, which I cover in the next section.

8. **Press the Shutter button halfway and start taking pictures.**

   As long as you see the GPS signal in your viewfinder (or on the LCD panel) and it's not blinking, you'll record GPS information with the images you photograph. When you create images with GPS enabled, the information can also be seen when you review images on your LCD monitor (see Figure 12-33).

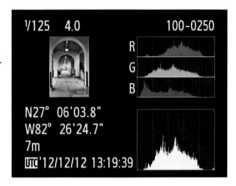

Figure 12-33: I knew this wasn't the legendary Atlantis.

GPS is a wonderful option; keep in mind, however, that it does drain the battery. Many photographers will enable GPS, shoot some images, put the camera in the camera bag, stow it away in the closet, and then not use the camera for a week. This drains the battery; even though the camera's not in use, the GPS is still acquiring a signal at the specified update time interval. When you're not using GPS, disable it. It would be wonderful if Canon had a switch on the camera that disabled GPS, but unfortunately they don't — which means you'll have to access the camera menu to disable GPS and stop the drain on the battery. Alternatively, you can remove the battery from the camera.

Mapping Your Day

When you use GPS, you can enable an option that logs the GPS coordinates of every place where you capture an image with your camera. You can download this information to your memory card and use it in conjunction with Canon's Mapping Utility to create a map that shows the locations where you created photographs. To map your day with GPS:

1. **Enable GPS as outlined in the previous section.**

   Don't leave the camera menu yet. There's one more thing you have to do before you can log the GPS information.

2. **Use the Multi-controller or the Quick Control Dial to highlight GPS Logger (see the left image in Figure 12-34), and then press Set.**

   The GPS Logger menu appears.

3. **Use the Multi-controller or the Quick Control Dial to highlight Enable (refer to the right image in Figure 12-34), and then press Set.**

   The GPS Logger is enabled. When the GPS Logger is enabled, you see the LOG icon displayed on your LCD monitor and on your LCD panel.

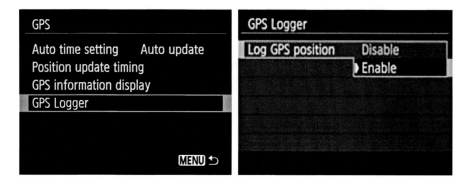

Figure 12-34: Enabling the GPS Logger.

4. **Press the Shutter button halfway to return to picture taking mode and shoot up a storm.**

   When you're done with your photo shoot, you need to transfer the GPS Log to your memory card.

5. **Press Menu.**

   The last-used menu is displayed.

6. **Use the Multi-controller to navigate to Camera Settings 3 tab, use the Multi-controller or the Quick Control Dial to highlight GPS Logger, and then press Set.**

   Now the GPS Logger can download log information, and also can delete data.

7. **Use the Multi-controller or the Quick Control dial to highlight Transfer Data to Card (see the left image in Figure 12-35), and then press Set.**

   The menu refreshes and a progress bar appears, showing you the download status (see the right image in Figure 12-35). At this stage, you may be tempted to delete the log data, but I always prefer to play devil's advocate, assume that the transfer failed, and keep the log on the card until I'm sure I've got it on my computer.

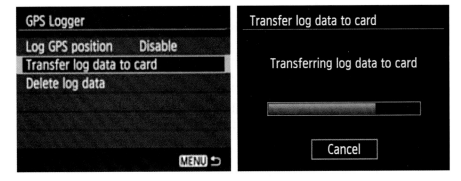

Figure 12-35: Downloading data to the card.

8. **After the data has transferred to the card, power off the camera and remove the card.**

You're now ready to map your day.

After you remove the card from your camera, you use the Canon Map utility to create a map that uses the GPS log to show all the places where you took pictures. The Map utility is included with the software that shipped with your camera.

If you didn't install the software, do so before attempting to use the GPS log information. You will need Internet access to install the Map utility.

To map the GPS log information, follow these steps:

1. **Download the card to your computer using the ImageBrowser EX or your favorite image editing application.**

When you use ImageBrowser EX to download the images, you're prompted to download the GPS log information as well (see Figure 12-36). If you use another application to download images, you'll have to use the Windows Explorer or Macintosh Finder to locate the log file and download it to your computer. The log files you downloaded to the card are found in the GPS folder, which is a subfolder of the MISC folder. The log files have the .LOG extension.

2. **Launch the Canon Map Utility.**

On a Windows machine, you find the file on the All Programs part of the Start menu. Click Canon Utilities and then click the Map Utility icon.

On a Macintosh machine, go to the Canon Utilities folder, which is in the Applications folder.

In the Canon Utilities folder, you find a MapUtility folder. Click MapUtility.app to start the application (see Figure 12-36).

3. **Click the folder icon and then locate the images you want to map.**

   The images are imported. The position of each image is noted with a red dot (see Figure 12-37).

4. **Click an image in the Images tab to see a thumbnail of the image on the map (see Figure 12-38).**

   You can also click a dot on the map to see the image that was photographed at that location.

5. **Click the GPS Log Files tab.**

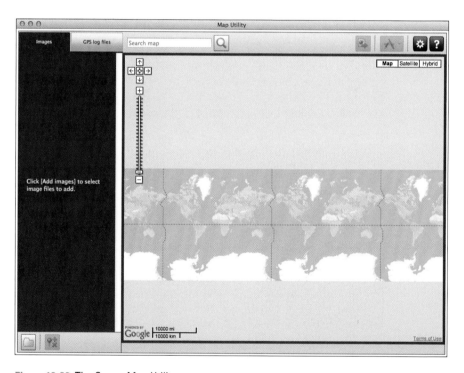

Figure 12-36: The Canon Map Utility.

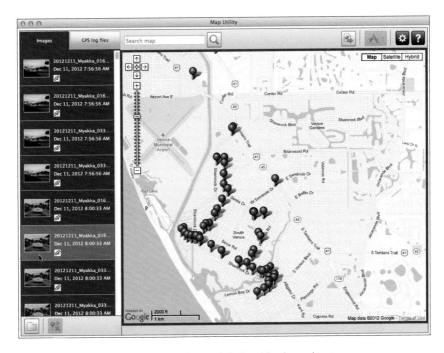

Figure 12-37: Wow. I covered a lot of ground during this photo shoot.

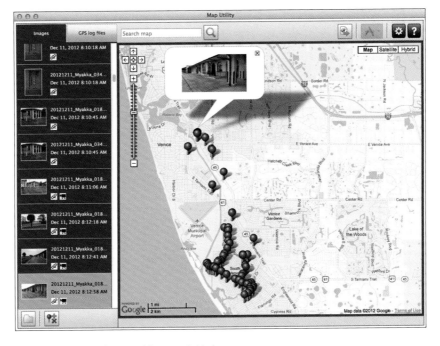

Figure 12-38: I was here and I created this image.

6. **Click the Import from File icon and then import the applicable log file.**

   If you use ImageBrowser EX to download your files and import your log files:

   - On a Windows machine, you find the log files in: Documents⟹ Canon Utilities⟹GPS Log Files.

   - On a Macintosh machine, you find the log files in: Documents⟹ Canon Utilities⟹GPS Log Files.

   After you import the log file, your photo shoot is mapped out (see Figure 12-39).

When you use the application to record multiple shoots, the log from each shoot is identified by the date the images were photographed appears in the GPS Log Files tab. When you click the icon for the log you want to review, it appears on the map.

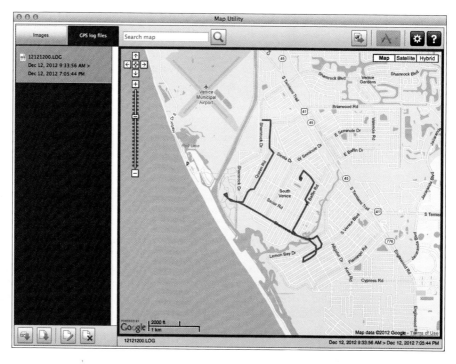

Figure 12-39: Geez, now I know where to look for that lens cap I lost.

Appendix

Digital SLR Settings and Shortcuts

*M*any people graduate to a digital SLR and think it's the ticket for creating great photos. Well it is, but there's a bit of technique involved. Part of that is your creativity and the way you see the world around you. You translate the vision that is in your head into an image when you capture it with your digital SLR.

To fully master your digital SLR and create compelling photos, you have to venture forth into a brave new world that involves making decisions about settings that will enable you to capture the images you see in your mind's eye. This does not happen when you shoot in your camera's automatic mode. When photographers have the urge to branch out, they turn to the manual for help. And then they get more confused. Which is where this appendix comes in. My goal in writing this appendix is to demystify taking photographs with a digital SLR.

Capturing Sporting Events

Photography is a wonderful pastime. You can use your camera to capture memories of the things that interest you. If you're a sports fan, you can photograph your favorite sport. You can photograph individual athletes, but sports have more to them than just the athletes. Whether your favorite sport is football or auto racing, each one has its own rituals. And every sport includes a supporting cast. When you photograph a sporting event, you photograph each chapter of the event, from the pre-games festivities, to the opening kick off, to the winning touchdown. Your creative mind, a knowledge of the sport, and the information in this section give you all the tools you need to tell a story. You begin at the beginning, before the athletes flex their muscles or the drivers start their engines.

Setting the camera

This section gives you a couple of different shooting scenarios. When you're photographing the pre-event festivities, you shoot in Aperture Priority mode. When your goal is to photograph an athlete preparing for the event, you want a shallow depth of field, therefore, you choose a large aperture (a small f/stop number). When you want to photograph the crowd, or a group of athletes practicing, you use a small aperture (a large f/stop number) to ensure a large depth of field. When your goal is to stop action, you shoot in Shutter Priority mode at a speed fast enough to freeze the action. For an athlete, you can freeze motion with a shutter speed as slow as 1/25 of a second. To stop a racecar dead in its tracks, you need a fast shutter speed of 1/2000 of a second. To capture the beauty of a speeding racecar with a motion blur, you pan the camera and shoot with a shutter speed of 1/125 of a second. The focal length you use varies depending on how close you can get to the action. If you're photographing a large crowd before the event, use a wide-angle focal length of 28 to 35mm. If you're photographing individual athletes, zoom in.

Taking the picture

When you photograph a sporting event, you have to be in the moment. Before the event starts, you can capture interesting pictures of the crowd, the athletes performing their pre-event rituals, and the athletes warming up. When the event starts, you can capture the frenetic action. When the event is well and truly underway, keep alert for any interesting situations that may arise and, of course, any team player who scores. If you're photographing an automobile race, be sure to include pictures of pit stops and other associated activities. And you probably want a picture or two of the winning driver spraying the champagne.

1. **Arrive at the event early and take pictures of anything that interests you.**

   You have to change settings based on what you're photographing.

2. **Photograph the pre-event activities, such as the introduction of the players, the coach meeting with her team on the sidelines, or if you're attending a race, pictures of the drivers getting ready.**

   You can get creative with your composition when you photograph the pre-race events. Don't be afraid to turn the camera diagonally or venture to an interesting vantage point. Let your inner child run amuck and capture some unusual pictures.

3. **Photograph the start of the event.**

   The action can get a little crazy. Each team is trying to gain an advantage over the other. If you're photographing a race, drivers may battle fiercely to achieve the lead by the first corner. You never know what might happen. Stay alert for any possibility. Hold the camera and be ready to compose an image when you see something interesting about to happen. Be proactive: Have the camera to your eye a split second before the crucial moment.

4. Photograph the middle of the event.

The middle of any event is a great time for photographers. If you're photographing an event such as a basketball or football game, you can get some shots of substitutions. You can also photograph the fans to capture their reactions to a winning score and so on. If you're photographing an auto race (as shown in Figure A-1), the cars are now a little battle weary, with tire marks, racer's tape, and other chinks in their armor.

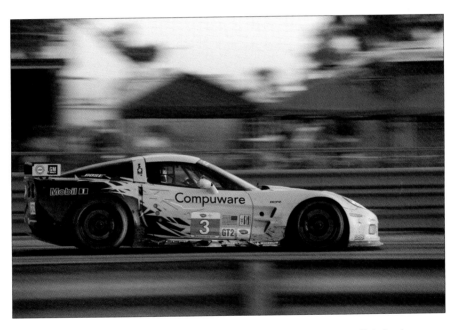

Figure A-1: Photograph the middle of the event when the participants are a little battle weary.

5. Photograph the end of the event.

Be on your toes, especially if the score is close. In the final minutes or final laps, it's do or die. Athletes give their all to win the event, which gives you opportunities for some great pictures.

6. Photograph the post-event activities.

Take photographs of the winning team celebrating and capture the glum looks of the losers. Take photographs of any award ceremonies. Tell the complete story of the event.

TIP

Photograph an athlete going through his pre-event ritual. Figure A-2 shows champion driver Allan McNish with a mask of concentration at the drivers' meeting.

Troubleshooting

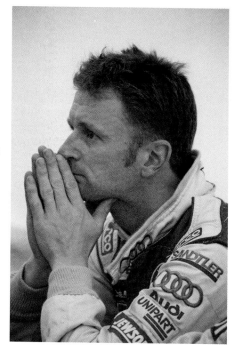

- ✔ **I don't know which mode to use.** If you're photographing athletes in motion, use Shutter Priority mode to freeze motion. If you're photographing people and things before the event, use Aperture Priority mode to control depth of field.

- ✔ **The picture isn't level.** This problem often happens when you're photographing people in motion, especially when you're panning the camera. Make sure that you're standing straight and that you don't lean when you pan the camera. You may also want to use the grid that's built into many cameras as a guide.

Figure A-2: Photograph athletes performing their pre-event rituals.

- ✔ **I can't get close to the action.** When you photograph a spectator event, sometimes you just need to wait for someone to move. Of course, always try to get a good seat ahead of time. If the event doesn't include assigned seating, arrive early.

Photographing Animals in the Wild

If you live near a state park or wilderness area, you can capture some wonderful photographs of animals such as deer, raccoons, and otters in their natural surroundings. You can easily spook these kinds of wild animals because they're relatively low in the food chain. They have a natural fear of people, which means you have to be somewhat stealthy to photograph them; patience is a virtue. If you're patient and don't do anything startling, you can capture great images of animals such as the one shown here.

If you live near a state park, go there often to find out in which areas of the park you're likely to find your subjects and to get to know the habits of those animals — including their feeding habits. After you know the habits of the animals you want to photograph, get familiar with the lay of the land, and use the settings I recommend, you can capture some wonderful wildlife images.

Setting the camera

The goal of this type of photography is to capture a photograph of an animal in the wild. You use Aperture Priority mode for this type of photography to control depth of field. The animal is the subject of your picture, therefore you use a large aperture to create a shallow depth of field and draw your viewer's attention to your subject. Continuous Auto-Focus mode enables the camera to update focus while the animal moves. You also use Continuous Drive mode to capture a sequence of images of the animal as it moves through the area. The focal length you use depends on how close you can safely approach the animal. Use image stabilization if you have to shoot at a slow shutter speed.

The slowest shutter speed you should use when handholding your camera is the reciprocal of the 35mm-equivalent focal length. For example, if your camera has a 1.6 focal length multiplier and you're using a 50mm lens, the slowest shutter speed you should use when holding the camera by hand is 1/100 of a second ($1 \div 50 \times 1.6$).

Taking the picture

When you're taking pictures of animals in their natural habitat, you have to stay out of the open so that you don't frighten the animal. I also recommend wearing clothing that helps you blend in with the surroundings.

1. **Go to a place where you've previously sighted the species you want to photograph, hide behind some natural cover, and wait.**

   Photograph during the early morning or late afternoon when the light is better and animals are out foraging for food.

2. **Switch to the camera settings mentioned earlier in this chapter.**

3. **When you see an animal, zoom in until the animal fills the frame, and then zoom out slightly.**

4. **Position the auto-focus point over the animal's eye, press the shutter button halfway to achieve focus, move the camera to compose the picture, and then press the shutter button fully to take the picture.**

   When you use Continuous Drive mode, the camera continues to capture images as long as you have your finger on the shutter button.

Zoom in tight on the animal to capture an intimate portrait and compose the image according to the Rule of Thirds. This kind of photo is as close as you'll get to shooting a portrait of a wild animal (see Figure A-3).

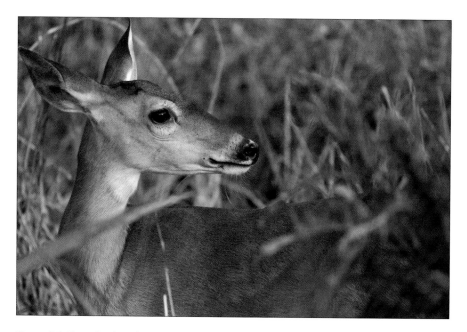

Figure A-3: Zoom in close for an intimate animal portrait.

Troubleshooting

- **The image isn't sharp.** Make sure you're shooting at an ISO that's high enough to enable a relatively fast shutter speed, and use image stabilization if your lens or camera has this feature. If you don't have the image stabilization feature, mount your camera on a tripod or monopod.

  Don't use image stabilization if the camera is mounted on a tripod because you may get undesirable results as the camera or lens attempts to compensate for operator motion when in fact the camera is rock steady.

- **The animal blends into the background.** The coloration of some animals causes those animals to blend into the background. Try shooting from a different angle. You can also use the largest aperture to blur the background as much as possible. If you use a large aperture, make sure you get the animal's eyes in focus. If you don't, the entire picture appears to be out of focus.

- **The animal disappears before I take the picture.** Make sure you're well hidden and not upwind from the animal.

Shooting Landscapes

No matter where you live, you can find lovely landscapes, usually within a few miles of your home. Landscape photography done right is stunning. It captures the mystery and grandeur of the place where you took the picture. When you photograph a landscape, your vantage point and the way you compose the photograph go a long way toward creating something that's a work of art and not just a snapshot. You want to draw viewers into the picture so that they take more than just a casual glance.

Setting the camera

When you photograph a beautiful landscape, you want to see every detail, which is why you use Aperture Priority mode and a small aperture. A wide-angle focal length lets you capture the majesty of the landscape in your photograph, and a low ISO setting gives you a noise-free image. However, if you're photographing landscapes on overcast days, you may have to increase the ISO setting to maintain a shutter speed of 1/30 of a second. If you don't want to increase the ISO setting, use image stabilization if your camera or lens has this feature, or mount your camera on a tripod.

When you photograph a landscape, you photograph the big picture: a wide sweeping brushstroke that captures the beauty of the area. So, you want every subtle detail to be in focus, which means you want a huge depth of field. In addition to a large depth of field, composition also plays a key role when you photograph a landscape.

 Being a great landscape photographer requires practice and a bit of study. Shoot landscapes whenever you have the chance and study the work of master landscape photographers, such as Ansel Adams, Clyde Butcher, and David Muench. Studying the work of the masters can help give you an eye for landscape photography and, after much practice, develop your own unique style. Google these photographers to see samples of their eye-popping work.

Taking the picture

You can photograph a landscape whenever you see one that strikes your fancy. However, whether you're photographing landscapes on vacation or at home, try to set aside a block of time in which to photograph landscapes. Travel to your favorite area, or spice things up and travel to a place you've never visited before. Then, you just need to embark on your quest to capture the perfect photograph of the area you're in.

1. **Enable the camera settings discussed previously in this chapter.**

2. **When you find an area that you want to photograph, find the ideal vantage point.**

Don't place the horizon line in the middle of the picture. Place the horizon line in the upper third of the image when the most important part of the landscape you're photographing dominates the bottom of the scene, such as when you're photographing sand dunes in the desert. Place the horizon line in the lower third of the image when the most important part of the landscape dominates the upper part of the scene you're photographing, such as when you're photographing a mountain range.

3. **Press the shutter button halfway to achieve focus, and then compose the image.**

If you're photographing with a zoom lens, zoom out until you see something you like in the viewfinder.

4. **Take the picture.**

To get the best shot possible, keep these points in mind:

✔ When you find an interesting element in the landscape, such as a photogenic rock or dead branch, move close to the object, zoom in, and then move around it until you see an interesting composition in your viewfinder (see Figure A-4).

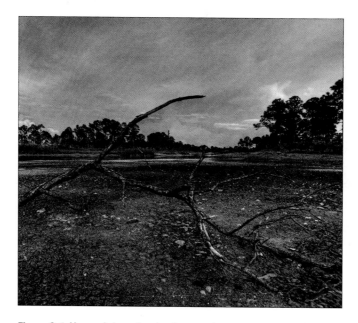

Figure A-4: Use an interesting landscape element to create an interesting picture.

- Many landscape photographers have tunnel vision and look straight ahead. Notice what's both above and below you. You may find an interesting photograph hiding there.

- Some people litter everywhere. Before taking your picture, take a good look at the area you have framed in the viewfinder to make sure there isn't any litter, such as empty soda cans or candy wrappers, that can ruin an otherwise great image.

- The best time to take great landscape pictures is early in the morning, just after the sun rises, or late in the afternoon, when the light is pleasing. The first hour and the last hour of daylight are known as the *Golden Hours,* times when you have great light for photographing landscapes because the light accentuates forms such as rocks and trees.

Barren landscapes can be saved with dramatic clouds. If you live near a place that's beautiful but stark, visit it when there are some moody clouds or thunderheads in the distance. Make this the focal point of your photograph by placing the horizon line in the lower part of the image (see Figure A-5).

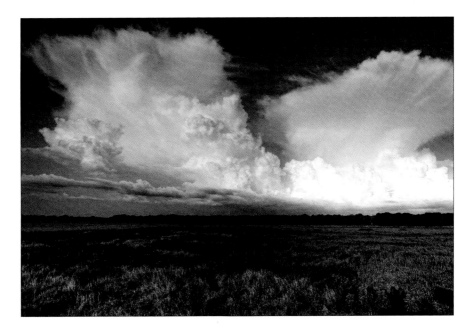

Figure A-5: Barren landscape and brooding clouds equals a compelling photograph.

Troubleshooting

- **The foreground is too busy.** If the picture has details such as twigs, vines, or branches that detract from the overall picture, move to a slightly different vantage point to remove the offending details from the image.

- **The background doesn't seem sharp.** When you're photographing a huge landscape that goes on for miles and miles, atmospheric haze can cause distant details to look soft. If you encounter this problem, consider purchasing a UV filter for your lens.

If your lenses have different accessory thread sizes, purchase filters for the largest-diameter lens you own, and then purchase a step-up ring for the smaller-diameter lenses. For example, if your biggest lens accepts 77mm filters and you also own a lens that accepts 58mm filters, buy a 58–77mm step-up ring, which is much cheaper than the cost of another filter.

- **There are telephone lines and houses in the picture.** Sometimes, you can't avoid getting a bit of civilization in your nature photos, but at other times, you can change your vantage point slightly to remove the offending elements from the picture. Alternatively, change your vantage point until a tree or other landscape element hides the objects.

- **The sky is boring.** If the scene you're photographing would benefit from a few clouds, patiently wait a few minutes for some clouds to drift into the scene. Alternatively, you can come back to the area on a different day, when atmospheric conditions are more conducive to a picture-perfect sky.

Photographing Horse Racing

The fluid motion of a horse and her rider are all the ingredients you need for an exciting picture. There are many forms of horse racing. When you photograph an event like steeplechase or barrel racing, you can hone in on the rider and her trusty steed as they negotiate the obstacles. If you photograph an event on a 5/8-mile course, you can photograph many racers at one time. This section focuses on events where a single rider and horse are racing against time. The rider is focused on making the horse do something that is not second nature to the animal. The pictures you capture show the interaction between the rider and her horse as she guides the animal around the obstacles.

Setting the camera

When you photograph a horse race, you want to capture a slice of action, a frozen moment in time when horse and rider act in unison. To achieve this, you use Shutter Priority mode and a relatively fast shutter speed. If you're photographing a steeplechase or barrel race, you can use the slowest setting when the horse slows and navigates an obstacle. For other horse racing events, where the horse is going flat out, you need a faster shutter speed.

If you want to capture a sequence of images as horse and rider negotiate obstacles, choose Continuous Drive mode. The ISO setting you choose will be dictated by the amount of light and the aperture the camera dials in. Because the horse and rider are your main subjects, you can get a good, crisp photo with an f/stop of f/5.6. Use Continuous Auto-Focus mode and the camera updates focus as the horse and rider move through the frame. Image stabilization is a plus because it ensures a sharp image if your arms get tired and your hand isn't as steady as it was at the start of the event. If you don't have image stabilization, and the light gets dim, you'll have to increase the ISO.

Taking the picture

To create a compelling photo of a horse and rider at a horse race, your focus has to be spot on. You want to set up the shot before you take it. This involves a bit of thought and anticipation on your part. It's a good idea to watch a couple of racers negotiate the course before you take a picture.

1. **Move to an unobstructed vantage point and enable the camera settings discussed previously in this chapter.**

   Choose a vantage point where there's a lot of action, such as a place where the racers are jumping a hurdle or negotiating a barrel. (See Figure A-6.)

2. **Adjust the ISO setting until you have an f/stop of f/5.6 or smaller (meaning a larger f/stop number).**

   If you're shooting in overcast conditions, or at a night race, you may have to use a very high ISO setting. This adds the risk of noise to the equation, but it's better than not getting the shot.

3. **Aim the camera at the horse and rider as they race toward the place where you're going to take the picture.**

   The camera updates focus as the team moves toward or away from you. If the horse and rider are parallel to you, you'll have to pan. The alternative is to prefocus on a horse and rider that negotiate the obstacle before the subjects you want to photograph get there.

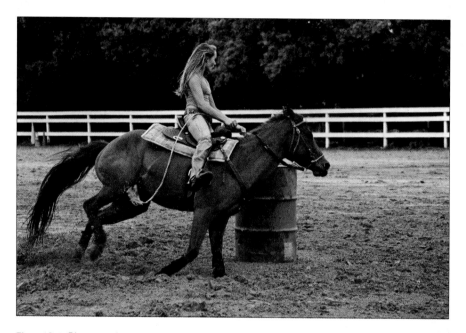

Figure A-6: Photographing horse and jockey as they approach an obstacle.

4. Zoom to the desired focal length.

Leave some room in front of the racers to give viewers the impression that horse and rider are going somewhere.

5. Press the shutter button halfway to achieve focus.

6. Press the shutter button fully to take the picture.

If you're photographing in Continuous Drive mode, release the shutter button to stop taking pictures. Review the images on your LCD monitor to make sure the image is properly exposed and that your subjects are in focus.

If you're photographing on an overcast afternoon, or at night, switch to a slow shutter speed of 1/6 or 1/15 of a second. Pan with the horse and rider to capture an artistic impression of speed, as shown in Figure A-7.

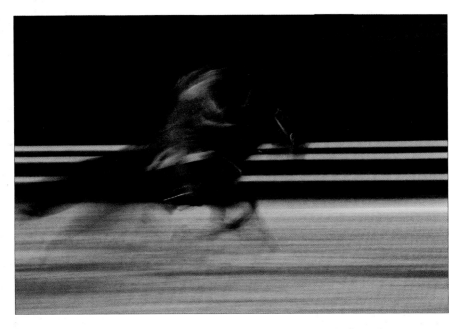

Figure A-7: Use a slow shutter speed to capture an artistic impression of speed.

Troubleshooting

- **The largest f/stop number is blinking.** This happens when you switch to a slow shutter speed in bright light. There's too much light to properly expose the image. Switch to your lowest ISO setting. If this doesn't solve the problem, place a neutral density filter over the lens.

- **The horse and rider are not in focus.** Make sure the camera is in Continuous Auto-Focus mode. If it is, make sure the auto-focus point is over the horse and rider when you press the shutter button to achieve focus.

- **The horse is in focus, but the rider isn't.** This happens in low light conditions. The camera chooses a large aperture to accommodate for the low light, which gives you a limited depth of field. The first cure is to increase the ISO setting until you get an f/stop of f/5.6 or larger (smaller aperture). The other alternative is to position the single auto-focus point over the rider. Many cameras give you the option of moving a single auto-focus point to a different part of the viewfinder other than dead center.

Capturing a City Skyline

Every city has a unique skyline comprised of landmark buildings that form a shape anyone who has visited the city can readily identify. Big cities such as New York City have skylines that are indelibly etched into the memory even of people who have never been there. If you live in or visit a city that has an interesting skyline, you can capture some wonderful pictures by using the settings in this section.

Setting the camera

When you photograph a skyline, you want to capture every subtle detail. Therefore, use Aperture Priority mode and a fairly small aperture because these settings give you a large depth of field, especially when you use a wide-angle focal length. The suggested focal-length range lets you either capture a wide expanse of the skyline or zoom in to photograph a single landmark building. The suggested ISO range lets you capture photos in bright sunlight or bright overcast conditions. If you photograph a skyline at dusk or during a dark day, you have to increase the ISO setting or use a tripod.

Taking the picture

Some photographers get in too much of a hurry when they take a picture. When you want to photograph a city skyline, you may be tempted to take a photograph from the first vantage point that shows the entire skyline. But if everyone else photographs the skyline from the same vantage point, people viewing the photo may think it's nice, but they don't spend much time looking at the image. If you slow down and photograph the skyline from several different and perhaps unique vantage points, you end up with a few images that stand out as different from everybody else's.

1. **Drive to the area from which you want to photograph the skyline.**

   You can see a lot more and locate interesting points from which to photograph the skyline if you're a passenger, rather than the driver.

2. **Enable the settings discussed previously in this chapter.**

3. **Find an interesting vantage point from which to photograph the skyline, and then press the shutter button halfway to achieve focus.**

4. **Compose the image and, if necessary, zoom in to crop out extraneous details.**

   If you're photographing a specific set of buildings, such as New York's Empire State Building and the surrounding area, rotate the camera 90 degrees so that you can match the format of the image to the shape of the building, like I've done here with the Bank of America building in Tampa, Florida (see Figure A-8). Notice how the bridge and reflections lead your eye to the building.

5. **To take the picture, fully press the shutter button.**

To create a unique photo of a landmark building in a city skyline, travel to a neighborhood that's readily identifiable to people who know the city and explore until you find a unique vantage point. Wait until one of the locals walks into the scene and take the picture (see Figure A-9).

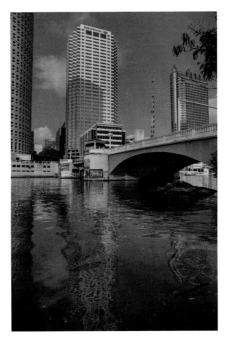 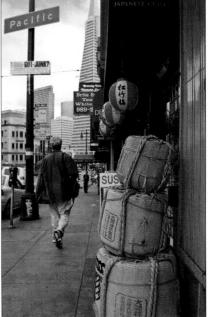

Figure A-8: Rotate the camera 90 degrees to photograph tall buildings from the skyline.

Figure A-9: Photographing a landmark building from a unique vista.

Troubleshooting

✔ **The buildings aren't level in the photo.** When you photograph a city skyline, you may not have a horizon for reference and therefore end up with an image that's off kilter. Take the picture again and pay attention to the vertical lines in the center of the image: Make sure they go straight up and down, and aren't slanted.

- ✔ **The buildings appear distorted in the photograph.** You run into this problem if you photograph the scene with a wide-angle lens from up close. Back up a little bit and take the picture again.

- ✔ **The buildings appear to be falling over in the picture.** This problem happens when you're close to the buildings and tip the camera up to get everything in the frame. Back up until you can get everything in the frame without tilting the camera.

Index